*Around the World
with the U.S. Navy*

# AROUND THE WORLD
# WITH THE U.S. NAVY

*A Reporter's Travels*

Bradley Peniston

Naval Institute Press
Annapolis, Maryland

Naval Institute Press
291 Wood Road
Annapolis, MD 21402

Library of Congress Cataloging-in-Publication Data
    Peniston, Bradley, 1968–
Around the world with the U.S. Navy : a reporter's travels /
Bradley Peniston.
        p.  cm.
ISBN 1-55750-665-5 (alk. paper)
1. United States.  Navy—History—20th century.  2. United States.
Navy—Sea life.  3. Peniston, Bradley, 1968–   .  I. Title.
VA58.4.P46   1998
359'.00973'0904–DC21                                          99-27320

Printed in the United States of America on acid-free paper ∞

06 05 04 03 02 01 00 99    9 8 7 6 5 4 3 2

First printing

For my parents, of course

# CONTENTS

# ACKNOWLEDGMENTS

It takes vision and faith to dispatch a reporter from a small newsroom for more than two months—vision to predict that the return will justify the investment, faith in the reporter and in the staff members who must cover his absence.

This book owes its existence to Tobias Naegele. As editor of *Navy Times,* Tobias conceived the idea of sending a reporter around the world to document the U.S. Navy's global reach. That trip and other assignments produced dozens of articles for the newspaper, and also the raw material for this volume. Tobias was also the first to encourage me to make them into a book.

His initial conception of the venture—a trip of two or three weeks' duration—had dissolved on broaching the subject in December 1997 with Rear Adm. Kendell Pease, then the navy's head of public affairs. Admiral Pease thought the idea a capital one, and his support made possible everything that followed, but he assured the editor that a circumnavigation of that speed was simply not going to happen aboard navy transport.

As plans came together in the spring of 1998, the itinerary stretched to four weeks, then six. Its several legs eventually consumed nearly three months in June, July, August, and September. Fortunately, Tobias was promoted over the summer to executive editor of the whole *Army Times* newspaper group, where he suddenly had more to worry about than a single reporter running amok.

After Tobias moved up, *Marine Corps Times* editor Phillip Thompson temporarily took over *Navy Times,* editing the stories that winged their way back to the newsroom via e-mail. The author of a forthcoming novel, Phillip offered thoughtful commiseration throughout the writing process.

Taking the next stint in the editor's chair, Times News Service managing editor Patrick Pexton midwifed the "Global Navy" series that appeared in *Navy Times* in November 1998. This package of sixteen articles, the major fruit of my summer's travels, was immeasurably improved by Pat's attention to craft, detail, and accuracy.

Alex Neill, who took the paper's helm in late November, was tremendously patient as I have worked toward completing the book.

Three *Navy Times* photographers came along on trips that provided material for this book: Rob Curtis, Jud McCrehin, and Steve Elfers. Each is competent and imaginative in the exercise of his professional duties; each is also a fine traveling companion.

Other colleagues at *Navy Times* have my gratitude for picking up the slack while I traveled, and for their daily dollops of inspiration. A sailor's sailor, retired Master Chief Journalist's Mate (SW/AW) John Burlage infuses his work with a chief's dedication to his bluejackets. Reporter-turned-editor B. J. Ramos brings to the newsroom unstoppable energy, a clear head, and a kind heart. And it's hard to find a marine who hasn't met or heard of Gidget Fuentes, whose incomparable roll of sources is matched only by her prodigious output of stories.

This book could not have been written without the assistance of the navy's public affairs corps. Scores of officers and enlisted people have devoted time and energy to this project. Pease retired from the navy in early 1998, but his successor, Rear Adm. Tom Jurkowsky, grabbed the ball and told his staff to run with it.

Lt. Bob Mehal was appointed point man and spent untold hours wrangling times and commitments from fellow public affairs officers on five continents. Bob gets the thinking-outside-the-box prize for plotting a circumnavigation that crossed the Atlantic Ocean three times. Capt. Steve Honda and other members of Naval Forces Europe exercised much creativity in showing off navy activities. Among those who helped in Europe were Lt. Carla McCarthy in Iceland; Lt. Curtis

Jenkins in London; Lt. Cdr. Ed Buclatin aboard *Vella Gulf;* Lt. William Breyfogle aboard *Halyburton;* Lt. Cdr. Bill Spann, Lt. Jeff Gordon, and Chief Journalist's Mate (SW) Eric Sesit in Naples, Italy; Lt. Cdr.–select Greg Geisen aboard *Wasp;* Cdr. Brian Cullen aboard *La Salle;* speedy Photographer's Mate 3d Class Renso Amariz in Calcavecchia, Italy; Lt. Dave Schontz in La Maddalena, Italy; Lt. Cappy Surette and Journalist's Mate 1st Class (SW) Anthony Falcone at Naval Air Station Sigonella, Sicily; erudite Senior Chief Journalist's Mate (SW) Dave Lovato in Romania and Italy; and Lt. Cdr. Ernest Duplessis aboard *Dwight D. Eisenhower.*

Many more people provided unstinting aid in North America, South America, and Asia, including Lt. Tom Kennedy from Naval Air Station Willow Grove, Pennsylvania, all the way to Hawaii; inexhaustible Capt. Kevin Wensing, Cdr. Betsy Bird, Jon Yoshishige, and many others in Honolulu; Cdr. Terry Sutherland and Interior Communications Electrician 1st Class Matt Green aboard *Independence;* Cdr. Fred Henney, plainspoken Jon Nylander, and Michael Chase in Yokosuka, Japan; Cdr. Greg Smith and Lt. Jeff Davis aboard *Blue Ridge*; Geralyn Noah at Naval Air Station Atsugi, Japan; Lt. Cdr. Cate Mueller in Singapore; Cdr. Gordon Hume and Lt. Brenda Malone in Manama, Bahrain; Cdr.-select Scott Harris aboard *Abraham Lincoln,* who uttered the line, "CHINFO hates it when we kill reporters" while supporting a lengthy embark; and Lt. Jud Shell everywhere from Naval Air Station Roosevelt Roads in Puerto Rico to Talcahuano, Chile.

Not all of the events recounted in these pages took place during the round-the-world trip. Many more members of the navy public affairs community provided invaluable help with stories in the months before and after, including Cdr. Jack Papp, Cdr. Bruce Cole, Lt. Cdr. Jim Fallin, Lt. Cdr. Jeff Alderson, Lt. Dee Dee Van Wormer, Lt. Christy Sheaff, and Master Chief Journalist's Mate (SW) Doug Gorham in San Diego; Dennis McGrath at Naval Air Station Lemoore, California; Capt. Joe Gradisher, Cdr. Roxie Merritt, and Senior Chief Journalist's Mate Ted Brown in Norfolk; and Cdr. T McCreary and Cdr. Frank Thorp in Washington.

Each step of my journey was facilitated by skippers and commanding officers who allowed me to visit their ships, squadrons, and support facilities. Many of these extraordinarily busy people spent precious hours to enrich my understanding of navy life and work. Thanks also go to the various fleet commanders who supported this effort by granting personal interviews and travel privileges throughout their domains.

All but a handful of the round-the-world trip's fifty-nine destinations were reached aboard military transportation, and this hitchhiker extends hearty thanks to the navy's C-9 and C-20 logistics squadrons. Navy, marine, and coast guard helicopters; air force tankers; and Air Mobility Command–chartered planes also provided much-appreciated lifts.

From seamen recruits to command master chiefs, from midshipmen to admirals, the sailors of the U.S. Navy were overwhelmingly generous in sharing their time and thoughts with me. They lead lives of sacrifice and toil, of duty and danger and honor. It is the landscape of their works that I have tried to paint in this book.

At the Naval Institute Press, *Proceedings* editor Fred Rainbow was unswervingly enthusiastic about this project, and his support and encouragement were instrumental. Press chief Ron Chambers and acquisitions editor Mark Gatlin risked a departure from Naval Institute Press business-as-usual to take this book from idea to reality in less than a year, and they have my gratitude for it.

Several people were kind enough to look over parts of the book and provided invaluable advice, including Capt. Kevin Morrissey, Lt. Wesley Price, Leah Gaffen, Mark Santangelo, and Amy Argetsinger.

This assistance not only made this project possible, it saved me from innumerable pitfalls, wrong turns, and dead-ends. Any errors that remain are mine alone.

Last on this list but first in my heart, my family fortified my spirit throughout the book's gestation. My brother James Peniston, sister Christy Myer, and brother-in-law Jeff Myer steadied my resolve with enduring faith. My mother, Mickey Peniston, continues to nourish my soul with love. This book is dedicated to her and to my father, William Peniston, who lived to see this book's genesis but not its publication.

*Around the World
with the U.S. Navy*

# INTRODUCTION

As the setting sun poured across the calm Adriatic Sea and into the hangar deck, Aviation Structural Mechanic (Structures) 2d Class Ralph Scott worked to mend the corroded skin of a strike fighter jet.

His ship, the aircraft carrier *Dwight D. Eisenhower,* had hustled halfway across the Mediterranean Sea in late June 1998 to take up station off Yugoslavia. The ninety-thousand-ton instrument of national policy readied for possible action over the breakaway province of Kosovo.

Preparing *Ike* for battle requires the teamwork of some five thousand sailors and airmen aboard the carrier, plus uncounted thousands in a global trail leading back through oilers, support bases, fleet headquarters, and myriad navy bureaus and offices. But the payoff is monumental.

"This is like a magic carpet, and we're ready to move anywhere on earth to do our jobs," Scott said.

From the frigid airstrips of Iceland to the volcanic tip of South America, from Japan to the Persian Gulf to the Black Sea, U.S. Navy sailors perform a mind-boggling array of missions: air strikes, covert operations, humanitarian aid, peacekeeping, and showing the flag a hundred ways in a hundred countries.

No one else does this. No one else can.

Pentagon maps divide the world's surface among the navy's fleets, taking for granted their power to ride the seas as obedient packhorses. Nature is not so easily tamed. Sailors fight an endless war against the constant corrosion of wind and water. Against the mightiest storms, there is nothing to do but run.

All the while, the seafarers remain vigilant against enemies armed with cheap mines and Mach-3 missiles. They learn to fight with the world's most complicated weapons. They train, and train, and train, forging teams that can fight fires as well as fighter jets.

It adds up to a globally diverse, nearly endless list of jobs: salvage diving in Singapore, computer programming in Naples, retrieving sonobuoys in Chile. And much of it is done by people too young to drink in Norfolk.

"Sometimes I'm not sure enough credit is given to the nineteen-year-old humping fifty pounds of chains, standing in what can be long chow lines," said Cdr. Thomas A. Cropper, the commander of a fighter jet squadron. "It's a spartan life, drawn down to the essentials: a rack, a very large roof over their heads, three squares, and something else: the feeling of being in an elite unit."

Even in peacetime, their jobs take them in harm's way. "What we do is inherently dangerous, whether it's arming jets on the big deck or sailing in a tin can below the waves," said Cdr. Mike Zieser, skipper of the attack submarine *Houston.*

In November 1998, four aviators died aboard the carrier *Enterprise* when their four-seat electronic-warfare jet, landing after a nighttime training mission, roared onto the flight deck, clipped the tail of an anti-submarine plane, and plunged over the side of the ship. It was one of the worst naval aviation accidents in two decades.

If the navy offers days of danger and nights of toil, it also offers travel and responsibilities that can stir the soul. Sonar Technician (Surface) Seaman Apprentice Rick Brown was a new member of the crew of the guided missile cruiser *Vella Gulf* when it sailed to the Baltic Sea in June. "No one in America can say they've been there unless they have a job like this. One year ago, never did I think I'd be riding a boat in the mid-Atlantic, heading for Ireland and Poland. A lot of people don't even make it to Mexico."

For Cdr. James Stewart, it was watching the guided missile frigate *Doyle* come pierside to an old wharf on Chile's Talcahuano Harbor. The sun sparkled on the trombones and trumpets of a Chilean naval band as they stoutly rendered "Anchors Aweigh." The frigate's even coat of fresh paint caught Stewart's eye, and the *Doyle*'s soon-to-be commanding officer nodded with satisfaction as the boatswain's mates made the ship fast to the foreign dock.

"It's a real joy when you get the opportunity to take an outstanding ship and keep the momentum going," said Stewart, who would complete the ship's Unitas cruise around South America. "I was ready for anything. If it was taking a bad crew and making her good, I could have done that too."

Stewart stepped into his new job three days later in a ceremony on the ship's fantail. The crew assembled in ranks, and the outgoing skipper made a small speech. Stewart made a few remarks, read his orders aloud, and took command. The formal change of command is one of the traditions that binds the naval service's men and women through time and space.

Half a world away, Navy Counselor 1st Class (SW) Charles Clarke worked in a corner of a cramped office, its window shuttered against the Mediterranean sun. The ancient building stood on a tiny island between Sardinia and Corsica, not far from a bearlike rock outcrop Homer mentioned in his *Odyssey*. Clarke's base, Naval Support Activity La Maddalena, helps support the navy's nuclear submarines. "The navy's the navy, no matter where you put it," he said.

The pages that follow tell the stories of American sailors in the U.S. Navy's Second, Third, Fifth, Sixth, and Seventh Fleets—that is, of sailors everywhere. The product of more than a year of reporting, they offer glimpses of the sailors who give the navy its global reach.

The events recounted in this book took place between September 1997 (the "smart ship" *Yorktown* cruising up the Chesapeake Bay) and March 1999 (combat aboard the cruiser *Philippine Sea*). But most of them occurred in the summer months of 1998, during which I undertook a round-the-world journey for *Navy Times*. (A weekly newspaper that covers the sea services, *Navy Times* is unaffiliated with the navy.)

In June of that year, a photographer and I left Washington, D.C., on a dream assignment: find the far-flung fleet and describe it at work. Our itinerary traced a pile of spaghetti on the European map, then drew a wobbly line all the way around the globe. Crossing the Atlantic a second time, we hitched a ride aboard a navy logistics flight out of suburban Philadelphia and proceeded through Hawaii, Guam, Japan, Singapore, Bahrain, Egypt, Italy, and Ireland. A Latin American swing through Puerto Rico, Panama, and Chile topped it off.

The trip eventually covered more than fifty-nine thousand air miles and some thirty-six hundred more at sea. Important lessons were learned, such as "Don't sit in the captain's chair" and "Don't stand up in the rigid-hull inflatable boat, no matter how calm the water looks." Flying off aircraft carriers became a little less unroutine. More precisely, we got used to being dragged backward like cargo when the mail plane exploded from standstill to flight in two seconds. The passenger seats in C-2 Greyhounds face aft, which eases the shock of smacking into the flight deck on landing but makes taking off a bug-eyed, painful, circulation-cut-off-by-the-shoulder-straps experience.

The trip illustrated that, in important ways, 1998 was little different from the previous two centuries of the American naval experience. Sailors still went to sea and risked their lives to protect those they left behind. But in ways just as vital, the year was a watershed for the sailors of the modern U.S. Navy.

When the curtain rose in January, ships were already massing in the Persian Gulf. The carriers *George Washington* and *Nimitz* and seventeen smaller ships prepared for combat. American troop strength in the region mounted to numbers unseen since the Iraqi military was chased from Kuwait in 1991's Operation Desert Storm.

This year's problem was more of the same: Saddam Hussein. After the Gulf War, the United Nations had begun sending inspectors into Iraqi to prevent Saddam from building an arsenal of chemical and biological weapons. In turn, the Iraqi leader had harassed the inspection teams, taking liberties when he sensed the world's attention wandering.

In late 1997 Saddam halted cooperation with the inspection teams altogether. The White House responded with naval sabers at full rattle—"maximum military presence," as Secretary of Defense William Cohen put it. In February, a third carrier, *Independence,* steamed into the gulf with three amphibious landing ships in tow.

Several weeks passed. United Nations secretary-general Kofi Annan negotiated a deal that allowed the weapons inspectors to resume their work under new restrictions. Although UN and U.S. officials professed guarded optimism, perhaps not even Annan himself actually believed this was a permanent solution. One *Nimitz* airman later recalled steamy days and nights of drilling for chemical attack in the gulf. Nobody likes combat, he said; "but we were ready to go and put an end to this mess. When they said, 'Not this time,' we said, well . . ."

*Indy* and its battle group departed in May, reducing the gulf presence to a single carrier for the first time in seven months. As if on schedule, a new crisis erupted to demand the navy's attention: Kosovo. Confronted by a separatist movement in rump Yugoslavia's southern province, the country's Serbian leaders had ordered a violent crackdown on ethnic Albanians. The death toll vaulted into the thousands. Many more were driven from their homes. By mid-year, President Bill Clinton worried that the killings would plunge the fragile region into war. It was time to send a message, the administration decided.

The White House yanked *Wasp* from a port visit in Turkey and sent the amphibious assault ship to the Adriatic Sea. On 15 June, four Harrier attack jets took off from *Wasp's* flight deck to join other NATO aircraft in an aerial show of force along the Yugoslav border. More ships, including the carrier *Eisenhower,* soon arrived to underline the threat of air strikes. Destroyers and submarines stood by with batteries of Tomahawk cruise missiles. The fighting ebbed, then rose again through the autumn, when renewed threats by NATO leaders persuaded Serb forces to begin a withdrawal from the province.

The navy received its chance to fire Tomahawks soon enough. In August, terrorist bombs exploded outside U.S. embassies in Kenya and Tanzania. Two weeks later, Clinton ordered retaliation. On 20 August, warships in the Persian Gulf launched more than seventy cruise missiles at a terrorist training camp in eastern Afghanistan. Six more Tomahawks destroyed a pharmaceuticals plant in Sudan that the White House had labeled a chemical weapons factory.

Meanwhile, Kofi Annan's deal with Saddam was unraveling only six months after it was signed. Iraqi troops began to interfere with UN weapons inspectors, and in late October Saddam blocked the inspections entirely. Once again, Clinton dispatched navy ships to the troubled area. *Eisenhower,* the amphibious assault ship *Essex,* and nineteen other warships were already in the gulf when the carrier *Enterprise* and eight more ships arrived at high speed. Three amphibious ships stuffed with marines joined them on Thanksgiving Day.

On 23 November, Clinton directed U.S. military forces to prepare to strike. Sailors around the gulf programmed Tomahawks to hit a multitude of Iraqi targets. Air force B-52 bombers, their bellies filled with ordnance, lumbered airborne and headed for Iraq. Faced with this imminent threat, Saddam signaled a renewed intent to cooperate. Fifteen minutes before the Tomahawks were to fire, Clinton canceled the attack.

One month later, the UN's chief weapons inspector reported that Iraqi troops were again denying inspectors access to suspected weapons plants; 1998 had improved the quality of Saddam's promises not a whit. In Washington, meanwhile, Congress was trying to decide whether to impeach Clinton for lying under oath about his affair with a young White House intern. As the House debate began on 16 December, the president ordered the attack he had called off a month before. This time, the *Enterprise* and *Carl Vinson* battle groups were on the scene: twenty-six ships, 194 warplanes, and some twenty-one thousand troops. Dubbed Operation Desert Fox, the four-day campaign opened with the largest cruise missile bombardment in the weapons' short history. Led by the attack sub *Miami,* eight ships rained more than two hundred Tomahawks—one-tenth of the navy's inventory—onto Iraqi targets. A torrent of U.S. and British planes followed, hammering more than a hundred antiaircraft missile sites, radar stations, weapons plants, military command posts, airfields, and more. Cohen and other military officials hailed the strikes, saying that they had "substantially degraded" Saddam's power to threaten neighboring countries with conventional or chemical weapons.

"But from the deck plates overlooking the Persian Gulf, 1998 ended much the way it began," reporter Bill Matthews wrote in *Navy Times.* "A powerful armada was marking time in the Persian Gulf and the United States was waiting for Saddam to make his next move."

In the new year, the situation in rump Yugoslavia deteriorated into war. The fragile cease-fire ended with the massacre of forty-five Kosovar civilians in January 1999. Two months later, NATO forces began bombing Serb military targets in an effort to put an end to the slaughter. American cruisers, destroyers, and submarines launched Tomahawk strikes while aircraft from the carrier *Theodore Roosevelt* flew hundreds of combat strike missions into Yugoslavia.

At this writing, the conflict, dubbed Operation Allied Force, was still raging. But something had begun to change for the U.S. Navy, stretched thin at the turn of the twenty-first century. Prodded by Congress and the fleet's overworked sailors, its leaders began to say, "Enough."

To look at the navy in 1998 was to see an organization still wrestling with the aftermath of the cold war. For decades, American warships, weapons, and tactics had been developed to fight the Soviet Union at sea. U.S. Navy submarines shadowed Russian subs through deep waters; carrier battle groups practiced for massive battles in the Arctic Sea. When the enemy collapsed in 1991, so did a world of assumptions about naval combat.

Left without its giant rival, the U.S. Navy sought new missions, finding them in the unfamiliar waters of the littoral, the fringe of the world's oceans where sea meets land. Here were the seeds of future conflict, especially in the coastal cities of the Third World. The navy's new goal, its leaders declared in 1994, would be "influencing events at sea and ashore."

The fleet began to prepare for low-intensity conflicts in which ship-on-ship battles gave way to a new kind of gunboat diplomacy. Turning to meet the new winds was difficult. Every ship in the fleet had been built to counter the Russian threat. Inevitably, there were problems. For example, the navy's sonar devices, designed to detect enemy subs in deep oceans, worked poorly in sonically hazy shallows.

In the meantime, America decided that the cold war military was too large for whatever came next. Budgets plummeted. Thousands of sailors were encouraged to leave the service. Ships were decommissioned in droves. By 1998, the 550-ship fleet was down to 320 and still falling.

Stung, and threatened by the downsizing, the navy began the pursuit of efficiency in many forms, but budgets fell even faster than force structure. Ships and squadrons in home ports suffered first. Traditionally, the military has employed "tiered readiness"; that is, units on deployment get first crack at parts and funds, units in final training come second, and those that have returned last get least.

The executive officer of a strike fighter squadron likened the flow of money and troops over a training cycle to a bathtub's long curve. When the VFA-83 Rampagers ended their previous six-month deployment, funding dropped like water rolling down toward the front end of the tub, said Cdr. Pat Rainey. The level rose very slowly over the next year, then started climbing vigorously near the end of the cycle. By the end of the decade, it took longer and longer for the predeployment increase to kick in. "Now we're not fully manned until one month before cruise," Rainey said. "It's harder than ever to make that climb."

Meanwhile, a strange thing happened: the navy got busier. The cold war's end uncorked dozens of local conflicts long kept bottled up by superpower politics. Some were deemed of little import to U.S. interests, but many others required military action—usually naval action. In 1998, admirals were showing charts that illustrated navy participation in a "real-world operation" every five weeks. By the time the Persian Gulf buildup started in January 1998, the strain on the navy's personnel and materials was visible.

When the White House asked the navy to keep a pair of carriers in the Persian Gulf for months on end, planners scrambled to fill the order. Erasers were worn to nubs on much-altered deployment schedules. Finally, the navy conceded defeat. It was either tell the president "no can do" or exceed self-imposed operating limits. The latter option would mean breaking one of the modern navy's most sacred troths with the troops—if you go out on deployment, you *will* be back six months later—and the navy refused to do that.

It was hard for Adm. Jay Johnson, the chief of naval operations, to admit that. Being in the military means hating to say, "I can't," especially to the commander in chief. But in May, Johnson and other military chieftains told Clinton that keeping the large force in the gulf was eroding combat fitness and hurting morale. The message got through. Soon afterward, *Indy* pulled out. (However, Secretary Cohen insisted for a week that the United States still had a two-carrier "policy" in the gulf.)

Later, in September, Admiral Johnson and the service chiefs reprised their new song for Congress, telling the Senate Armed Services Committee that they were having problems maintaining proper "readiness" for combat. Worse yet, they were mortgaging future needs to pay for current readiness. The lawmakers responded: Last year, you said everything was fine. What happened?

To some extent the problem had become obvious even to outsiders. Too many tales of fighter squadrons starved for parts had reached congressional ears. Simple arithmetic showed that the navy's shipbuilding budgets would not much longer sustain a three-hundred-ship fleet. But the new year had also brought new evidence of a mounting problem. By mid-1998, the fleet had twenty-two thousand more jobs than sailors to fill them.

"We don't have the people we need, simple math, simple fact," said Master Chief Machinist's Mate (SW/AW) Bernard L. Heffernan Jr., echoing a lament heard around the fleet. "Here's what really hurts: it's not unusual to have a third-class petty officer filling slots on the mess deck, and that's become the rule rather than the exception," said *Ike's* senior enlisted man. "I like to have a huge wall between [seaman] and [petty officer]. If there's no difference, it's hard to convince them to stay in the navy."

Navy personnel directors were in a bind. For a decade they had encouraged sailors to leave the service as the fleet shrank in accordance with Congress's dictates. As the fleet prepared to move from shrinking to stable by 2000, however, retention levels had to rise. They didn't. The navy had been blindsided by a stunningly good economy that tempted potential recruits and old sailors alike.

And money wasn't the only thing. Sailors who said they had joined the navy for the travel found themselves returning to the same sun-scorched Persian Gulf ports. Many were frustrated by personnel shortfalls and parts shortages that made a tough job tougher. A recent reduction in retirement benefits rankled as well. Traditionally, a service member's pension was half his final pay. Now it was less. "I love the corpsman rating," said one of *Eisenhower's* hospitalmen. "I don't even mind being shot at. That's my job. But 35 percent isn't worth twenty years."

Especially prevalent among junior officers was the feeling that the job just wasn't as much fun anymore. There were too many inspections to pass, too many hoops to jump through. "We're a peacetime navy, which means we stand inspections and do paperwork," one submariner said.

Worst of all, a navy survey found that fewer junior surface warfare officers aspired to command at sea—traditionally the naval service's highest calling. "I look at my boss, and I don't want his job," one young officer said. The heirs of John Paul Jones, some felt, had to take too much crap for too little glory.

In the fall, Admiral Johnson made a decision that promised to change his sailors' lives more than anything else the CNO did in 1998. He slashed the number of inspections and "assist visits" required for ships in home port. This meant fewer "at-home" days spent cruising offshore sweating it out during inspections, and fewer weekends spent preparing for Monday's retests. It allowed many ships to cut back on in-port working hours.

Most important, it gave time back to captains and crews, encouraging sailors to feel like they strode the decks of warships, not the moving parts of a giant bureaucratic machine. "It's like you're regaining control of your own destiny," said sub skipper Mike Zieser.

Johnson and the other service chiefs also pushed for more money for the troops, securing the biggest military pay raises in eighteen years and persuading Congress to take another look at the retirement policy.

A new frank-talking navy secretary arrived in December. Richard Danzig, a smart former undersecretary who called himself an "activist," set out to correct a slew of problems: poor recruiting, low morale, operational-tempo woes. Some of his ideas, such as hiring civilians to paint warships, were simply attempts to ease the burdens of the American bluejacket's life.

Those were the big issues in 1998. In one way or another, they touched every man and woman in the fleet. But more interesting—and more the province of this book—are the stories on a smaller scale.

High above *Independence*'s busy flight deck, Aviation Machinist's Mate 3d Class Joe Taylor watched the "roof crew" scurry, prepping their growling warbirds for one last flight from the navy's oldest aircraft carrier. Steaming toward Hawaii under the bluest of July skies, *Indy* would soon tie up in Pearl Harbor, and Taylor and all but a skeleton crew would depart for the carrier *Kitty Hawk*.

Equipped with the navy's newest strike fighters and latest electronic gear, the younger carrier would head smartly for Japan to assume *Indy*'s duties in the forward-based Seventh Fleet. The elder flattop, in no hurry after four decades of service, would sail off to its rest in Puget Sound's ship graveyard.

The aviation machinist's mate mulled over his life as a sailor, and his thoughts drifted to family and friends in their civilian worlds. "I wish they could see what I see. You just can't explain it," the petty officer said.

Perhaps this book can help.

# 1. THE FRIGATES

Aboard the USS *Halyburton* in the Baltic Sea, June 1998

Enfolded by a moonless, starless night, six men in black prepared to shove off from the guided missile frigate *Halyburton* in a twenty-four-foot motorboat. Darkened, their own ship was all but invisible, but their objective—the Polish intelligence vessel *Hydrograf*—glowed brightly across a watery half mile. It was after midnight on the Baltic Sea, and the summer darkness, however abbreviated at northern latitudes, would conceal the boarding party's approach.

They mustered on the frigate's starboard weather deck, stepping over the transom of a watertight door and dogging it with a healthy shove of its long handle. They emerged on a long, narrow platform, squeezed between the looming superstructure and a twenty-foot drop to the dark water below, and gave their gear a last check. Each wore a .45-caliber pistol strapped to a Kevlar bulletproof vest and a radio headset clamped over a black knit cap. The sailors stepped through a gap in the safety cable at the deck's edge and wobbled down a rope ladder to the boat waiting below.

The black-clad men alighted on an inflated rubber pontoon epoxied to the powerboat's fiberglass gunwales. In high seas, the pontoon would give the little boat remarkable stability, but in tonight's calm it was simply a good foothold. Two of the boat's crewmen helped the boarding party into the hull. All aboard, they hunkered down and held on. The calm Scandinavian seas were running less than a foot, but the water beyond the boat's low sides was blacker than the velvet sky.

Standing amidships, a senior chief boatswain's mate goosed the throttle. The boat heeled toward the *Hydrograf* and accelerated to fifteen knots. A few sailors exchanged wicked smiles as the boat skimmed along. But as the distance closed between the vessels and the chief throttled back on the roaring diesel engine, the sailors applied serious miens. Like policemen everywhere, the boarders knew the value of first impressions.

"They respect you more if you're all uniform and squared away," said Gunner's Mate 1st Class (SW) Steve Dunham.

The boat came alongside the Polish vessel, and the boarders hailed the watch standers at the well-lit rail. The smaller vessel rocked against the warship's low-slung hull as a cargo net was lowered to the waterline. Two at a time, the American sailors clambered up the looped ropes.

This is the moment of maximum vulnerability during a boarding operation: the members of the boarding party, hands full, are spread out between boat and ship. The mission had been laid on quickly, and no one knew quite what to expect.

As it happened, *Halyburton*'s veteran team performed none of the choreographed contraband searches they had perfected during a previous deployment to the Persian Gulf. The effusive Polish crew simply swept them away to the bridge to receive their skipper's good wishes and a box of cookies. The Poles seemed thrilled to see such an operation up close; the Americans said later that it didn't compare with the real thing.

"It's a lot more fun when you're going to a vessel you don't know anything about and they don't speak English," Dunham said.

As actions went, *Halyburton*'s wee-hours "boarding" was no big deal, a demonstration ginned up to demonstrate American capabilities to a Polish crew. But in many ways, it was an archetypal mission for the navy's frigate sailors in 1998.

*Halyburton* and its numerous sister ships in the *Oliver Hazard Perry* class were designed in the 1970s as inexpensive sub hunters. One and one-half times the length of a football field, *Halyburton*'s graceful hull swoops in a single long curve from high prow to low fantail. The boxy superstructures rising above the ship's rails look something like cargo plopped down on the main deck.

Sensitive sonar microphones embedded in the hull and towed astern help the crew find enemy submarines. There are six deck-mounted torpedo tubes, but the frigate's main antisub weapon is the pair of SH-60 Seahawk helicopters that travel with the ship.

To protect themselves from air attack, the crew has air-search radars, a seventy-six-millimeter gun, and a missile launcher that can whirl around to bring its deadly rockets to bear. But the ship lacks two features of the navy's more modern surface combatants: the powerful Aegis combat system with its revolutionary radar, and the vertical missile tubes that fire Tomahawk cruise missiles. The forty-one-hundred-ton *Perrys* are headed for the ship-breaking yards or the auction block, perhaps just after the turn of the century. In 1998, however, they remained the most numerous surface ships in the navy. Indeed, the three dozen frigates served as the fleet's utility infielders, ever flexible, ever on the move.

The boarding of the *Hydrograf* was a good example. It took place during the naval exercise called BALTOPS, an annual gathering of allied warships in the Baltic Sea. During the exercise, *Halyburton* and its crew hunted diesel submarines, tracked swift patrol boats, picked paths through simulated minefields, and erected invisible umbrellas of air defense radar. The boarders' brief visit had a purpose beyond the strictly military. Along with the port visits and diplomatic receptions that were part of the two-week exercise, it was a chance for Americans and foreigners to get to know one another. By using naval vessels to knit the fabric of international community, BALTOPS 1998 was a classic example of what navy officials call "engagement." Like social networking on a global scale, engagement is intended to turn strangers into acquaintances, acquaintances into friends. Frigates may not be the navy's most capable ships, but they are great at showing the flag.

Nevertheless, the exercises illustrated the difficulties in adapting cold war procedures and equipment to the 1990s. Like the rest of the navy, frigate crews have spent the last decade rewriting their mid-ocean playbooks for operations in shallower waters. The boarding party was one example; BALTOPS 1998 would provide more of them, as *Halyburton*'s crew adjusted to unfamiliar waters, unfamiliar team-mates, and unfamiliar tactics.

A wet, early-summer haze obscured the chilly Baltic sky, and some-times the radio conversations flying between the warships below weren't much clearer. Although English is the operational lingua fran-ca of the North Atlantic Treaty Organization, the foreign accents often baffled the American sailors, who strained to interpret the static-laced voices in their headphones.

There were plenty of different accents to puzzle over. Many be-longed to longtime allies: Denmark, France, Germany, Holland, Nor-way, and the United Kingdom. But the airwaves carried the voices of crews from non-NATO countries as well: Estonia, Finland, Latvia, Lith-uania, Poland, and Sweden. BALTOPS 1998 was one of a series of NATO exercises designed to help bring former Eastern bloc countries into the international fold. Such events, called Partnership for Peace exercises, were first staged in the mid-1990s. The first week of BALTOPS 1998 would help treaty members get to know the non-NATO participants, while the second would be a NATO-only event.

Maneuvering in formation with ships from a dozen Baltic navies requires more than careful diction. It also takes a bit of extra thought. *Halyburton*'s gas turbines—essentially a pair of diesel-fuel jet engines whose compressors drive the ship's propeller—made the frigate the nimblest warship around. It could gain or shed speed more quickly than steam-powered squadron mates such as the German destroyer *Moelders*.

The difference showed during even the most elementary ma-neuvers. "If we're in front of the *Moelders,* I have to tell my guys that if we're going to slow down, you have to think of steam plants. Be care-ful or we're going to get run over," said Cdr. Kevin Morrissey, *Halybur-ton*'s skipper.

But the Americans had other problems as well. The territory used for the BALTOPS exercises extended miles beyond the Danish island of Bornholm, into the Baltic Sea—terra incognita for the U.S. Navy. Dur-ing the cold war, few American ships ventured east of Bornholm, just fifty miles from the Polish coast and less than two hundred from the Soviet Union itself. Not even Morrissey, a navy officer since 1978, had ever operated so close to Soviet territory. "I don't think anybody felt comfortable poking the Bear with this frigate back then," the skipper said.

Predictably, the European subs that played the "enemy" in the exercise pushed their home-field advantage. The diesel-powered boats made tough targets for the Americans, who usually practiced hunting their own, slightly louder nuclear-propelled subs.

Right at home, the foreign subs ducked between thermal layers in the water and darted down gullies in the seafloor. Sometimes they sat on the seabed itself, rigging their diesel engines for ultraquiet operation. The salty, noisy, cold water twisted their faint aural telltales into unrecognizable noise, wrapping a damper around *Halyburton*'s sensitive sonar microphones.

The ship's active sonar system was faring even worse. Active sonar is usually the undersea warfare equivalent of hitting the light switch in a darkened room. The system sends powerful pulses of sound into the water and listens for their echoes. But *Halyburton*'s "pings" were simply disappearing into the underwater murk of the Baltic Sea.

In the frigate's darkened sonar room, Seaman Apprentice Rick Brown stared at a speckled green computer screen. "The water sucks here. Passive's going OK, but we can't hear what the active's doing," said Brown, one of *Halyburton*'s sonar equipment operators.

The crowd of ships in the pocket-sized sea didn't help things much. Their noises flooded Brown's headphones, interfering with his attempts to pick out a sub's distinctive signature. The ship hadn't received authorization to use the towed array to track the foreign submarines, forcing Brown and his shipmates to use less capable sensors within the hull—the so-called Helen Keller system. Meanwhile, the crew was simultaneously pressed to monitor every blip in a galaxy of green twinkles, lest a sneaky submarine use the confusion for cover. "I want to know what every surface contact is because there might be a sub right next to us," Morrissey said.

Eventually, *Halyburton*'s crew adjusted their entire approach to antisubmarine warfare, or ASW in naval parlance. U.S. ships customarily play the game at arm's length, striking with torpedoes, missiles, and depth-bombing helicopters before submarines get close. The Baltic navies have a different philosophy: Get on top of the underwater threats and pound them. After a few days, the American sailors, flexible and well trained on their equipment, got the hang of Baltic-style ASW. "When the Swede was the submarine, we kicked her around like kids with a soccer ball," said Lt. Cdr. Lloyd Brown, *Halyburton's* executive officer.

The exercise allowed skipper and seamen alike close inspection of their counterparts' seagoing skills. Morrissey called the French and German mariners "the consummate professionals," citing their crisp radio calls and sharp ship maneuvers. He judged the two Polish ships to be coming on strong. "They obviously have been planning a lot," Morrissey said. "They're going to be members of NATO, and you can tell they really want to."

The day that ended with the *Hydrograf* boarding had featured a wild and glorious afternoon of ship handling; there weren't many aboard the American frigate who recalled its like. The European sailors who regularly plied the Baltic were accustomed to operating half a dozen warships at close range, but some of their freewheeling maneuvers left *Halyburton's* crew openmouthed.

Standing on the frigate's starboard bridge wing, the small platform outside the bridge, Morrissey could see a dozen naval vessels near and far. Under swirling clouds and a threatening sky, ships slid into line abreast, broke into a torpedo screen, then wheeled about, practicing convoy formations and antisubmarine maneuvers. It was all basic stuff—division tactics, or "divtacs" in surface warfare lingo. But nothing is simple with so many vessels, and the frigate's bridge buzzed as officers and sailors worked to keep a handle on the situation. "The more ships you have, the more difficult it gets," said Brown, the exec.

*Halyburton* prepared to come about, working into position to rendezvous with an oiler. Suddenly, another smallish warship sliced across *Halyburton's* bow. It was the Danish frigate *Falke*, passing within a narrow nautical mile.

"What the hell?" escaped several throats. Someone on the bridge wing yelled out, "What is this, McHale's Navy?" Boatswain's Mate 2d Class Quilici Brumfield shook his head and weighed in on *Falke*'s seagoing manners. "That ain't the way to do business," said the ten-year veteran.

But Brumfield and the other bridge watch standers soon returned their concentration to the upcoming refueling. A seafaring pit stop minus the pit and the stop, "underway replenishment" brings a warship alongside a fleet oiler to take on fuel and lubricants, even small quantities of food, spare parts, and supplies. The technique gives American and allied warships unparalleled range and flexibility. It is a tricky operation that the Soviet navy never really mastered.

Attempting a full stop amid heaving seas and blowing winds would invite disaster, so the ships keep moving during the replenishment, which allows for quick evasive action. The "unrep" remains one of the most hazardous of naval maneuvers, putting hundreds or thousands of lives at risk of a collision at sea. A ship might unrep dozens of times during a six-month deployment, but the procedure never really becomes routine.

Under Morrissey's watchful eye, Quartermaster 1st Class (SW) Troy Valahos prepared to conn the ship through the unrep. The petty officer had earned the status of officer of the deck—unusual for an enlisted person—through months of study and instruction. It was testament to the petty officer's competence, but also to the opportunities afforded an enterprising sailor aboard a small ship. There is no end to the work aboard a frigate, so the commissioned officers welcomed the opportunity to spread the load among more hands.

The frigate, like every navy vessel bigger than a powerboat, required several people to steer it. Valahos issued his commands to a helmsman at the center of the bridge's wide control panel, and that sailor turned the saucer-sized steering wheel that controls the electric motors that move the ship's rudder. With crisp orders, Valahos conned *Halyburton* into a twenty-two-knot turn that left a wake like a frothy letter S. The ship slid smartly along the port side of the Dutch oiler *Zuiderkruis*. "We like to go up to station fast because we like to impress people with our gas turbine," he said later.

Now it was time to throttle back. "Ahead two-thirds for eleven knots," Valahos said.

"Ahead two-thirds for eleven knots, aye," the helmsman responded, pulling the speed indicator.

On the sloping deck forward of the bridge, a boatswain's mate in an orange life vest and slate blue hardhat lifted an air rifle toward the oiler. He pulled the trigger and a red weight, trailing a thin line, arced across the hundred-foot gap to *Zuiderkruis*. A trio of Dutch sailors scrambled to pull it taut across the gap. Marked at ten-foot increments with colored plastic plaques, the cable would help Valahos keep an even distance from the oiler as the ships heaved through the sea.

Amidships, sailors from *Halyburton*'s deck division fired another line, which the Dutch sailors attached to an inch-thick manila rope. Taking a strain on the rope, the American blueshirts hauled across the gap a flexible, foot-thick pipe that dangled from the oiler's extendible derricks. They wrestled its nose cone into a matching receptacle on the main deck. The oiler began pumping fuel into the frigate's tanks.

Ten minutes later, the destroyer *Moelders* moved onto *Zuiderkruis*'s starboard beam for its own unrep. For a few minutes, the crews of three ships exulted in the drama of thousands of steel tons sailing in close formation. "People have no idea how difficult this is," noted Lt. William Breyfogle, a reservist doing his annual two weeks' service aboard *Halyburton*. "You do not stop a four thousand, one hundred–ton boat on a dime, and these ships can swing together in a heartbeat."

Fuel tanks topped off, the deck sailors unplugged the fuel hose, sent it back to the Dutch vessel, and reeled in their lines. At a word from Valahos, *Halyburton* departed the unrep at twenty-eight knots. In a navywide custom, music blared from topside loudspeakers. Executive Officer Brown had selected Wagner's triumphal "Ride of the Valkyries."

"Outstanding job, QM1, outstanding," the skipper said, wiping spray from the lenses of his navy-issue plastic frames, called "birth control glasses" for their sheer unattractiveness. "Secure from operational maneuvering."

A few minutes later, Morrissey's voice broke from the ship's public address system, describing the maneuver for sailors inside the ship's skin. "At ten to fifteen knots, we had fifteen thousand tons of ships within two hundred and fifty feet," he said. "That was one of the finest deck seamanship evolutions I have ever seen. Congrats to the deck team."

For all the hard work, BALTOPS's two weeks offered *Halyburton's* crew a break from their usual hectic schedule: port visits in Poland, Sweden, Lithuania, Holland, and, on the way home, northern Ireland. Inspections and training and exercises had kept the ship and its crew on the go for almost two straight months.

The journeys hadn't been easy on the crew, who were working hard to cover gaps in their ranks. The shortages were wide as well as deep. With few exceptions, every specialty onboard was short of skilled sailors. For example, the gas turbine repair shop was staffed with nine mechanics during a recent Persian Gulf deployment, but it carried only three for BALTOPS. In all, *Halyburton* was missing a body for nearly one of every six billets.

It was a depressing fact of life in the navy of 1998. In order to keep ships on six-month deployments manned up to 90 percent or so, ships between "cruises" were shorted on sailors, parts, and operating funds. This practice kept tip-of-the-spear units as ready as possible but ran the rest of the fleet ragged. It angered sailors, who found BALTOPS and other exercises just as demanding as duty in the Persian Gulf. "We're still held to the standards of a fully-manned ship," XO Brown said. "If we'd wanted to launch a helo alongside the oiler, we wouldn't have been able to."

The frigate's top enlisted man was just as frustrated. "I shouldn't have to be running around out here 15 percent undermanned," said Master Chief Machinist's Mate (SW) Mark Butler. As *Halyburton's* command master chief, Butler worked as the skipper's top enlisted adviser and a link between captain and crew.

Deployed frigates sometimes find it just as hard to hang onto sailors. Skilled technicians are often yanked for duty in the higher-tech combat centers aboard carriers, cruisers, and destroyers. And the frigates are ineligible to carry about 15 percent of the navy's sailors, for they lack separate berthing spaces for mixed-gender crews. "There are bodies out there," Brown said, "but they're female."

Even the relentless enthusiasm of the navy's World Wide Web site flags when it comes to the *Perry*-class ships. "The guided missile frigates bring an anti–air warfare capability to the frigate mission, but they have some limitations," it says. "Designed as cost-efficient surface combatants, they lack the multi-mission capability necessary for modern surface combatants faced with multiple, high-technology threats. They also offer limited capacity for growth."

Ask the crew, and they'll tell you they get short shrift from the media as well. Operations Specialist 2d Class Brandon Moore recalled a bit of galling television coverage after his crew performed a daring high-seas rescue. When the cruise ship *Achille Lauro* caught fire off the Somali coast in 1994, *Halyburton* and the guided missile cruiser *Gettysburg* arrived on the scene within hours. The ships sent sailors to fight the flames and helicopters to ferry the passengers to safety. The next day, Moore watched a television news anchor name the cruiser while mentioning the frigate only generically. "We're the USS Other Ship, basically," the sailor said.

All this doesn't stop navy brass from sending the "figs" on utility-man missions all over the globe. "We're perfect for things like this," said Brown, citing the frigate's thrifty fuel consumption and shallow draft. The weary XO admitted there was probably another motive as well. "We're rapidly approaching obsolescence. It's okay if we're off on this and the world goes to crap, because our contribution is probably pretty little," he said.

Yet even frigates are precious in a shrinking fleet. Pacific Fleet commander Adm. Archie Clemins noted in May that his forces had little leeway for the unexpected. "The value of even a single unit is now clear," Clemins said. "If scheduled maintenance for a ship gets delayed, it directly impacts the maintenance, training, or at-sea time of other ships."

One week later, the frigate *Jarrett* suffered damage to its sonar dome when its heavy anchor came free and plunged into San Diego Harbor. The anchor chain scraped across the sonar dome, puncturing the bulbous dome and requiring five days of repairs with metal plates and epoxy. The frigate was scheduled to sail with the aircraft carrier *Abraham Lincoln,* but instead wound up chasing the carrier across the Pacific Ocean. Had *Jarrett* suffered more grievous injury, the incident could have left the eight-vessel *Lincoln* battle group light one warship.

---

Aboard the USS *Thach,* Manama, Bahrain, August 1998

While *Halyburton* was demonstrating boarding operations to friendly vessels, its sister ship *Thach* was doing it for real, thousands of miles away in sweltering desert climes.

As the Gulf War dissolved into smaller operations designed to contain Saddam Hussein, American warships began enforcing a United Nations embargo on trade with Iraq. Since 1991, sailors from *Thach* and dozens of other navy warships have boarded thousands of merchant ships. The American sailors search for contraband, especially oil, Iraq's most valuable export.

In the days of sail, the boarding of hostile vessels was a standard part of every sailor's duties. Today, the navy's boardings are called VBSS operations, which stands for "visit, board, search, and seizure." The sailors who perform them get several weeks' training in maritime law enforcement and a mix of high- and low-tech equipment. When *Thach*'s crew go looking for smugglers along the gulf's northern coast, they make good use of the electronic gear aboard the ship's helicopters: radar, infrared cameras, and night vision goggles. "Any kind of gee-whiz tool you want," said Aviation Warfare Systems Operator 1st Class (AW) Jim Toler. With its three full aircrews and two "birds," *Thach* can keep an air search going around the clock.

Just as only infantry can hold hostile ground, however, it takes sailors with decidedly unsophisticated equipment—sounding cords and grappling hooks—to inspect ships. Finding contraband means peering into dark cargo holds and deep ballast tanks. That means sending *Thach*'s sailors across the gulf's tepid water in rubber boats with nothing but sidearms, pepper spray, and good judgment to protect them. Plus bulletproof vests and the M-60 machine gun in the helicopter circling above.

Patrolling the busy gulf, thick with tankers and cargo vessels, is a full-time task that continually occupies several warships. *Thach*'s skipper, Cdr. Thomas D. Goodall, reckoned his crew would use most of their four months in the area to seek, stop, and inspect suspicious vessels.

Actual "bad guys" are needles in a haystack. "My sense is that 98 percent of these guys are real, honest businessmen," Goodall said. In four months of searching in summer 1998, the entire *Lincoln* battle group boarded 185 vessels and found only half a dozen smugglers.

Pierside in Bahrain for a few days of maintenance and resupply, several of *Thach*'s boarders dissected their jobs, describing the process and mulling over its various satisfactions. Some liked the speedboat rides best. Others simply relished the chance to get off their ship. Seaman Mike Hylton claimed to get his adrenaline rush during the actual boarding. "Climbing up, you don't know if the ladder's going to fall apart," said Hylton, who handled security on one of *Thach*'s two inspection parties.

A typical vBSS operation begins with a radio call to the target vessel. Where are you going? What are you carrying? The frigate's crew may send up its helicopters to see whether ships that claim to be empty are riding low in the water. Or they compare a ship's purported destination with its current speed and heading. If anything feels suspicious, they put the rubber boat in the water and order the foreign vessel to heave to and prepare to be boarded.

The vast majority of vessels comply. A few don't. In January 1997, the frigate *Reid* attempted to halt an oceangoing tug. Instead, the tug rammed the warship, cut its oil barge, and escaped. The collision punctured *Reid*'s hull, leaving an inch-wide, two-foot-long crack near the starboard bow. The frigate still sports a square steel patch about ten feet above the waterline—but also a deployment record for seizing contraband: 1.5 million gallons of embargo-busting oil and 650 tons of other illicit cargo.

After *Thach*'s calls bring the target vessel to a halt, a team of six to twelve sailors—depending on the size of the vessel and the anticipated belligerence of its crew—head over in their motorboat. Alongside, Hylton and a security teammate go up first, take a split-second look around, and post themselves fore and aft of the ladder. Like *Haly-burton*'s boarders, Hylton and his mates know the value of projecting authority and establishing control. But *Thach*'s boarding team eschews the all-black, special-ops look. For their missions, they don a clean set of standard issue, royal blue coveralls.

Following the security team aboard, the rest of the boarders spread out across the ship, rounding up the crew, checking the ship's seaworthiness, and collecting weapons. In a month of boardings, *Thach*'s sailors hadn't found anything more dangerous than a knife.

After the crew is marshaled in some comfortable, preferably air-conditioned space, the boarding team splits up. An engineman heads off to make sure the ballast tanks hold water and not smuggled oil. He also checks the engine room, no quick task. Commercial diesel engines can be massive—up to four stories tall. "You can barely see across some of these spaces," said Engineman 2d Class (SW) Daniel Wilbanks, a team leader.

Other team members head for the cargo holds. Most of the world's solid cargo is shipped in containers forty or eighty feet long. Gulf traffic is no different. The sailors often find the containers stacked five high or more, so they bring ropes and climbing harnesses. They tie into the top container and rappel down the colorful steel walls. Using bolt cutters, they sever the containers' lead-and-plastic seals. "They're not the easiest things to break, especially when you're hanging off the cargo, bouncing off them," said Gunner's Mate 2d Class (SW) Shawn Snyder. "Just doing five, your arms are dead, like Jell-O."

In the course of verifying dozens of manifests, Snyder and his company have picked through everything from agricultural tractors to forty-five-kilogram bags of black tea. "You don't think that's heavy—you try it," he said. If nothing is amiss, they reseal the containers and head home. Vessels that are found to be carrying illegal shipments are diverted to a gulf port, their cargo removed, and their fate determined by UN officials.

*Thach* left its Yokosuka, Japan, home port on 8 June and arrived in the gulf one month later. In three weeks of searching, the frigate's sailors hadn't uncovered a speck of contraband. They had, however, seen all manner of vessels: cockroach-infested hulks whose crews wore flip-flops, spanking new boats that could pass for floating hotels. "It's kind of fun to see how other ships live," one sailor said. "You realize you really have it good aboard your U.S. ship."

The inspectors get no additional pay and no respite from their regular shipboard jobs. It's not uncommon for them to return from a twelve-hour boarding mission just in time to stand watch. But sailors treasure any opportunity to get off their ship for a few hours. Besides, the extra duty offers the chance to learn new skills, see other ships, and, most of all, have some fun.

Even their failure to turn up any contraband hadn't dimmed the boarders' enthusiasm for their part-time job. "At times, you feel like a pirate, going across to someone else's ship," Snyder said. "It's a sailor thing, I guess."

---

Aboard the USS *Kauffman* in the Black Sea, June 1998

Several miles off the crushed-shell beaches of Romania's Black Sea shore, Chief Gunner's Mate Bob Cottone leaned from *Kauffman's* bridge wing to watch his sailors unlimber a small deck gun. His ears were plugged with yellow cylinders of foam. He was grinning hugely.

Ahead and astern of the guided missile frigate, a multinational flotilla of small warships was preparing to take potshots at an inflatable target floating a thousand yards away. "This is where it's at," Cottone declared. "This is the real navy."

The gunnery exercise that so delighted the gunner's mate was part of Exercise Cooperative Partner 1998. Another Partnership for Peace event, the exercise included ships, marines, and soldiers from Bulgaria, Romania, Georgia, France, Italy, Greece, and Turkey. The two-week schedule included maritime interdiction, explosive ordnance disposal, and humanitarian assistance. The curriculum would gird the participants for "peace enforcement" missions such as the ongoing NATO operation in Bosnia.

*Kauffman's* skipper found it all a bit amazing. "Ten years ago, if you were tasked to go into the Black Sea, you were headed into the Bear's den," said Cdr. George J. Karol III, a well-built man the crew was wont to call "Gorgeous George."

Out on the narrow starboard deck, Sonar Technician (Surface) 2d Class (SW) Joe Stump belted himself into one of the frigate's twenty-five-millimeter Bushmaster deck cannons. Firing such weapons isn't in the sonar tech job description, but Stump had volunteered for gunnery school and had returned fully qualified for the job.

His target floated a mile to starboard: a red ball the size of a Volkswagen Beetle. Crews call it the "killer tomato." Stump waited as the line of ships passed by, firing all manner of small-bore weapons at the ball. It was still floating when *Kauffman* pulled abreast.

An automatic weapon akin to an eight-foot machine gun, the Bushmaster rests on an electrically powered mount. The gunner swings the barrel into position with switches that control elevation and rotation. Yet this electrical assistance doesn't make shooting easy. The tracer rounds don't fly laser-straight. Over a twenty-five-hundred-yard range, their vague spirals add up to a lot of slop.

The sonar tech sighted down the barrel. Squeezing the trigger, he unleashed earsplitting four-shell salvos—*pow-pow-pow-pow, pow-pow-pow-pow*. Geysers erupted around the distant target. With corrections after each burst, Stump soon began putting the one-pound shells on target. The tomato began to deflate.

Karol nodded his approval with a tight movement of his jaw. An exacting commander, *Kauffman's* skipper had sharp words for sailors whose performance he deemed lacking. But polished brass junction boxes gleamed in the passageways, and the ship's spaces were spotless—bellwethers of the crew's pride in their vessel and faith in their captain.

Command at sea is ever one of the loneliest of jobs, and 1998 put a lot of pressure on Karol. He commanded his warship in a year of personnel shortages. Predeployment inspections seemed endless. The exigencies of world politics yanked his ship around on a two-week chain. But the skipper was as relaxed in his stateroom as he was stern on the bridge. He ticked off a long list of rewards accorded the skipper of "the navy's finest ship."

"The fun part is seeing young men come from the Midwest without any education, and then signing, as I did this morning, four diplomas for having completed a college course at sea," Karol said. "It's seeing a young man up to his ass in dirt because I gave him the parts to fix his diesel. It's standing up on the bridge, tossing a smoke flare overboard, yelling at the top of your lungs, 'man overboard, starboard side,' and the guy in the combat information center, who doesn't know anything except that there's a man overboard, calls in the helo from five miles away, and it flares out over the smoke and there's a guy in the door ready to jump in the water."

Karol evinced satisfaction with his crew's military prowess, but took pleasure in their human gestures as well—particularly in "seeing the guys engaging with people less fortunate than they are," Karol said.

A few days previously, a few dozen *Kauffman* sailors and airmen devoted a sunny liberty morning to an orphanage in the shabby port of Constanta. Home to some fifty HIV-positive children, the Casa Speranta orphanage consists of one khaki-colored concrete building, a playground, and a small grassy yard. The sailors brought paint, brushes, and a will to work. In a few hours they had Casa Speranta as shipshape as their frigate. "If for whatever reason my kids wound up in someplace like this, I'd want people to spend time with them," said Aviation Electronics Technician 1st Class (AW) Ken Deaton, a father of two.

The home's director, a Texas native named Marolen Mullinax, declared her undying gratitude. "This place is kept together with masking tape, chewing gum, and the workforce of the navy," she said.

The orphanage has received much tender loving care from American service members who come through the Black Sea area, largely because reserve Cdr. Robert Tate steers them toward Mullinax. "We can do more than shoot guns and missiles. We can also work with people, and what better way to show the flag in a positive way," the American naval attaché said.

"If nothing else, that is what the legacy of this deployment is going to be," Karol said. "That is what people are going to remember."

---

Aboard the USS *Doyle* off Chile, September 1998

Ruffled seas were running a few feet high and the mountains of the Chilean coast were barely visible to starboard as the frigate *Doyle* moved up to lead a flotilla of American and Chilean vessels. The U.S. ships had already come halfway around South America on the annual deployment called Unitas.

For this exercise, the frigate would be point guard for a screen around the tank landing ship *La Moure County.* The convoy would protect the troop transport during a sprint through an imaginary choke point.

On the frigate's bridge, Lt. Cdr. Ivan Aguilar conned his gray warship into position ahead of a pair of Chilean destroyers. There was no nervousness in the officer's calm commands, but his accented speech hinted at his foreign birth. Indeed, Aguilar was an officer in the Colombian navy. His place on the American bridge was unusual but hardly unique—hundreds of foreign officers have served yearlong tours under the Stars and Stripes.

Such exchanges represent another kind of "engagement," but serve a tactical purpose as well. In future coalition operations, navy officials say, it will be invaluable for officers of other navies to have firsthand experience with American operational procedures.

Aguilar's Colombian superiors value that knowledge but also have other designs on his invaluable expertise. After his tour of duty aboard *Doyle,* Aguilar will help change his country's naval culture.

Trained as an engineer, Aguilar had fifteen years of sea service under his belt, but until he boarded *Doyle,* he had spent almost none of it on the bridge. Colombian midshipmen learn to run engines or fight ships—rarely both. American surface warriors, by contrast, are generalists who learn something of the bridge, the engine room, the combat center, the supply department, and so on. Aguilar will be the first of Colombia's American-style surface warriors. "It's opening up a new frontier for the engineers behind me, fifty or sixty guys," he said.

The Colombian had also found a new use for his native tongue: hosting Latin American officers who visited *Doyle* as it slowly circled South America. The frigate was participating in the navy's longest-running annual exercise. For thirty-nine years, U.S. naval squadrons have circumnavigated the continent on journeys that are part serious training, part goodwill tour, part get-to-know-you networking.

The proportions have varied from one year to the next. Many sailors fondly recall their Unitas cruises, recounting tales of days and nights on Latin beaches, liberty languorously savored between a slow samba of naval exercises. The whirl of official and unofficial parties have led to its reputation as the navy's premier "cocktail cruise."

Three months into *Doyle's* deployment, the ship's public-address system told a different story. "This is turning into the trotting tour of South America," Cdr. Earle S. Yerger told his crew as *Doyle* headed for sea after a one-night pit stop in southern Chile's Talcahuano Harbor. With ten countries, eleven exercises, and twenty port visits squeezed into the cruise, there hadn't been much time to lie around.

"A lot of people think this is the liberty cruise to get, but in the Med you're pulling into Palma for a week. Here we're pulling in for one or two days," said Aviation Warfare Systems Operator (AW) 2nd Class Chuck Harders. "It's been a lot more work than people thought it was going to be, a lot more time on the water."

Still, the helicopter crewman treasured the memory of volcanoes, icebergs, and seals spotted off the continent's frozen southern tip. "And the ports are good. Nothing wrong with twenty-five- or fifty-cent beers," he said.

The spring air held a tang of eucalyptus and naval pomp as Destroyer Squadron Thirty-two pulled into Talcahuano on 16 September. Besides the frigate and troop transport, the unit included a destroyer, *Moosbrugger,* and the attack submarine *Boston.*

A Chilean brass band thumped out "Anchors Aweigh" as *Doyle's* sailors made the frigate fast to the cobblestone pier. On the bridge, the mess specialists laid out cheesecake and Swedish meatballs for the foreign brass who would come aboard during the stop.

But there was to be little liberty on this overnight port call. On arrival, some crew members broke out paint rollers and began to touch up the ship's hull. Others began to load the huge pile of supplies waiting on the pier. On *Moosbrugger,* American and Chilean officers cemented plans for the coming week. It was a typical stop for the 1998 version of Unitas.

"You get off the ship and the guys have five hours to find the closest beer joint," said Chief Aviation Electronics Technician (AW) Craig Gaines.

Early the next morning, *Doyle* shoved off from the pier and followed several Chilean warships out of the harbor. Over the shipboard loudspeaker system—the "1MC"—Yerger laid out a rapid-fire schedule for the two days ahead. During their transit north to the Chilean naval headquarters at Valparaiso, the combined forces would hunt down the submarine *Boston,* take gunnery practice at the frigate's jet-powered drones, defend against a trio of Chilean fighter jets, and more. First up: antisubmarine warfare. "We're going to try to spank the *Boston* today," Yerger said.

It was to be a full day, fuller than the crew knew. As *Doyle* worked to find the sub, Yerger announced that the ship had been struck by a missile, and then a mine. The damage control drill tested the crew's ability to save their ship in combat, pushing their skills to the limit as other shipmates kept up the pursuit of the sub.

Yerger wanted to make sure the busy schedule wasn't dulling his crew's fire-fighting skills. Even war-fighting abilities can suffer, despite Unitas's never-ending exercises, because the U.S. Navy's sophisticated sailors are restricted for five months to the more basic tactics of the South American navies. Local pride can also get in the way of useful practice. Helicopter crewman Harder was eager for the rare opportunity to hunt foreign diesel submarines but found that some of the Unitas navies weren't playing by the rules, which insist the subs keep moving. "It's all pride," the helicopter sensor operator said. "If they're on battery sitting on the bottom, I'm not going to get them."

Still, there was plenty of opportunity for basic military training, such as shooting at the stubby-winged, jet-powered drones embarked aboard *Doyle.*

In this exercise the drones were operated by Fleet Composite Squadron Six, a Dam Neck, Virginia–based squadron that has for decades sent a detachment along with the ships of the Unitas cruise. The stars of the modern VC-6 hangar are "Big Orange," thirteen-foot drones that resemble cruise missiles painted for Halloween. They fly about forty minutes on a tank of JP-5 jet fuel. Crews can mount nose reflectors to return fighter jet–sized radar signatures, or tape the aircrafts' metal seams to produce blips the size of cruise missiles.

Ships' gunners don't need to destroy the $300,000 drones to get good practice; their computer-guided guns can be programmed to fire behind the expensive aircraft. Over the years, drone crews have lost a few birds to the wayward shells of South American gunners. Later explanations about malfunctioning offsets didn't completely dispel speculation that the gunners simply wanted to blast something out of the sky.

Halfway to Valparaiso, the drone crew launched a Big Orange cylinder from *Doyle*'s flight deck. With a heart-stopping blast from its rocket booster, the drone leapt from the ship and streaked away to invisibility. In seconds, the unmanned aircraft accelerated to five hundred miles per hour. Fifteen hundred feet above the swelling Pacific, the jet-propelled target rolled toward the line of ships, whose gunners waited with itchy fingers. In the frigate's hangar, Gaines twisted a pair of dials, steering the drone toward *Doyle* as if drawing on an Etch-a-Sketch.

Amidships, the frigate's radar-guided, remote-controlled seventy-six-millimeter gun came alive. Its barrel began tracking, jerking up and down to compensate for the ship's roll. Coolant water poured from the rifled metal tube like a predator drooling after its prey. A salvo of ten rapid-fire rounds ripped from the gun, deafening onlookers. Foot-long brass cartridges spilled onto the deck.

"We'll go anywhere to do this," said Lt. Cdr. Jeff Hamman, the drone detachment's officer in charge. "Guam, the gulf, the Med."

## 2. THE CARRIERS

Aboard the USS *Abraham Lincoln* in the Persian Gulf, July 1998

The fighter pilot headed back to the aircraft carrier, another uneventful patrol over southern Iraq almost complete. In moments, his F-14 Tomcat would cross *Lincoln*'s fantail, its tail hook questing for the four cables that stretched across the gently pitching flight deck. If the hook caught a wire—its target was number three—the thick steel cable would bring the plane to a halt in two seconds of neck-snapping deceleration.

Several decks below the tiny runway, a quartet of sailors eyed a leaking hydraulic cylinder and prayed that just this once the Tomcat's landing would be a few feet shy of perfect.

A minute earlier, Aviation Boatswain's Mate 1st Class (AW) Dennis Prazeau had opened a check valve on the giant machine that controlled the third cable and found a thin trickle of ethylene glycol—a dangerous sign. If too much of the green liquid had escaped, the hydraulic brake would not stop the Tomcat before it plunged over the side of the *Lincoln*.

Prazeau's supervisor, Chief Aviation Boatswain's Mate (AW/SW) Mike Brown, hustled over for a look. Eighteen years of experience told him repairs could wait—if none of the three remaining aircraft caught the number three wire.

The sailors held their breath, listening through their headphones as a shipmate on the fantail called out the fighter's approach. "Groove . . . short . . . ramp!"

Thunder boomed through the aft bulkhead. An arresting cable engine whined in the next space. The Tomcat had flown in two feet too low, catching the number two wire. Belowdecks, the number three crew sweated in 103-degree heat. As the approach calls started again, they braced for the next landing. Again, a muted eruption from the second engine. Another strike fighter, an F/A-18 Hornet, had undershot its landing.

The sailors exchanged hopeful looks as the approach calls began a third time. An explosion of noise welled from engine number four: a bang and a whir beyond the forward bulkhead. The last Tomcat had come in high.

The crew—and the carrier—had lucked out. Quickly, the sailors began to dismantle the balky engine, racing the clock against next morning's flight operations.

The repairs forced yet another sleepless night for the ABEs, the navy designation for the aviation boatswain's mates who operate and maintain the carrier's launch and recovery equipment. It's a tough job, but most who do it carry themselves with tremendous pride. "The aviators may get the glory," the ABEs like to say, "but not a one flies on or off this boat without us."

With a crowd of family, friends, and onlookers waving from the pier, *Lincoln* left its home port of Everett, Washington, in June 1998, sailing down Puget Sound toward the Pacific Ocean. Its commute to work, including stops in San Diego and Hong Kong, took six weeks.

On 23 July, the carrier passed through the Strait of Hormuz, the narrow body that connects the Indian Ocean to the Persian Gulf. Its crew quickly set to work. Some of the carrier's aircraft patrolled the skies over southern Iraq, enforcing the United Nations–mandated no-fly zone. Others scanned the seas, helping *Thach* and other allied vessels with their intercept-and-board operations. For old hands, the missions were all too familiar. Over the long summer, Lt. Brian Burke spent hours in the sky above Iraq's marshes and deserts. Through his bubble canopy, the Hornet pilot often spotted the detritus of Operation Desert

Storm. The years had not yet filled the bomb craters, nor buried the twisted carcasses of tanks and trucks. Burke, who had watched the Gulf War's televised images in a Naval Academy dorm room, found the situation quite eerie. "It's hard to believe that eight or nine years later, we're still out here," he said.

His was a common sentiment aboard the carrier. This was *Lincoln's* third gulf cruise in five years. Iraq's provocations had continued, and so had U.S. leaders' reliance on the navy's twelve aircraft carriers for on-call military force.

Stretching 1,092 feet from stem to stern, the *Nimitz*-class carriers are the largest warships ever built. Their enormous flat-bottomed hulls displace ninety thousand tons. Measuring four-and-one-half acres, their flight decks are at once vast seagoing platforms and postage-stamp airfields. Powered by a pair of nuclear reactors, the vessels can travel far faster than the officially given "thirty-plus knots." Their unrefueled range is measured not in miles but decades. When *Nimitz* pulled into a Virginia shipyard for new reactor cores in May 1998, it was the twenty-three-year-old ship's first nuclear "fill-up."

Combined with midair refueling techniques, this mobility allows navy aircraft to operate almost anywhere in the world. Standing on the cramped bridge of the carrier *Dwight D. Eisenhower,* Capt. Greg Brown surveyed a flight deck abuzz with sailors and deadly flying machines. "I would think nothing of launching an air strike over St. Louis," the skipper declared. At the time, *Ike* was off the Virginia coast, eight hundred miles east of Missouri.

The ships themselves are armed only lightly: four missile launchers to shoot down enemy aircraft, and three or four Gatling-style guns to take out incoming missiles. Their air wings are their swords and shields. For its 1998 deployment to the Persian Gulf, *Lincoln* embarked the seventy-three aircraft of Carrier Air Wing Fourteen.

The wing included about four dozen strike fighters—thirty-six F/A-18 Hornets and thirteen F-14 Tomcats—equipped to attack targets on land, in the air, and at sea. On strike missions, the fighters are usually accompanied by one of the wing's four EA-6B Prowlers, electronic shield bearers that carry jamming equipment to confuse enemy radar stations and radar-tracking missiles to knock them out.

On this trip, *Lincoln* brought along eight S-3B Vikings for protection against enemy ships and subs. These twin-jets with comically large tails usually carry missiles, mines, bombs, and torpedoes. Two other S-3s, stuffed with electronic eavesdroppers and redesignated ES-3 Shadows, scooped up and analyzed enemy communications.

Four propeller-driven E-2C Hawkeyes gave *Lincoln* its long-range eyes and ears, keeping tabs on friend and foe alike with saucer-shaped dorsal radars. A pair of C-2A Greyhounds—the Hawkeye's close cousins—flew thousands of passengers and parts on and off the ship. They also flew most of the mail, which made them the crew's favorite aircraft, hands-down. Rounding out the air wing were four Seahawk helicopters to handle antisubmarine and search-and-rescue operations.

This vast airborne armada required a small oceangoing metropolis to keep it in fighting trim. Each squadron had at least a dozen officer and enlisted fliers: pilots, navigators, sensor operators, aircrew. And for every aviator there were ten or more deckbound maintainers: mechanics, machinists, technicians, and electricians. In all, the ten squadrons brought more than two thousand sailors and airmen aboard when the carrier deployed.

Yet, big as it was, the air wing was smaller than *Lincoln's* own company. Nearly three thousand sailors strong, the crew drove the ship, cooked the meals, husbanded the supplies, and generally supported the air wing in uncountable ways. The list of jobs ran literally from A to Z: airframers, barbers, cryptologists, dentists, electricians, firefighters, gunners, hospitalmen, intercom techs, journalists, legal specialists, munitions experts, network managers, optical grinders, postal clerks, quartermasters, reactor technicians, storekeepers, torpedomen, upholsterers, weather forecasters, x-ray technicians, yeomen, zone inspectors, and hundreds more.

Charged with the care of two nuclear reactors, the reactor department alone employed more than four hundred sailors: machinists, electricians, electronics techs, and enginemen, plus yeomen to handle the paperwork. The reactors turn the four giant propellers, provide steam for the catapults, and generate electricity for a ship whose power needs, for starters, include thirty thousand light bulbs. The reactors require large volumes of pure water for cooling, so the department also handles the ship's desalinization needs. On an average day, the ship uses four hundred thousand gallons of fresh water for cooling, cooking, cleaning, showers, laundry, aircraft washes, and endless other needs.

A corps of chaplains served the spiritual needs of the crew—and hundreds more souls in the ships of the associated battle group. The battle group chaplain, Lt. Jim West, compared himself to the traveling preachers of the Old West. "When the U.S. was being settled and there weren't enough chaplains to go around, they put you on a horse with a saddlebag," he said. "Instead of a horse, I have a small boat and a helo." The deployment was the chaplain's first, although he had been a commissioned officer for more than five years. "They told me that eventually I'd get a ship. They just didn't tell me how many," he said.

For those who might go astray, there was the brig—now available for male or female miscreants. *Lincoln,* which has carried mixed-gender crews for several years, sailed in 1998 with female guards for the first time. "The co's general idea is that it's not fair for male prisoners to face the brig, while females only get restriction," said Aviation Electronics Technician 2d Class Lance Hunziker, a guard instructor and navy reservist. "Three days' bread and water really tends to bring someone around."

Navy regulations require female guards for female prisoners during bathroom breaks, showers, and strip searches. So in April, as the crew prepared for deployment, Hunziker came aboard the ship to train a dozen women in guard techniques. On bright blue exercise mats set amid the hangar bay's fighter planes and bomb racks, the guards-to-be practiced the fine art of subduing rowdies with precisely applied pain. "If they're chasing you, you give them knuckles to the rib. That's my favorite one," said Mess Specialist 3d Class Sherl Craft.

Craft and the others had already spent two weeks ashore for special training in the rules and regulations on the treatment of prisoners. By the time it sailed, *Lincoln* had enough qualified women to staff a confinement cell. The volunteers would get a call only if a female sailor got into major trouble, which had happened three times in three years,

Hunziker said. In that time, about forty-five men were similarly disciplined.

Operations Specialist 3d Class Brook Desrosiers said she volunteered to learn a new skill, see a different kind of work, and participate in something just a bit historic. "We're the first ones, and that's pretty cool," said Desrosiers. "And you can use some of these in the real world if you get into trouble."

The medical department also included a few new specialists for the cruise. An aviation optometrist came aboard for the deployment, and a psychologist and a physical therapist began two-year tours aboard *Lincoln*. Navy officials authorized the groundbreaking assignments in hopes that on-scene experts would cut down on costly medical evacuations. At midsummer, all three specialists said it seemed to be working.

Flat on his back in the hospital ward, Dental Technician 3d Class Mateo Hernandez grimaced as Lt. Cdr. Scott R. Jonson flexed his right knee upward, then lowered it to the mattress. Hernandez had torn some connective tissue during a "field day"—an all-hands ship-cleaning session—and after two weeks in a leg brace was working to regain his knee's range and strength. Without Jonson aboard, Hernandez would have been flown off to a shore facility. "You do the math as far as the lost work hours, the travel costs, and the rest, and it's much more efficient, effective, and advantageous for us to come to the fleet than for the fleet to come to us," the physical therapist said.

Psychologist Lt. Brian Hershey saw himself less as a therapist than a gatekeeper, a local mental health professional to answer the question: Does this guy have a major problem that we can work with here, or do we need to send him off? "We don't generally do long-term treatment. We basically do evaluations," Hershey said.

A former enlisted marine and civilian policeman, Hershey became a psychologist after working with cops who had been involved in shootings and other high-stress situations. Since coming aboard in May, he had seen some sixty sailors, mostly referrals from the ship's doctors and chaplains. "You don't want someone checking an aircraft who's really upset about something," Hershey said.

An aircraft carrier might seem a natural place for an aviation optometrist, but Lt. Cdr. Mitch Brown waited impatiently a decade for the naval medical community to agree. "Why join the navy if you're not going to do something like this?" Brown said. "Of course, it's terrible timing. For ten years, I was single. Now I'm married and my first kid will be born while I'm under way."

The eye business was booming. The ship's optician, Hospitalman 2d Class Eric Johnson, had already ground out three hundred pairs of glasses—five or six times as many as on *Lincoln's* last cruise. With appointments booked nearly a week in advance, Brown expected to top a thousand by deployment's end. About 30 percent were emergencies—chemical spills, metallic particles caught in eyes, and so on— but the rest were routine checkups. "I figured, might as well take advantage of this. It's been four years since I had one," said Aviation Structural Mechanic (Safety Equipment) 1st Class Paul Jung, waiting for his pupils to dilate under the influence of Brown's eyedrops.

Like the others, Jonson was adjusting to working a hemisphere removed from mail-order catalogs. "In the U.S., you can pick up the phone and you can call folks, and you can arrange things," the physical therapist said. "At sea, it's very difficult to coordinate with the equipment companies."

Specialists aside, the preeminent medical problem faced by *Lincoln's* crew was heat stress. They had the misfortune to arrive during the hottest summer in three decades. On the greasy tar of the flight deck, where blasting jet engines sent rivers of boiling air down the decks, the heat index—air and surface temperatures and humidity— easily reached 140 degrees. The flight deck workers, clad for safety in long-sleeve turtlenecks, life vests, helmets, and goggles, returned belowdecks soaked with sweat.

"Every time I hear 'medical emergency, medical emergency,' I run to the phone to see if it's one of our guys," said pilot Burke, who oversaw the flight line maintainers for his squadron, the VFA-113 Stingers. "It's brutal out there. There's no shelter. I have no idea how they do it. They're superhuman. I'm just flying over the desert, but they're the guys who are making the sacrifice."

Even when the gulf weather isn't breaking meteorological records, heat is an omnipresent enemy. The summer air averages 110 degrees, and nightfall brings not relief but humidity. "It is more than just proximity to the equator," the ship's newspaper—*Penny Press*—wrote one day. "Dry air heats up as it passes over the desert of Saudi Arabia and comes up from the south and west. It warms as it passes through the mountains of Iran from the north. The Gulf is a basin where the sea and air are relatively still, and it holds that heat in." The only breezes drift in from the northwest, wafting down Iraq's Tigris and Euphrates River valleys. Even the seawater is ninety-plus degrees, and swimming in its brine is like bathing in uncongealed gelatin.

Keeping hydrated becomes a way of life where the sun can cause heat stroke and muscle cramps in hours. Everyone who went out on the carrier's sweltering deck was issued a backpack canteen—a "CamelBack"—and ordered to sip liberally. Still, more than a dozen *Lincoln* crew members received medical attention for heat-related problems in the first few weeks of the gulf cruise. One went down in a fetal position with dehydration-induced muscle cramps.

It takes most people eight to ten miserable days to get used to the heat and to drinking massive amounts of water. No one wants to eat much, which is why Ens. Jennifer Blakeslee stocked her tiny freezer with flavored ice pops. The air transfer officer, Blakeslee was in charge of moving cargo and passengers on and off the ship. Her cramped little office was one of the main passages to the flight deck. "I'm like the mom, always checking to see if everybody's got Camelbaks, see if they're eating," she said. "It's sugar, so it's not the best, but it's cold and at least it's something."

The canteens were popular as well with those who toiled in the un-air-conditioned spaces belowdecks. Standing watch by a massive arresting gear piston, Aviation Boatswain's Mate 3d Class Chris Semanko worked in noise and sweat to bring twenty-ton aircraft to a halt above his head. "Some days I'll go through four of these," Semanko said, biting down on the tube that ran from his 70-ounce canteen.

Clad in the green turtlenecks of their trade, Semanko and his fellow "gear dogs" risked death and dismemberment a dozen ways to give the navy its airborne punch. Gear dogs creep beneath screaming jets to hook them into the catapults, or wait, unflinching, by cables that can snap under the impact of a speeding tail hook.

But like the pilots, the aviation boatswain's mates live with torpor sandwiched between frenzy. Between landing cycles, the gear dogs grab catnaps, sprawling on the linoleum floors by the cable engines. No one begrudges the greenshirts their daylight rack time. Flight operations can last eighteen hours a day, forcing the ABEs to wait until the wee hours to fix their vital machines. "We try to get them to bed," said Chief Brown, the arresting gear machine supervisor. "But if it's something major, we keep them right here."

It would have helped if the arresting gear watch had been fully manned, but like the rest of the ship—and the navy—the team was somewhat short of sailors. *Lincoln's* ABES compensated by cross training, making sure everyone could fill every slot. "These guys can do just about anything," Brown said.

The day after Prazeau and his team spent the night repairing the leaking arresting gear engine cylinder, *Lincoln's* number three wire was in action. Around 4:00 P.M., the first Hornet of the afternoon roared in along the starboard beam. The strike fighter banked hard across the carrier's bow and circled aft to land. Lowering tail hook and landing gear, the pilot steered into "the groove," the invisible path that begins a mile behind the giant ship and ends at its arresting cables.

Getting the fast jet onto the carrier's tiny runway requires control of mind, muscle, and machinery in the cockpit and on the ship. The gear dogs went to work.

On a cramped catwalk by the fantail, the arresting officer and an aviation boatswain's mate peered at the incoming aircraft. "Sir, Hornet battery," the deck edge operator cried. Like everyone else on the flight deck, he wore goggles and skull protector, an inflatable life vest, and a colored turtleneck. The ABE's was green. "Hornet battery," confirmed the officer. He wore a plane handler's yellow shirt.

Belowdeck, four teams of greenshirts pressed rubber-sheathed buttons, setting their arresting gear engines for the coming impact. *Lincoln* has one engine for each wire, and one for the thick nylon net that can be raised when a damaged plane cannot make an arrested landing.

The engines are essentially hydraulic shock absorbers connected to immense block and tackles. Like an angler's thumb on a reel of fishing line, the machine allows the wire to run when hooked—and stops it before the aircraft falls off the flight deck. They are adjusted before each landing so that a relatively light Hornet gets the same 340-foot runout as a heavy Tomcat. This minimizes the stress on airframes and arresting gear, extending their lives.

There's another reason for the caution. Every "trap" is haunted by the specter of a broken wire. A tail hook can snap the cable, transforming it into a pair of fifty-foot whipsaws. Such accidents are extremely rare but can have horrific results: decapitation or dismemberment for the firefighters, mechanics, chock-and-chain runners, and other flight deck workers.

At the mere mention of the possibility, the color drained from Brown's face. "I've been in eighteen years and only seen it once," he said, looking at the steel ceiling, "and if it never happens again, that'll be too soon."

As a precaution, the ABEs replace the cables frequently. The majority of each wire—several hundred feet—is "engine cable," measuring one and seven-sixteenths inches thick. The gear dogs swap it out every two thousand traps in a process that takes eight hours.

The hundred-foot sections that cross the deck are slightly thinner, at one and three-eighths inches. But these "cross-deck pendants" are built to withstand 188,000 pounds of pressure—and are never allowed to take more than a hundred traps before being tossed overboard.

Even the engine rooms are dangerous. Valves and cams have been known to blow—right through bulkheads. Between each landing the operators adjust the heavy machinery, placing their hands in dangerous proximity to its moving parts. They rely on the deck edge operator's approach calls to withdraw before a trap sets the giant block and tackle in furious motion.

When the Hornet roared over the fantail, the arresting officer and deck edge operator ducked to avoid the shower of cinders kicked up by its jet engines. As the landing gear struck the deck, its pilot threw the throttle wide open against the possibility of "boltering"—missing all four wires. The hook grabbed the number three wire, which dragged the fighter to a halt fifteen yards from the edge. Down in the engine room, the impact sent a loud boom echoing through the space. Ship scuttlebutt had it that sound technicians for the movie *Star Wars* used a recording of the noise to accompany the explosion of the Death Star.

A greenshirt ran in front of the roaring aircraft, which was still straining at its steel leash. The sailor raised and crossed his wrists, signaling the pilot to cut the engines, raise the hook, and clear the landing area. As the Hornet taxied away, the ABE signaled to the deck edge operator, more than a football field's length away.

The deck edge operator stomped on a pedal, and the number three engine began to reel the wire in, sending the thick cable skittering across the flight deck. Yet another greenshirt stepped in with a four-foot iron bar to keep the cable on track as it sprang back into place. By the fantail, the deck edge greenshirt was calling the approach for the next jet, now just forty-five seconds away.

For *Lincoln's* ABEs, landing the planes is only half of the work. The other half takes place forward, where the greenshirts use the ship's four catapults to fling its aircraft aloft. Immensely powerful, the catapults can accelerate a thirty-ton aircraft to more than 150 mph in seconds.

A "cat shot" is a marvel of teamwork. It takes more than a dozen greenshirts, plane handlers, ordnancemen, and others to get a bird into the air. Amid the sound and fury of the flight deck, they work largely with hand signals. The whine of jet engines, the thrum of turboprops, and the keening of auxiliary generators overwhelm human voices.

The first morning in August brought typical gulf weather: ninety hazy degrees by 9:00 A.M. The flight deck had been busy for hours, preparing to launch the day's first wave of aircraft.

A voice boomed from the loudspeakers mounted on the "island," the starboard-side superstructure that is bridge, control tower, admiral's observation deck, and antenna platform. "Heads up in the bow, heads up in the waist. Launching aircraft off catapults one, two, and three. Shoot 'em up, shoot 'em up!" the voice cried.

The crew of number three, the inner waist cat, fired one Hornet aloft, sending it hurtling from the port deck edge. The entire ninety-thousand-ton ship shuddered. Not even a Tomcat smacking into the deck at the three wire imparts as much force as a cat shot. A second Hornet taxied into place. Walking alongside the rumbling fighter jet, Airman Gary Harrison lifted a black, shoebox-sized device toward the cockpit. White digits on its face showed "42000," the plane's takeoff weight in pounds.

Receiving a confirming thumbs-up from the pilot, the weight-board operator trotted over to show the weight to the jet-blast deflector operator, Aviation Boatswain's Mate Airman Ronnie Kennedy. Perched on the greasy nonskid lip of an open hatch on the flight deck, Kennedy passed the word to the catapult control room below.

In a hot little space dominated by pipes, dials, and controls, Aviation Boatswain's Mate 2d Class Todd Gray conferred by microphone with the catapult officer and then carefully punched a steam pressure order into the system. Too much steam, and the powerful catapult could rip the aircraft's nosewheels off. Too little, and the plane would simply roll off the bow and plummet into the ocean.

On deck, the Hornet swung toward the rear end of the catapult. A yellow-shirted "cat spotter" stood astride the catapult's three-inch-wide track, motioning the jet forward with precise gestures. Once the jet was properly lined up, the pilot would lower its tow bar into the catapult's grip. The trick was getting the aircraft lined up with the track, and the bar directly above the insertion point.

Seated in the cockpit, pilots are directly above their nosewheels and cannot see to steer this last little way. A greenshirt must crabwalk under the moving jet to guide the plane into position.

Keeping one hand on the nosewheel strut for balance, Aviation Boatswain's Mate 2d Class Joseph Breaux scuttled sideways as the Hornet crept forward. He gestured to the cat spotter, who relayed the signal to the pilot. The jet inched forward. Its wheels rolled up and over the catapult shuttle, the metal box that would pull the plane forward. The topside petty officer signaled again. The pilot set his brakes and lowered the tow bar into the shuttle's throat.

Another greenshirt, Airman Mike Nelson, ducked beneath the

fighter and inserted a holdback bar into a pincers behind the nose-wheel strut. Locked into the deck, the bar would keep the plane on deck while the jet's engines revved up to takeoff power.

Behind the aircraft, a trio of giant metal panels ascended at Kennedy's command. Lifted on hydraulic pistons, the jet-blast deflectors rose out of the deck to sixty-degree angles. The seawater-cooled deflectors would keep the fourteen-hundred-degree exhaust from blowing people and machines off the flight deck.

Now halfway through the launch process, the greenshirts sprinted away from the fighter jet, following curved paths to avoid engine intakes and exhaust pipes. A pair of red-shirted ordnancemen approached to arm the air-to-air missiles on each wingtip. In a few seconds, the Sidewinders were live, ready to shoot down anything that emitted heat.

At a sign from the safety officer, Breaux returned to the nosewheel to check the tow bar's descent into the shuttle. Throwing his arms in a wide circle, he signaled the panel operator to draw the shuttle forward a few inches. Under the tension, the nosewheel strut compressed. The Hornet squatted like a runner at the starting line.

There are few jobs anywhere more hazardous than Breaux's. Were the holdback mechanism to fail, the twenty-one-ton aircraft would run over the petty officer, maul him with an external fuel tank, and scorch him with blazing-hot exhaust. A moment's inattention, and he could be sucked into a jet or pureed by propellers. After a final check, Breaux emerged from below the Hornet, giving the intakes a wide berth and the catapult officer a thumbs-up.

The "shooter"—carrier lingo for catapult officer—now took control, shaking two fingers at the sky. On the shooter's signal, the pilot shoved his throttles forward, bringing the engine's roar to an earsplitting scream. Fifty feet away, on the lowered catwalk girding the flight deck, Aviation Boatswain's Mate 1st Class Javier Medina pressed the "military power" button on a gray steel box. The pilot rotated the control stick, flapping the Hornet's ailerons and elevators to give everyone a last chance to find problems. Satisfied, he snapped a salute to the catapult officer and passed control of the process back to the deck crew.

The shooter returned the pilot's salute, peering into the cockpit to confirm that the pilot had leaned back on the headrest and taken his hands off the stick. The Hornet's digital controls would handle the plane in the first seconds of flight.

Out on the catwalk, Medina—the deck edge operator—pushed the "final ready" button and held up both hands. A trio of green-shirted safety observers held up their thumbs: blast deflectors up, power at full, and no one under the aircraft—time to fly. Squatting down, the shooter touched the deck and pointed down the track.

Medina made his own quick safety scan, counting the upraised thumbs. The deck edge operator pushed a pair of buttons beside his panel's green lights and raised his hands once more.

In a flash, steam rushed from the reservoirs and pounded the catapult pistons, breaking the grip of the holdback bar. Propelled by pent-up steam and blazing jet fuel, the fighter howled down the deck. Sailors along the track turned away from the scorching exhaust.

In 310 feet and two seconds, the jet accelerated to 150 mph, then soared free as the shuttle halted at the deck's edge. A visceral *whump* shook the immense ship. Steam vented from the piston chamber, boiled from the shuttle track. Before the white clouds melted away, Aviation Boatswain's Mate 2d Class Derrick Reeves was pulling the deflectors down, clearing the way for the next Hornet.

On a typical day, *Lincoln*'s air wing and crew repeat the dangerous, intricate process of launching and landing ninety or more times. "They can't get off the ship without us," Gray said later. "We're why the air wing does so good."

The ABEs will tell you that the best part of the movie *Top Gun* is the opening credits, which set the launch and recovery of aircraft to rock music. Their jobs are vital—and something few care to try. When *Lincoln*'s command master chief wanted to give a yeoman first class a quick lesson in "no whining," he dragged the sailor from his air-conditioned office into one of the arresting gear engine rooms, where they sat and sweated for fifteen minutes—long enough for the yeoman to get the point.

"I tell these guys, 'Even if you don't get much recognition, you are respected, because no one would do your job,'" Breaux said. Gray put it another way. "My job's a little too dangerous for anybody else," he said with a wolfish grin.

---

Aboard the USS *Independence,* West of Hawaii, July 1998

The aircraft carrier surged eastward at twenty-five knots, its freshly painted bow slicing through the azure seas. On the horizon, a pencil-thin wreath of clouds foretold smooth sailing. Pearl Harbor was just a day's steaming distant.

At 2:18 P.M., a twin-prop early warning plane with a big dorsal radar touched down to a noisy arrival on the flight deck. Like all carrier landings, it was hazardous. Like most, it went flawlessly. Unlike *Indy*'s previous half-million traps, however, this one was the last.

The E-2C Hawkeye taxied to an empty spot forward of the island, swung its nose toward the bow, and shut down, leaving an unaccustomed stillness on the flight deck. Its four-man crew climbed out. Scattered applause rose and died out, swallowed by the silence. None of the suddenly idled flight deck crew, standing around in headgear and colorful float coats, knew whether to laugh, clap, or cry.

"We're actually having a pretty sad day here," said Capt. Mark R. Milliken, *Indy*'s final commanding officer. A Hawkeye naval flight officer, he rode backseat for his ship's last trap. "It's kind of ripping your heart and stomach out at the same time."

In 1998, the fleet continued its post–cold war drawdown and decommissioned nearly two dozen ships. Ships are artifacts of steel, but their crews and naval tradition imbue them with souls. With rare exceptions, their passings are noted with sadness.

"You get to know every nuance of the ship, the creak of the engines," said Yeoman 2d Class (SW) Nathaniel Roundy, whose final task aboard was planning *Indy*'s decommissioning ceremony in Bremerton, Washington. "She is everything to you, because every action the ship makes, you are part of."

*Independence*'s passing loomed larger than those of the various cruisers, destroyers, frigates, and submarines that left the fleet in the same year. For one thing, *Indy* was the fleet's oldest vessel. In port, the crew flaunted their pride of place, flying the "Don't Tread on Me" jack from a bow staff. Depicting a defiant snake on a field of red and white stripes, the banner dates to 1775 and the Continental Navy's first ships.

Commissioned in 1959 at New York Naval Shipyard, the eighty-thousand-ton *Independence* was built with a folding mast, a relic of the era when ships leaving the Brooklyn Navy Yard were required to pass beneath the Brooklyn Bridge. Only a few feet shorter than its *Nimitz*-class successors, *Indy* was much narrower, displaced ten thousand tons less, and sported a flight deck 10 percent smaller. Eight oil boilers could speed the ship at "thirty-plus" knots. On an average day, they burned 120,000 gallons of fuel.

*Indy* owned one of the fleet's proudest service records. The carrier served in the naval blockade of Cuba during the 1962 missile crisis and cruised off Vietnam two years later. In 1983, the ship saw combat off Grenada and Lebanon. In August 1990, *Indy* raced to the Persian Gulf after Iraq's invasion of Kuwait, becoming the first American flat-top in those waters since 1974. It returned in 1992, the first carrier to launch missions in support of Operation Southern Watch. In 1996, *Indy* was one of two big sticks on the scene when tensions flared in the strait between China and Taiwan.

*Indy*'s final cruise was meant to be a leisurely tour of Southeast Asian garden spots: Singapore, Hong Kong, Thailand. Instead, the ship and crew were sent to the Persian Gulf a fourth and last time, bearing to Iraq the two-carrier, we-mean-business message of early 1998.

When the orders arrived in January, boiler technicians and aircraft maintainers and the entire crew scrambled to prepare for sea. The change caught *Indy*'s administrative staff waist-deep in a task that, if left uncompleted, would ripple across the entire navy.

As decommissioning approached, the ship's twenty-six hundred sailors needed new assignments. The process of reassignment often takes months of exchanging telephone calls or e-mail messages with the navy's "detailers" in Washington, D.C. But if *Indy*'s crew couldn't wrap things up in a week—before the carrier left its Yokosuka, Japan, home port—hundreds of other ships and commands might be left without sailors in a few months. Lt. Cdr. John Oakes shuddered at the thought.

*Indy*'s administrative officer and his staff had spent months laying the groundwork for an efficient, orderly assignment process. Most of the big questions had been answered: How many sailors did *Indy* need for the journey to Bremerton? What specialties? How many people would go to *Kitty Hawk,* the carrier that would replace *Indy* in Japan?

In late 1997, Oakes and his team had interviewed every single sailor aboard about their assignment preferences. Most of the crew members were looking forward to getting back to the States after several years abroad. "It's kind of tough, especially for these younger guys who come over here and aren't married," said Master Chief Aviation Boatswain's Mate (SW/AW) Michael Knight. The Pentagon, however, requires most troops sent abroad to remain there for three years, a cost-saving measure. Those who had completed less than two years of their overseas tour were likely to be sent back on *Kitty Hawk.*

About five hundred crewmen had volunteered to ride back to Japan to complete their tours or begin new ones. Some would return to Japanese spouses. Others, like Roundy, enjoyed the Far East's combination of exotic travel and professional experience. Roundy believed practice with the paperwork unique to a forward-based ship would serve him well the next time he took the advancement exam.

In January 1998, Oakes sent Knight and twenty shipmates to Washington to hammer out final details with representatives from *Kitty Hawk,* the Pacific fleet, the Pacific naval air force, and the navy's Bureau of Personnel. No sooner had they returned than the gulf orders came.

*Indy*'s administrative staff took a collective deep breath and plunged ahead. The staff began to connect sailors with detailers in D.C. via innumerable conference calls. Each sailor got about a three-minute call to review his assignment options—then made the decision that would chart his life's course for the next three to five years.

The marathon detailing session lasted three straight days: seventy-two hours of around-the-clock frenzy. When it was over, all twenty-six hundred sailors in the ship's company had their orders.

"Most carriers take three detailers' conferences. It was unbelievable to do it in one," Oakes said. Planning for the decommissioning, he said, was the biggest accomplishment of his career.

*Independence* sailed on time, taking its place on station during a moment of international tension. The unexpected cruise eventually lasted five months. The skipper called it a fitting finale. "The morale ran high. The crew were excited that there was a real, no-kidding mission for her last deployment," Milliken said.

After the gulf cruise, *Indy* returned to Yokosuka to say good-bye for good in July. The carrier departed its home port of seven years as a sea of family, dignitaries, and media watched from the pier. It would take ten days to reach Hawaii. As the ship made its way across the Pacific, the crew cleaned out their workspaces and packed up their gear. Ordnancemen cleared out the ship's magazines, stacking bombs carefully on the flight deck for airlift to a nearby combat stores ship. "We've been doing a lot of corrosion control, a lot of painting. The ship's going to be in really good shape to put her into mothballs," said Aviation Boatswain's Mate (Launch and Recovery Equipment) 2d Class (SW) Bobby Freeman.

Meanwhile, a team of personnelmen and corpsmen from *Kitty Hawk* helped the *Indy* staff to review twenty-eight document boxes stuffed with personnel and medical records. An assembly line of people ran for two days in the hangar deck as sailors lined up to double-check their records. "We're trying to make this seamless for the guys, so they can walk off the Indy and go to work on the *Kitty Hawk* and not have to stand in lines," said Ens. Bryan Catoe, the leader of *Kitty*'s "away admin team."

A team of historians from the Naval Historical Center in Washington was also packing things away during the trip to Pearl Harbor. Scores of items would go to the navy archives—everything from sugar packets with Arabic printing to the wooden Hard Rock Cafe sign from the crew's mess. The historians also taped thirty-four hours of interviews with the ship's crew for the oral history records.

Even the battle group commander put in hours preparing to shift his flag to *Kitty Hawk*. "We are literally packing things up, pulling computers out of the wall," said Rear Adm. Timothy J. Keating. "We will box them up, carry them over on our shoulders, and plug them back in." Keating said he was happy to trade the old carrier for the navy's newest command and control systems. "Nothing against the *Indy*. It's just that *Kitty Hawk* is a much more capable platform," the admiral said. "Unfortunately, I'm going to have to open up the books and read the manuals."

As *Indy* approached Pearl Harbor, most of Carrier Air Wing Five's planes and aviators hopped over to their new carrier, which was approaching from the eastern side of the island chain. Four squadrons of Hornets, Tomcats, and Hawkeyes remained behind. They would ride to San Diego for refurbishing.

The sixteenth of July dawned a perfect day for flying. A dozen aircraft took off for *Kitty Hawk.* Several of the pilots who remained behind took a few cat shots, a few traps, for practice. The very last hop didn't appear on the day's air plan.

Since the ship's skipper and air wing commander were both Hawkeye naval flight officers, it fell to pilot Lt. Brent Johnson of the VAW-115 Liberty Bells to fly *Indy*'s last cat shot and trap. "I was ecstatic when they told me four days ago," said Johnson, who got the nod because the squadron's three senior pilots were either sick or already aboard *Kitty Hawk.* "It's such an honor, especially for a lieutenant. They only decomm carriers every two years or so." The junior pilot launched, circled the ship, and brought the Hawkeye in for a picture-perfect landing.

He would soon return to the skies. The ABE who closed out *Indy*'s flight ops would never launch a plane again. "That's it for me," said Aviation Boatswain's Mate Airman Jason Beard, relaxing by the catapult's firing panel on the starboard catwalk. His enlistment up and college money socked away, the deck edge operator had plans to get out and go for his commercial pilot's license.

"I've done everything I wanted to do in the navy: I wanted to fight fires; I wanted to launch airplanes," Beard said. "That's the last time of my career. All we have to do now is clean up the grease, put everything away, and go home."

Lt. Rick Black was the catapult officer who gave Beard the last "shoot" signal. For him, the end of flight ops meant release from the bondage of a "disassociated sea tour." A naval flight officer, Black flew in P-3C Orions, the navy's shore-based, long-range maritime patrol aircraft. Like many of those who oversee carrier takeoffs and landings, he regarded his two-year tour aboard ship as a necessary but regrettable hiatus from flying. "Oh, hell no," said Black, when asked about plans to move to *Kitty Hawk.* "After two years on a boat, I'm going back to the VP Navy."

A few hours after flight ops ceased, *Indy* pulled up to the oiler *Guadeloupe* and off-loaded several thousand gallons of unused jet fuel. Below the stilled flight deck, sailors and airmen chewed over the day's significance. "Fifty or sixty years from now, I'll be able to go anywhere on this ship in my head," said Photographer's Mate 2d Class (AW) John Yoder, who came aboard *Indy* when it replaced *Midway* as the forward-based carrier in 1991.

The admiral pointed out that the ship was older than almost every car on the road but still conducting flight ops, still ready for combat. "It's a bittersweet occasion," Keating said.

Members of Air Wing Five seemed less sentimental about *Indy*'s passing. That warm afternoon, Aviation Electrician's Mate 3d Class Garrett Keaough waited stolidly for his F/A-18 to return from the skies. The tiedown chains slung over his shoulders rubbed rust into his brown plane captain's jersey. Sweat pooled behind his goggles. "It's just another day," said Keaough, a member of the VFA-195 Dambusters.

Others were not so unmoved. "It's kind of sad to see it go," said Aviation Machinist's Mate 3d Class Joe Taylor, a member of the VQ-5 Black Ravens. "We have it pretty good. All the shops are set up just the way we like it. But we're looking forward to it. That's one of the things about the navy: always something new."

In the forward wardroom, the "dirty-shirt" mess area where flight suits may be worn at meals, aviators coolly shrugged about the move from *Indy* to *Kitty Hawk.* "It's just another boat," said Lt. Dean Sibley, a Tomcat pilot with the VF-154 Black Knights.

Still, there would be one dividend, Sibley allowed. Switching from the navy's smallest carrier meant a fractionally larger postage stamp of a landing strip. On a perfect approach to *Indy,* a Tomcat passes a mere fourteen feet above the fantail. On *Kitty Hawk,* the margin is three comforting feet higher. "It gives you one last correction after you cross the ramp," Sibley said. "You feel much better."

As *Independence* pulled into Pearl Harbor at dawn the next day, the sailors lined the deck in white uniforms and silently rendered honors to the *Arizona.* Soon, *Indy* was tied up next to *Kitty Hawk* at a giant pier. Sailors began to stream from one flight deck to the other, taking along their seabags, their tools, and their memories.

A week later, the two carriers departed. *Kitty Hawk* steamed toward *Indy*'s old berth in Yokosuka, Japan. *Independence* and its crew—now 20 percent smaller—sailed for San Diego, the carrier's final stop before Puget Sound and the navy's West Coast ship graveyard. The carrier officially left the fleet when it was decommissioned on 30 September in Bremerton, Washington.

*Indy*'s last year was rough on the crew. Those who rode the carrier all the way to Bremerton spent three quarters of 1998 away from home. "People are relieved that it's over," said Journalist 3d Class Jason Moore. "Nine months out of the year is draining. But most people are glad they did the tour because a lot of people have a lot of pride."

When *Indy* left the fleet, the vast majority of its sailors didn't. Most went directly to *Kitty Hawk.* New hands aboard that carrier, they were nevertheless old hands in the Seventh Fleet. Most of *Kitty Hawk*'s sailors had never lived in Japan or worked under the forward-based fleet's rapid-fire operating tempo.

"We'll take them under our wing and show them what to do," said Yoder, who has spent almost a quarter of his twenty-seven years in Japan. "The guys on the *Midway* did the same thing for us, keeping us out of trouble, showing us what to do."

"This is the most squared-away crew, the cleanest ship I have ever seen. This ship knows what it's doing," said reserve Cdr. Byron King, one of the historical archivists. "They're going to get to the *Kitty Hawk* and kick some ass."

---

Aboard the USS *Dwight D. Eisenhower* in the Adriatic Sea, June 1998

If *Indy* represented the best of the fleet's history, the carrier *Eisenhower* offers a glimpse of the navy to come.

In a darkened room deep within the carrier's hull, new racks of computers and support gear stuck out like elbows. Seated at the watch desk, Lt. Steve Meade scanned a trio of huge projection-TV screens. A glowing schematic showed ships and airplanes spread across the Adriatic Sea, circles and squares moving slowly across the displays. The carrier's tactical action officer, Meade was keeping track of the scene over and around Bosnia.

The gear was part of the navy's Cooperative Engagement Capability system. Still under development, the system combines the radar, sonar, and weapons sensor data from a group of ships into a single tactical network. When completed, navy planners say, it will weld an entire carrier battle group into a single flexible weapon.

*Ike*'s networking gear, hastily installed before its most recent deployment, was still incomplete. No matter. Meade was already hooked. "The CEC's just awesome. If we could get the whole battle group on it, the air picture wouldn't be a problem," he said.

Navy war-fighting visionaries believe that network centric warfare is the key to the next century's military. The idea comes from a computer-age chestnut: networks are as powerful as the square of the number of their nodes. In military terms, that means two ships that share sensor data become not twice but four times as formidable a force.

The idea of combining radar pictures is not new. Every major American warship already has the ability to draw radar data from nearby ships, itself a remarkable achievement that increases tactical awareness tenfold. But the new system is a quantum leap ahead. The old systems have a time lag of up to thirty minutes. The CEC system sends data over the airwaves at fifty-six thousand bits per second, providing a real-time picture for every ship in the network.

The faster links allow the radars to work together automatically, resolving inscrutable radar returns into useful information. Meade pointed to a pair of circles: aircraft flying in close formation. With the old system, he said, "we'd never have been able to track them. Two right next to each other, we'd normally get them confused."

The unprecedented speed and accuracy translate into flexibility in firepower. Every radar in the network can be a targeting device for every gunner in the battle group. Using data from one ship's radar, another ship can fire on targets hidden from its own sensors.

That wasn't yet the case with *Eisenhower,* the first carrier to deploy with the new equipment, Meade said. The crew ran out of time before deployment and hadn't yet certified the system operational. Besides, the battle group included only two other CEC-capable ships: the guided missile cruisers *Anzio* and *Cape St. George.*

The CEC equipment wasn't even hooked into the carrier's main combat direction center. The only ones who could see the combined picture were Meade and the battle group commander's staff, embarked several decks higher in *Ike's* superstructure.

But there are plans to change all that—and eventually even to include the sensors aboard navy aircraft. "This is the way of the future," Meade said.

# 3. THE ORIONS

Aboard a P-3 over Bosnia, June 1998

A tattered blanket of clouds lay over Bosnia's ridges and rivers, making things tough for the aviators in the P-3C Orion high above. For nearly six hours, the plane and its twelve-person crew had crisscrossed the Balkan skies, prospecting for brief glimpses of bridge and highway traffic.

Equipped with a video camera, a telescopic lens, and a six-foot antenna, the Orion was feeding live black-and-white video images to American forces on the ground in Tuzla. Army commanders love the propeller-driven plane's unparalleled ability to keep an eye on the war-torn country, and the aircrews take pride in protecting the soldiers.

"When we're sending to a Humvee, that's when you really feel like you're doing your mission," said Lt. Cdr. George Sherwood, the commander of Combat Aircrew Nine, VP-26 Tridents. "Down on the ground in the army, they're really grateful."

But what are the navy's maritime patrol squadrons doing over Bosnia?

In the cold war days, the North Atlantic was the P-3's playground. In a deadly serious game of hide-and-seek, the Orions helped keep track of the Soviet submarine fleet. Creeping from their Arctic home ports to the Atlantic Ocean, the Red subs would pass through the briny gaps between Greenland, Iceland, and the United Kingdom. The

P-3 crews operating from a base near Reykjavik would pick up and tail them for days.

During the 1990s, Orions started showing up wherever naval forces faced trouble. "We started seeing a shift in the missions," said Cdr. Andy Johnson, VP-26's commander. "The planes had infrared and electro-optical sensors added. It allowed us to hunt on the water and over land."

During the Gulf War, P-3s tracked thousands of ships and boats off the Kuwaiti coast. They received credit for spotting more than fifty vessels that were eventually sunk by coalition forces. Today, VP squadrons routinely deploy to the Caribbean Sea for counterdrug operations and to the Mediterranean theater for just about everything.

The new camera gear has made the long-legged Orions the preferred eye in the sky for many ground operations. During the 1997 evacuation of the U.S. embassy in Albania, P-3 crews monitored city crowds, kept an eye out for trouble, and produced a wide range of helpful information. "You can look into embassy parking lots, see if there's room for helos to land," said Cdr. Ken Deutsch, the operations officer for the Sixth Fleet's maritime surveillance forces.

Some P-3 missions are not so dramatic. In 1998, the state government of Maine hired a reserve squadron to search out thriving blueberry patches in the forest. The July flight wasn't strictly agricultural in nature, however; it also gave the squadron a chance to test-drive its new sensors.

The venerable Orion, designed in the late 1950s as a dedicated sub hunter, is the modern navy's aerial workhorse. Today's P-3 crews handle maritime, littoral, and ground surveillance; antiship warfare; over-the-horizon targeting for other units; maritime command and control; search and rescue; minelaying; and more.

"My first tour, 60 to 80 percent of what we did was ASW," said Sherwood, whose squadron completed a deployment to Sigonella Naval Air Station in Sicily in August. "Now, 15 percent is."

Most of the P-3Cs flying today were manufactured in the 1970s and 1980s. Their flexible design and numerous upgrades have provided a longevity few airframes can match. Powerful yet fuel-thrifty, the

Orion's forty-six-hundred-horsepower turboprop engines and eighteen-thousand-pound gas tanks give the plane long legs. A P-3C crew can fly fifteen hundred miles at up to 450 mph, then turn off an engine and "loiter" above a target for twelve hours at 190 mph. The ceiling is officially twenty-eight thousand feet, although its pilots say it's at least five thousand feet higher.

The bomb bay and wing pylons can carry torpedoes, depth charges, mines, antiship Harpoon cruise missiles, and short-range air-to-surface Maverick missiles. A "Bullwinkle" pod under the left wing warns the crew of enemy radar. The pilot can jettison flares to deceive heat-seeking missiles or bundles of aluminum chaff strips to foil radar locks. Fire-fighting foam in the wing fuel tanks can help keep a hit from turning into a kill.

When the Orions entered the fleet in 1962, they were the first navy planes whose innards—rack after rack of sensitive electronic sub-hunting gear—cost more than the aircraft itself. Today's aircraft can drop up to thirty-two floating microphones to relay waterborne noises up to the circling plane. Two sophisticated acoustic processing stations help detect submarines' aural traces in the noisy seas.

There is a chin-mounted infrared camera for night flights and a short-range sensor that can pick out a sub's steel hull against the earth's magnetic field. A dozen antennae stud the 116-foot fuselage. The aircraft's most distinctive feature is the tail-mounted, pencil-shaped "stinger" that houses the magnetic sensors. A central computer compiles the sensor data into a murky picture of the underwater world.

Since 1994, new surveillance systems have dramatically broadened the Orion's usefulness. Officially, they are called "stand-off visual electro-optics packages"; in essence, they are video cameras on steroids, equipped with powerful telephoto lenses and the ability to broadcast their black-and-white pictures to earth. The video images that arrive on the ground are startlingly clear. "Some of them, their mothers would be able to say, 'Hi, son,'" said Cdr. Bing Lengyel, whose team at Sigonella's Tactical Support Center helped prepare Orion crews for missions in the Med.

The new cameras have turned P-3 flights over Bosnia into daily command performances. Aerial reconnaissance serves a number of needs: tracking the movement of armed groups, helping the ground troops monitor treaty compliance and elections, and keeping an eye on large gatherings of civilians.

"We'll watch soccer games if they think there's going to be a riot. Like if the British fans are there," Sherwood said. "Sometimes it's humorous. One time it turned out to be a wedding."

Sherwood, Johnson, and the rest of VP-26's 360 men and women began their 1998 deployment to Sigonella in February, arriving at the Sicilian air station in seven P-3s and a chartered airliner. They brought the squadron's Orions from their home field, Brunswick Naval Air Station in Maine, and inherited two more in "Sig": P-3s modified for the Med's overland surveillance missions. In all, VP-26 "owned" nine birds for its dozen aircrews. About 240 maintainers and other support personnel kept them flying.

The flight schedule on 21 June was fairly typical. One Orion supported the *Eisenhower* battle group, which had recently passed through the Strait of Gibraltar in its rush to the Adriatic Sea. The P-3's crew scanned the waters ahead of the carrier, keeping *Ike* informed about ships and subs.

Two ASW flights tracked the Med's submarine traffic, keeping tabs on the underwater operations of several different navies. A fourth aircraft dedicated the day to training, helping the squadron's junior aviators work toward qualification as prime pilots and plane commanders. A fifth was on call for whatever contingencies might arise on the longest day of the year.

Combat Aircrew Nine drew the day's sixth mission: a surveillance flight over Bosnia.

Since 1994, the navy's maritime patrol squadrons have supported United Nations efforts in the war-torn region once known as Yugoslavia. First came Operation Deny Flight, the no-fly enforcement in which air force captain Scott O'Grady was shot down. Operation Deliberate Guard put troops on the ground in 1996, an affair that had evolved into Operation Deliberate Forge in early June 1998. Bosnia and other areas watched by the blue-helmeted stabilization force were calming down.

But to the northeast, a new civil war was heating up. Armed rebels in the Serbian province of Kosovo had begun fighting against the Serbian military forces of rump Yugoslavia. No one knew how the conflict, yanking once again on twisted ethnic and territorial ties, might affect the rest of the region. Indeed, no one—NATO officials, the populace, nor the foreign and domestic press—was quite sure exactly what was happening.

Were Kosovar refugees flooding Bosnia? Were Bosnians—or ethnic Albanians and Serbs—sending soldiers or arms into the separatist province? As NATO commanders looked hungrily for information, Combat Aircrew Nine stepped up.

A few hours after dawn, the crew arrived at the Tactical Support Center, a windowless building across the street from the flight line. In a darkened conference room equipped with an overhead projector, the intelligence and support team flashed the weather forecast—cloudy —and a rundown of the day's observation targets, mostly bridges and highways. There was a bit of discussion of the big picture—How does this flight fit in with NATO's general objectives?—and details such as radio frequencies and identification channels.

The Orion waited on the concrete taxiway outside the hangar, its blunt nose pointed toward a ridge on Sicily's well-farmed western plain. As the aircrew arrived from the briefing, the maintainers finished up their preflight inspection.

On their way out to the flight line, the aircrew slipped "blood chits" into the lower leg pockets of their flight suits. For use in the event of a landing in hostile territory, the flat Ziploc bags contained survival maps and a multilingual plea for assistance—reward guaranteed. The aviators had long ago filed four "authenticating statements" that they would use to identify themselves over a survival radio.

At a quarter to nine, the crew mustered aboard the aircraft, squeezing into the cabin's midsection for a safety brief. Donning gray fireproof gloves for takeoff, Chief Aviation Warfare Systems Operator (AW/AC) Rich Kowalczyk ran briskly through parachute procedures:

don't forget to unfasten one, not two, of the leg loops just before you hit water, the better to get clear of the nylon chute's shrouds.

The crew took their stations for takeoff. Nose to tail, there were three pilots, a flight engineer, two tactical coordinators, a navigator/communicator, three sensor operators, and an in-flight electronics technician who doubled as an ordnance specialist.

Sherwood—the mission commander and primary pilot—pushed the four throttles to their stops. Laden with fuel for its nine-hour mission, the plane would need maximum power to get up to cruising altitude. As the Orion zoomed past the base's antiaircraft missile batteries and took off to the east, the cockpit windows offered spectacular views of orchards, quarries, and, finally, the smoking crater of Mount Etna.

"Nice-looking volcano," the pilot said.

Sicily fell behind and the instep of Italy's boot appeared below. Sherwood turned over the flight controls to Lt. (jg) Wesley Price, the crew's third pilot, or "three-p." On long missions, the trio of pilots rotates through the two cockpit seats: three hours on, ninety minutes off. Price took over as his boss headed aft.

Eighty feet from cockpit to crew lounge, the Orion's cabin was crowded with equipment: sensor stations, electrical panels, and racks of sonobuoys. Still, there was enough room to stand up, stretch, and move around a bit. And to the rear of the narrow fuselage were some bare-bones amenities: a small cooler, a coffee thermos, a convection oven, and a fair approximation of a restaurant booth. Above, where an airliner's overhead bins would be, was rack space for two people to catch naps. Comfortwise, Orion missions are akin to a twelve-hour ride in a half-full moving truck.

The P-3 pilots admit their craft is no strike fighter, but say it's still fun to fly, like the airborne equivalent of a sports car. The plane's stiff wings add maneuverability at the price of a rougher ride. "P-3's are kind of funny. The jet guys make fun of us. Actually, it's a lot sportier than it looks, and I'm happy about that," said Lt. Carol Prather, the number-two pilot.

The ribbing may have something to do with a photograph that seems to hang in every VP ready room in the navy. It's an image of an Orion rolling hard, diving away from the camera. Laden with wing-mounted missiles, the bomb bay doors wide open, the P-3 is loaded for bear and on the attack. "Everybody jokes about how big it is and how slow, but whoever it is [we're supporting], a guy in the water or on land, we give them a lot of options," Price said.

Sherwood settled into one of the booth's vinyl-covered seats and previewed the upcoming recon runs. Keeping the video camera on target and the plane inside friendly airspace would require some pretty fancy flying, he said.

In an effort to save money, navy program officials designed the electro-optical camera prototype, code-named "Cast Glance," to require a minimum of modifications to the aircraft. The system is bolted to the cabin deck, with the lens aimed through a porthole behind the left wing. The camera points horizontally while its subjects are thousands of vertical feet below.

The sensor operator can swing the lens around a bit, but in order to bring the camera to bear, the pilots have to wrench the whole aircraft into position. Usually, the aviator in the right seat takes the controls while the pilot on the left fixes the target in a window-mounted reticule. They fly together, the left pilot relaying instructions across the cramped cockpit to the right one.

The right-seater can monitor their progress on a small screen that presents the camera's view but is otherwise flying pretty blind. "Flying left seat is fun," Price said. "Right isn't, especially when we're flying close to someplace we're not supposed to go."

It takes about a twelve-degree bank to aim the camera at the ground, half again as steep as a normal turn. The right pilot stomps on the right rudder pedal and rolls left. The plane tilts and skids through the sky. And making everything just a bit tougher, the pilots usually shut down the outer left engine to save fuel and reduce exhaust haze in the camera images. "Showing the other pilots how we fly, they say, 'You're nuts,'" Price said.

The tight orbits force the plane into unnatural, undulating flight. "The crew gets used to it, but it's not very comfortable for the pilot," Sherwood said. "You're going to see us sweating pretty hard."

Out a porthole, Bosnia's rocky Dalmatian coastline appeared at the edge of the Adriatic Sea. "Pretty awe-inspiring, pretty rough country, especially the area around Sarajevo," Sherwood said. "This is the cloudiest country in the world. It'll be clear over Italy, clear over the Adriatic, and here it'll be cloudy."

The Orion arrived on station at 11:00 A.M. Price ran through one of aviation's omnipresent checklists and shut off the number one engine. To the rear, past racks of dark and silent sub-hunting apparatus, three people huddled around a rack of equipment the size of three microwave ovens.

Kowalczyk gripped the camera controller, a two-pound joystick scrounged from another weapons system. Back when the Orions were sub hunters, the crew's sensor controller used to spend most of his flight time helping the aircraft's three junior sensor operators pluck muted submarine noises from the waters below. Now he is a high-flying cameraman, working to keep his lens on target through the plane's twists and turns.

Next to the chief sat Aviation Warfare Systems Operator 2d Class Phillip Moss, the crew's "sensor one." Sensor one is trained to track underwater noises with the help of digital noise processors. Instead, perched on a metal folding chair stenciled "MWR," Moss waited with a notebook to log the visual contacts.

Lt. Bill Schreiber was the crew's sensor coordinator, one of three naval flight officers aboard. The NFOs don't fly the Orions, but they mastermind the complicated process of tracking and destroying their hidden targets. For this mission, Schreiber forsook his usual station beside the acoustic sensor displays to watch over the chief's shoulder.

The rack before them held the surveillance camera, its electronic drivers, two videocassette recorders, and a pair of seven-inch black-and-white monitors. One of the monitors showed the zoom view; the other, a wider field of vision. The system allows the sensor operators to send motion video or annotated still images. The transmissions go through a six-foot antenna that sticks through the aircraft's belly and arrive at dish antennae on the ground. The ground commanders can also use the link to send up their own still images.

"It's tailored collection," Sherwood said. "They'll tell us, 'You're one house off, one field off.'"

Thumbing a nickel-sized button on his joystick, Kowalczyk panned the camera left and right, probing for a cloud break. Schreiber spotted the day's first target: a highway bridge lightly dotted with tractor-trailers and cars. The road loomed large on the viewfinder, then wobbled and rotated away as the aircraft turned for a second pass.

The camera crew fell into a pattern: a few seconds of unobstructed view followed by a few minutes of cloud-enforced off time. The plane rose, fell, turned, and banked, giving its crew the sensation of riding an earthworm through its spiral hole. The camera focused on a road, slid forward too fast.

"Back, back, back," Schreiber ordered, but the road moved out of sight. As Kowalczyk stood up and leaned forward to review the videotape, a hard bank sent his folding chair sliding across the deck. Retrieving his seat, the chief gave some extra scrutiny to a truck parked near a bridge.

Steering the camera eye isn't hard, but it does require concentration to keep the picture stable. "You get it juking too much, you get people sick," Schreiber said. "We've gotten people sick looking at it on the ground."

More bridges, roads, and airfields. Between targets, Kowalczyk scanned the area's lakes. The avid fisherman was scouting for likely looking fishing holes. To the rear, other members heated up lunch in the oven. The smell of TV dinners and tomato sauce wafted through the chilly cabin.

Moss, who started his navy career aboard the carrier *Carl Vinson* in 1992 and reenlisted two years later, reflected on his sailor's life. "I love what I do: seeing the world, doing a job most people dream of doing. How many people can say they've seen six continents in six years?" he asked. "The recruiter was completely honest with me. He said, 'Your life for two years will pretty much suck, but if you like it even a little bit, stick around. It gets so much better.'"

Even the nature of the surveillance work appealed to Moss, who said he was considering a switch to nursing at some point in the future. "It's kind of nice to know that we work to deter people from having problems. I find that comforting. Instead of causing problems, we're preventing them."

Two o'clock P.M. found Schreiber, Moss, and Kowalczyk scanning up and down the banks of a river, panning for long seconds until the exhaust from the inboard engine clouded the camera's vision. As the hours passed, their vision began to get blurry from staring at the small screens. In the back, crew members racked out in the drop-down cots.

The cabin temperature had gradually dropped into the low fifties. This had two salutary effects: it kept the pilots alert and the electronics functioning well. The latter lightened the mood of Aviation Electronics Technician 2d Class Andrea Fowler Sr., whose job it was to fix problems with the avionics, sensors, sonobuoys, and ordnance. "If that air conditioner's not working, I'm facing a long day," the in-flight technician said.

At 4:30, just as life seemed ready to slow to a complete halt, Sherwood radioed for permission to leave station and head home. Hearing an affirmative, he goaded the feathered number one engine back to shuddering life.

On the way out of Bosnia, Sherwood radioed thanks to "Magic," the nearby AWACS early-warning and air-traffic-control plane. The air force radar operators aboard the big jet had helped coordinate the mission, keeping the Orion's patrol area clear of traffic and the patrol plane itself out of Kosovan airspace.

A few minutes past five, it was time for housekeeping. Aviation Warfare Systems Operator 3d Class David Chavez, a sensor operator, collected the blood chits, the emergency identifications, and the survival radios. The navigator, Lt. (jg) Brian Erickson, hauled a small vacuum cleaner from behind a gray metal panel and gave the cabin a quick once-over.

The curve of Italy's boot heel appeared out the cockpit windows an hour later, followed by Mount Etna and its long southern slope. Over the Sicilian coast, the aircraft climbed to avoid the commercial airport outside the city of Catania, then swooped down onto the Sigonella runway.

Nine hours after takeoff, the flight ended.

But the day didn't. The maintainers welcomed the aircraft back to the hangar and got to work putting the old bird in shape for another long mission tomorrow. The flight crew headed for the Tactical Support Center to chew over the mission. Debriefs can last ninety minutes; the workday, fourteen hours.

"Every once in a while, you're like, 'Why can we carry so much gas in this thing?'" Price said.

---

Aboard a P-3 above the Arctic Ocean, June 1998

A bit north of the Arctic Circle, another Orion twisted and turned above the slate gray water. Each steep bank dipped a wingtip within 150 feet of the waves—that is, less than two wingspans.

The members of VP-16's Combat Aircrew Three might have been nervous. Life expectancy, should they wind up in the thirty-three-degree water, would be a frigid four minutes. But as their P-3C Orion "yanked and banked" several hundred miles north of Iceland, no one had time to ponder the dangers. All ten crewmen were concentrating, working hard to draw a bead on their submerged prey. The intercom crackled.

"Stand by for attack," said Lt. Rob Hartman, the tactical coordinator. His finger hovered over a red button.

On this training flight, the VP-16 War Eagles were practicing for the oldest P-3 mission in the book: hunting subs.

Time was when the frigid waters around Iceland were the hottest place in the world for the VP Navy. If war erupted with the Soviet Union, the maritime patrol aircraft flying out of Keflavik Naval Air Station would have been charged with keeping the Red subs out of the Atlantic. Nowadays, fewer and fewer P-3s are sent to Keflavik. The airfield that once hosted full squadrons now sees detachments of four aircraft.

Nevertheless, there is important work to do in this frozen corner of the world. More and more navies are adding submarines—new and used—to their fleets, drawn by the cost-effective punch of stealthy underwater warships. Powered by ultraquiet diesel engines, today's subs are smaller and quieter than ever.

This makes the new diesels harder to track for American sub hunters, but so does another fact: the U.S. Navy gets most of its ASW experience from hunting its own nuclear subs, which emit subtly different sounds.

So even if the Soviets aren't threatening to break out into the Atlantic, there's another reason to fly out of Keflavik. Many of the world's exporters of diesel subs—Sweden, Holland, Germany, and Russia—operate in the northern seas. If their products are going to be out in the world making trouble, the VP Navy wants to practice on them first.

But on this breezy June morning the crew was taking some basic practice on a training drone. The Orion took off from Keflavik, left behind Iceland's lava spits, and headed north across the Arctic Circle. En route, they brought their steed's eyes and ears to life. A dozen green displays flickered and grew steady. The mission computer indicated ready to go.

Aviation Electronics Technician 1st Class (AW) Dan Cole knelt amidships, checking the quartet of six-inch tubes that descended through the cabin deck and out of the fuselage. Canted toward the rear, the chutes allow the in-flight technician to drop sensors, smoke flares, and other equipment into the water below.

Cole was also in charge of the aircraft's sonobuoys, the floating microphones that are ASW's electronic bloodhounds. During preflight, the ordnanceman had stacked sixteen of the white cylinders, each the size of a jumbo mailing tube, in a rack just forward of the drop chutes. Another sixteen were tucked into holes in the plane's belly, rigged for remote control.

Ejected from the plane with a small propellant charge, the deployed buoy free-falls to the water, where it rights itself and begins to float. A cable ringed with stabilizing fins descends from its underside, dangling an exquisitely sensitive omnidirectional microphone.

Some sonobuoys have a powerful speaker that allows them to send out bursts of sound—"pings"—and track the echoes. Active sonobuoys dropped near a sub can fix its position quite accurately, but are rarely used before the Orion is ready to strike. Finding and tailing a sub is easier when its crew doesn't know you're listening.

Passive or active, sonobuoys radio their data up to twin acoustic listening posts in the circling plane. On this mission, the seats were filled by Aviation Antisubmarine Warfare Operator (AW) 1st Class Kenneth Stringer and Aviation Warfare Systems Operator 2d Class Shannon Roy. Called "sensor one" and "sensor two," Stringer and Roy listened through expensive headphones to the song of the sonobuoys. The two sensor operators are the heart of the crew's antisubmarine efforts; it is their job to distill the sub sounds from the noisy seas.

When their Orion was built in the 1970s, the sound-processing computers were state of the art. Now, the gray panels and monochrome screens are dated. A home computer has more processing power. But the P-3's systems still do a creditable job of helping their operators wring hints of submarine from incoming signals. Displaying the feeds from four sonobuoys at once, each station can amplify, filter, analyze, and break them down into component frequencies. A twenty-one-track tape recorder allows the operators to replay suspicious noises, electronically slicing and dicing them a bit differently each time to deduce their origins.

"Everything that rubs, moves, bounces, or springs makes noise. The question is, can you hear it?" said Cdr. Chuck Martello, VP-16's executive officer, who had come along for the ride.

Across the aisle, Aviation Warfare Systems Operator Airman Aaron Butler presided over a miscellaneous collection of displays and sensor gear. The phone booth–sized sensor three position includes radios, weather radar, and an enemy radar and radio wave detector. A joystick controller swivels a hull-mounted infrared camera to help spot subs at night.

Butler also monitored the magnetic anomaly detector, which indicates when the plane flies directly over a steel-hulled sub. Like the active sonobuoys, the MAD is used to confirm the position of a sub just before attack. A successful overflight is marked with the cry "Madman! Madman!"

A few feet forward, navigator Lt. Brad Rosen updated the plane's position on a chart. The job—one of the most hectic aboard—has gotten much easier since Global Positioning Satellite receivers were grafted onto the Orion's avionics a few years ago, replacing the gyroscopic navigation system and the periscope-mounted sextant. Nevertheless, Rosen was keeping a dead-reckoning plot of the plane's course, and would soon add a track of the sub's suspected position.

Across the aisle and just behind the cockpit, Hartman studied a round fourteen-inch screen set into his own instrument panel. All of the sensor data on the plane flows into a central computer and onto the tactical coordinator's screen. Hartman would use it to stage-manage the three-dimensional hunt. A smaller display in the cockpit would show the pilots where to fly as the game became more and more rigidly geometric.

Meanwhile, the pilots had their own sensors—their "Mark 1, Mod 0" eyeballs. By day, the sight of dolphins—who love to play in a submarine's bow wave—can be a tip-off. At night, even a submerged sub often leaves a wake of sorts: a faint glow of bioluminescence from churned-up microorganisms. Even with all of the Orion's expensive gear, many subs are first spotted with sharp eyes.

As the Orion arrived on station, Cole slapped a lever on tube three. There was a muffled bang, and a small charge fired a five-foot tube into the water below. This training drone would be the day's quarry. Running below the water's surface, the tiny watercraft would simulate the noises, maneuvers, and even the sonar returns of a three-hundred-foot submarine.

While waiting a few minutes to give the drone a head start, Cole dropped an ambient noise detector into the water. Marine animals infuse the underwater environment with sound. So do surface ships. The detector would help Stringer and Roy set their computers to filter out the existing noises.

The ordnance specialist also dropped a bathythermograph, which radioed out the changing water temperature as it sank. Seawater seldom grows smoothly colder with depth. Instead, it forms discrete temperature layers, oceanographic detail that is vital to sub hunters. Like any material, water's ability to transmit noise varies with its temperature, and sound will refract—change direction—when passing from one isotherm to the next.

Submariners are trained to take advantage of this law of physics and slip between the layers to throw off their pursuers. Orion crews are trained to work the problem backward, adding or subtracting the angles to compute the sub's position in three-dimensional space.

In the Arctic, however, the water is usually fairly isothermic—that is, lacking distinct temperature boundaries. The bathythermograph indicated this was so. The hunting grounds were a bit less cluttered.

The plane circled back, ready to hunt.

The crew began dropping sonobuoys. Stringer and Roy turned to their headphones. The pilots buckled in and pulled the plane hard to port.

Through the cockpit window, the ocean tilted until the horizon was a sharply diagonal line. The plane leveled out, then banked right, then left. Hunting subs requires a lot more maneuvering than one might suspect.

The problem is sonobuoy drift. Like any untethered floating object, microphones tend to wander away from their starting places. But the crew has to know the buoys' exact positions in order to get useful bearings. The solution, developed in the days before GPS, uses two much older phenomena: the plane's engine noise and the Doppler effect.

Just as a car's engine noise seems to rise and fall as it passes, the roar of the Orion's propellers registers a frequency shift when the plane passes overhead. By marking the position at the exact second the sensor operators see the shift, the mission computer keeps track of the sonobuoys.

Making this happen is no mean feat for the pilots. Urged on by physics—and peer pressure—they pull the plane into hard banks, trying to come as close to the buoys as possible. Traveling over each of the sonobuoys in turn is called "flying a racetrack," and it feels like an aerial grand prix.

Ignoring the plane's twists and turns, Roy concentrated on the sounds flowing through his headphones and peered at the winking green display before him. Rotating knobs and punching buttons, he set his computers to filtering the sound. The first clue would be the appearance of various frequencies and harmonics common to sub engines. "You look for something really quick that shoots in and shoots out," Roy said.

A picture began to form on his speckled screen. The Orion's own engine noise, picked up by the buoys and radioed to the sensor stations, emerged as a flexing sine wave. Four smaller frequency spikes appeared in the fuzzy band of frequencies: noises from the drone.

Roy and Stringer queried the sonobuoys for bearings on the spikes, then triangulated and fixed the drone's position. A small circle appeared on Hartman's screen. They had found their prey. Now they would tail it for a bit.

An hour went by. The crew dropped a dozen more sonobuoys, creating "gates" by dropping them off the drone's forward quarters. On Hartman's screen, the green buoy symbols outlined a curving path.

Suddenly, the tactical controller gasped in surprise. "The sneaky little guy turned on us," the TACCO said. A few minutes later, he reported, "I'm not sure how close the sub track is right now."

But the drone's juking didn't shake the P-3 for long, and the crew decided to put some simulated bombs on their target. As the plane roared over the drone, Cole loosed an active buoy. A moment later, its sonar pings nailed down the target's position.

The pilots swung the Orion around again, this time lining up to drop a torpedo. They had to get the plane close enough for the torp to be able to find its target with active sonar. The imaginary circle defined by the limits of the torpedo's sensors is called "the basket."

Hartman ran through a checklist.

"Time to get jiggy with it," someone said over the intercom.

The TACCO opened the bomb bay door. "Bomb, bomb, bomb," he said, and hit the red firing button.

If there had been real torpedoes aboard the Orion, Hartman said, and a real submarine below, that sub would have been in big trouble.

In back, Cole punched a drop tube. A smoke flare shot out the bottom of the plane, marking the spot where the "torpedo" landed. Even with GPS, the old ways are still useful. If the plane had to come around for another shot, the smoke would make things a lot easier.

If a real torpedo had been dropped, Cole would have fired off a pair of buoys, one active, one passive, to catch the sub's reaction.

"When you drop, he's going to do something: evade, drop a noise-maker, something to compromise his position," Martello said.

What about staying still?

"That's very risky," the XO said with a smile.

The plane flew home over ice floes spotted with the brown teardrops of seals in repose. A few miles later, the Orion passed a group of killer whales headed north, swimming just below the water's surface.

A few weeks after the practice mission, VP-26 pilot Wes Price offered an assessment of the Orion's sub-hunting abilities from a unique point of view. For a dozen years Price fought the other side of the underwater battle, sailing aboard subs as an enlisted fire controlman. He left the sub community to finish up his bachelor's degree—as an environmental science major at the University of Virginia—and earn an officer's commission. As a new ensign, Price was selected for flight school. He earned his wings in 1996 and was assigned to P-3s.

Back when he was a practitioner of the black art of underwater stealth, he figured submarines held the advantage in oceangoing hide-and-seek. "I came and I was a big nonbeliever," said Price, who enjoys the irony of hunting his old shipmates. Now, he said, "I'm quite impressed. We get ahold of a guy, and unless he does something spectacular, he is not getting away."

Aboard a P-3 over the Black Sea, June 1998

Price's squadron got a chance to show off their skills in hunting surface ships later that summer. The Tridents dispatched Combat Aircrew Twelve to Romania for Exercise Cooperative Partner 1998. Another NATO Partnership for Peace event, the exercise was designed to introduce Black Sea naval forces—ships and marines from Romania, Bulgaria, Georgia, and Ukraine—to NATO operations.

For the handful of Romanian and Bulgarian ships, the exercise offered a rare opportunity to work with a maritime patrol aircraft. For Lt. Sal Contreras, a VP-16 pilot, it brought a dose of aviation culture shock. Home field for the exercise was the municipal airport at the Black Sea port city of Constanta. In the days of Soviet leader Leonid Brezhnev, the city's strand of resort hotels was a favorite summer getaway for Communist Party bigwigs, who came nine hundred miles south from Moscow to walk the beach of crushed seashells.

The airfield was well inland, amid wheat fields worked with tractors and oxen. On 24 June, the American aircrew checked out their aircraft on the cracked tarmac, then headed to the somnolent terminal for a preflight weather brief. The Romanian weather forecaster was somewhat more concise than a typical American meteorologist. In fact, his report gave a new meaning to the word *brief.* "He said, 'It's a fine day to fly.' That was it," Contreras said. He chuckled and strode out to his plane. It was 8:00 A.M.

An hour later, Contreras and the rest of the crew were two thousand feet above the Black Sea. For the moment they idled, drawing giant rectangles in the sky. Below them, the frigate *Kauffman* and a half dozen European ships practiced basic destroyer squadron maneuvers.

After a while, the ships formed a defensive screen and called in the patrol aircraft. The next few hours went like this: Frigate calls P-3, gives bearing to unidentified patrol boat. P-3 flies over and begins circling the "enemy." Repeat.

The Tridents were veteran teachers of this kind of introductory lesson, having flown similar missions in the Mediterranean. "We were working with a Spanish frigate," recalled third pilot Lt. (jg) Dan Jurta. "We said, 'We're here,' and they didn't know what to do with us. So we said, 'Do you have a surface contact that you want us to find?'"

They did, and vectored the Orion ahead. In minutes, the patrol plane was circling over the target, feeding gunnery information back to the frigate.

"They caught on quick," Jurta said. "They were saying, 'This is great.'"

The Black Sea sailors seemed to share the Spaniards' sentiments, dispatching the Orion here and there.

By 11:00 A.M., however, Jurta and the rest of the P-3 crew were bored stiff. "If we're not doing something, then we're just wasting gas," someone said over the cockpit intercom. When the next lull arrived, the crew jumped on the opportunity to hunt—just for practice.

Revving the engines, the crew set up mock attacks on the vessels below. In the span of seventeen minutes, the crew dropped four sonobuoys, locked a pair of frigates in their crosshairs, and "took them out" with imaginary Harpoon missiles.

"Nice setup, TACCO," Jurta said over the intercom circuit that fed the crew's headsets. Over the next two hours, the crew methodically pretended to kill off every other ship in the vicinity.

At some point in the six-hour flight, a section of Greek fighter jets streaked into the area, burning hot circles in the sky. Safe being better than sorry when dealing with "fast movers" and "pointy-nose guys," the Orion climbed to put some airspace between it and the jets. An air controller on the ground asked the fighters about their fuel reserves.

"Jason Alpha, call your state."

"Fifteen minutes," the flight leader responded.

Someone in the P-3 cockpit let out a howl of derisive laughter. The fuel-thirsty fighters bugged out. The Orion flew on and on and on.

The P-3s won't last forever, of course, but some of them will be four decades old by the time their replacement—the not-even-on-the-drawing-board Multi-Mission Maritime Aircraft—arrives around 2015. This is not necessarily a problem: today's P-3s were designed to fly for thirty-eight years. Still, even the best-designed aircraft gets balky with age. Many of the fleet's 241 Orions are slated for service life extension programs, overhauls that will add a decade to each airframe's life.

Meanwhile, the navy is transforming the venerable P-3 yet again, updating it with a package of improved sensors, communications gear, and weapons controls called the Anti-Surface Warfare Improvement Program. By 2002, more than half of the Orions will emerge as more capable hunters of surface ships and gatherers of littoral reconnaissance. Five of the improved aircraft were deployed in fall 1998: four to the VP-9 Golden Eagles in Diego Garcia, and one to the VP-5 Mad Foxes who relieved VP-26 in Sigonella.

The new equipment will make the Tridents' fancy flying largely a memory. The synthetic aperture radar can pierce clouds to count trucks hidden under camouflage netting and ships moored at piers. The electro-optical camera—a production version of the Cast Glance system—peers conveniently out the bottom of the fuselage.

The package also includes a new infrared camera and better gear to detect and classify incoming electronic signals. Its digital radios allow secure voice and image exchanges via satellite. And the Orion can strap on a new weapon: the Maverick, a short-range air-to-ground missile that uses infrared, lasers, or television to home in on its targets.

Computer upgrades make things easier on the crew. Full-color displays replace the TACCO and navigator's cryptic green-on-black screens, allowing the naval flight officers to keep track of targets almost effortlessly. Simplifying things for the sensor operators, the new devices are controlled by computers that run the Microsoft Windows operating system. A navywide trend, the switch from specialty systems to the PC standard makes maintenance and upgrading cheaper and faster. Operationally, Windows will soon make it possible to split the duties of the sensor three position among the other two sensor operators.

VP-5 was supposed to deploy with four improved P-3s, but production delays slowed delivery of three of them. One glitch has so far emerged: The automatic satellite communication system had a tough time hooking into the *Eisenhower* carrier battle group's net. Sixth Fleet officials fault the ships' older, analog systems and say the problem will be resolved as they upgrade to digital gear.

The Mad Foxes' skipper said the new gear's advantages vastly outweigh any new-car problems. "We're very excited about it," Cdr. Mark Ensor said. "You can find a tank on the ground day or night, in bad weather or under cloud cover." And the beefed-up infrared targeting camera has been "a pleasure to watch and see."

The whole plane is so much more effective, Ensor said, that the navy might have to rethink training and assignments for Orion crews. "It is a new breed," he continued. "We are learning lessons every day. You really don't know about the depth of the technology until you use it tactically."

In November 1998, the NATO-enforced pullout of Serbian military forces from Kosovo put the Mad Foxes' Orions on the front pages of the world's newspapers. Supplementing the intelligence coming from satellites and air force U-2s, the navy aircraft helped NATO officials keep a close eye on both the Serbs and the advancing Kosovo Liberation Army.

Meanwhile, VP-5 continued to support peacekeeping operations in Bosnia, surface surveillance around the Med, and exercises throughout the Sixth Fleet theater. Ensor said he had never flown more in the first three months of a deployment.

Cdr. Ken Deutsch, "ops O" for the Med's maritime surveillance forces, confirmed the rising demand for the P-3s. "Now we have an aircraft that's able to do the job at night, and when you have that ability, everybody wants to use you," Deutsch said.

This extra demand comes after years of cuts to the Orion flock. As the Soviet submarine threat receded in the early 1990s, the navy responded by reducing active-duty VP squadrons from twenty-four to twelve. The thirteen naval reserve units shrank to eight.

The result: VP-5 wasn't the only squadron whose aging birds were seeing more airtime. One June week, nine VP-26 crews flew on detachments to four different countries. "We do get more [requests] than we can handle," VP-26 skipper Johnson said.

On their summer 1998 deployment, the Tridents wound up flying about thirty plane-hours a day. Pilots had trouble keeping their flight hours under 130 per month, as required by regulations. "The VP community is really having to maximize their flight hours. Five or six years ago we didn't have to worry about that," Sherwood said. The commander of the navy's air forces in the Mediterranean has said that he is "well aware of the problems" and is keeping a close eye on the situation.

Cdr. Andy Johnson, for one, wasn't much surprised at the evolution of the P-3. "If you take the skills associated with finding a submerged submarine, it translates very well into a formula for finding anything anywhere," he said. "Now we are hunters of information."

# 4. THE CRUISERS

Aboard the USS *Princeton* off San Diego, January 1998

Flag in one hand, lanyard in the other, Signalman Seaman Apprentice Zach Bursnall cocked an ear at the loudspeaker mounted behind the bridge of the guided missile cruiser *Princeton*. Several decks below, his shipmates cast off the lines that bound the warship to the pier at Naval Station San Diego.

The 567-foot vessel inched away from the concrete mooring. The command "Break ensign" burst from the speaker. Yanking the lines, Bursnall ran the Stars and Stripes smartly up the mast. Then the young sailor headed forward to watch San Diego Harbor slide by. "I've never been to sea, so I'll see if I get seasick," said the eighteen-year-old Bursnall.

The three-day workup would barely take the guided missile cruiser over the horizon, but the Denver native was about to voyage into a whole new world. The grandson and stepson of sailors, the slim, bright-faced young man was several months into a six-year hitch that had already given him his first train ride and airplane flight. Outfitted in a brand-new nylon jacket and "*Princeton*" ball cap, Bursnall was having the time of his life.

On the bridge, his skipper was murmuring reminders to the junior officer who was conning the ship toward the harbor's mouth. "Watch the tide and the wind," cautioned Capt. James Moseman. "Now, one prolonged blast." The cruiser's foghorn let loose with a single note of mind-numbing volume.

The only visible cloud was a mile away, a very localized blob of water vapor kicked up by one of the navy's amphibious landing hovercraft. In *Princeton's* pilothouse, the quartermasters and other watch standers pretended to navigate through solid fog. They furiously exchanged position fixes and sailing directions.

Two small boats came alongside the cruiser, skillfully maneuvering through swells that threatened to toss them against the ship's massive hull. The deck crew lowered a pair of lines to the boatswain's mates on the captain's gig, winched the boat fifty feet up, and lowered it onto a cradle on *Princeton's* deck. They repeated the process for the second boat, plucking the rigid-hulled inflatable utility craft from the water and settling it into a second cradle. It was the kind of thing that could have been accomplished more safely at pierside, but this way was better practice.

"The basics are still important. If you can't do the basics, you can't get under way. Sometimes we kind of forget that," said Cdr. Randy Hill, the ship's executive officer.

The next three days aboard *Princeton* would be all about the basics: getting under way, setting watches, fighting fires. It had been nearly half a year since the cruiser returned from a six-month counternarcotics deployment off Central and South America. The interval had been spent profitably. Many crew members had journeyed for training to navy schools near and far. Others, aided by navy workers and civilian contractors, had tended to machinery and equipment worn by the long equatorial cruise. But sailing and fighting a warship is a complex endeavor, "a complicated team sport," as Moseman liked to put it. Crews that are razor-sharp at deployment's end lose their edge within months.

The problem on *Princeton* wasn't just the frailty of human memory. On any ship, a large portion of the crew leaves for good after each deployment. Enlistments end, promotions are granted, sailors move on to shore commands or other ships. One quarter of *Princeton's* four hundred crewmen had come aboard since the cruise ended in July 1997.

Few were so junior as Zach Bursnall, but forging an effective team would take the attention of youngsters and veterans alike. "One of the biggest challenges is taking those guys and teaching them to fight fires and not hurt themselves," Hill said. "When they step onboard, I tell them, 'This will be the biggest physical and mental challenge of your life.'"

A few days earlier, Hill had dispensed a welcome-aboard tip to Bursnall: Don't be afraid to ask for help. "The xo told me that in 'A' school, in boot camp, they expect you to fail, and if you fail, it's no big deal because they haven't lost anything. Here, everybody'll help you out because if you fail, we all fail," Bursnall said.

*Princeton's* departure from San Diego marked the crew's first step toward its next deployment. Over the next six months, the crew would learn to drive the ship, find potential threats, and take them out. Then *Princeton's* attention would turn toward the rest of the *Carl Vinson* battle group. Five more months would be spent learning to operate in close harmony with nearly a dozen other ships. Finally, in November, *Princeton* and the rest of the group would sail for the Persian Gulf.

Moseman would need every day of those eleven months to prepare his crew. Launched in 1987, *Princeton* is one of the navy's twenty-seven *Ticonderoga*-class guided missile cruisers. Enormously capable, they are correspondingly complex.

The ninety-five-hundred-ton cruisers were built around the Aegis combat system, which knits the ship's computers, radars, guns, and missiles into an unparalleled surface-to-air defense network. *Princeton's* massive aluminum superstructures bear the distinctive hexagonal panels of the world's best air-search system. Unlike traditional rotating radars, the arrays project hundreds of narrow beams, reaching out like fingers over vast volumes of airspace. Its operators track scores of airborne contacts at once, from high-flying bombers to sea-skimming cruise missiles. They boast they can spot a tossed quarter miles off.

The radars feed a fire-control system that governs the largest variety of weapons available on an American warship. After World War II's battleships were retired, the "*Ticos*" became America's most heavily armed surface combatants—navy jargon for warships that don't carry fighter planes and don't submerge. Eight Harpoon missiles can take out enemy ships up to seventy-five miles away. Six torpedo tubes can launch lightweight torps against submarines. Like the frigates, each *Tico* carries a pair of antisubmarine helicopters that greatly increase the ship's hearing and reach.

The cruisers carry a pair of five-inch guns, one mounted on the forecastle and the other on the fantail. Firing shells weighing up to seventy pounds, they can strike ships or shore targets fourteen miles away. The dual-purpose guns can also bring down aircraft flying as high as forty-eight thousand feet. For close-in defense against antiship missiles, *Tico*s have a pair of modern-day Gatling guns called Phalanxes. Firing fifty rounds per second, they can rip "leakers" to shreds with heavy slugs of depleted uranium. The cruisers also carry flares and chaff to foil missile locks.

But a modern cruiser's biggest punch is hidden under the deck: the batteries of antiaircraft and cruise missiles. Like frigates, the first five *Tico*s still carry trainable launchers, but *Princeton* and the rest of the class are equipped with vertical launch boxes. Mounted fore and aft of the superstructure, 122 missile cells are sealed under twin grids of trapdoors that resembled the snap tops to giant pillboxes. Each cell can disgorge its missile in seconds, sending it hurtling off in a rush of flame and smoke. The supersonic Standard rocket can destroy a missile or airplane up to forty miles away, while the jet-propelled Tomahawk can hit a building at a thousand.

The *Tico*s were designed in the late 1970s as bodyguards for the fleet's aircraft carriers. No flattop deploys anywhere without escorts, and certainly not to the Persian Gulf. There's precious little space to hide a thousand-foot aircraft carrier in the small sea. Traffic is heavy on, above, and possibly below the waves, and there is no way to tell which craft holds prying eyes or hostile intent. In the upcoming deployment, *Vinson*'s crew would rely on *Princeton* to keep them safe.

But in one way, cruisers are no different from frigates: the cold war's end has changed and expanded their mission. Today, *Tico*s use their sensitive radars to find airborne drug couriers in the Caribbean or oil smugglers in the Persian Gulf.

Cruise missile strikes have become increasingly common over the past decade. Ever since it was first used in combat during 1991's

Persian Gulf War, the Tomahawk has often been the Pentagon's strike weapon of choice. *Princeton* and six other *Tico*s launched 105 Tomahawks against Iraqi targets during Operation Desert Storm, more than a third of the total. In 1993, President Clinton picked the cruise missile to punish Saddam Hussein for an assassination attempt aimed at former president George Bush. In 1995, the cruiser *Normandy* fired thirteen Tomahawks at Serbian emplacements in Bosnia. One year later, U.S. leaders punished Baghdad's violence against Iraqi Kurds with Operation Desert Strike, which included six missiles from the cruiser *Shiloh.*

In 1998, *Shiloh* was again the ship on the scene when Clinton ordered strikes against suspected terrorist camps in Afghanistan and a pharmaceuticals factory in Sudan in retaliation for the August bombings of two American embassies. The year ended with the largest missile bombardment in the Tomahawk's two-decade history. In December's four-day air strike campaign, *Tico*s fired some two hundred cruise missiles into Iraq. Combined with launches from subs and destroyers, Operation Desert Fox used up 10 percent of the navy's Tomahawk inventory.

Decision makers in Washington see two major virtues in the Tomahawk: its precise delivery of a thousand-pound warhead helps avoid civilian casualties and "collateral damage"; and it keeps American aviators out of harm's way. For the *Tico*s that launch the Tomahawk, the new policy has meant a whole new importance.

In January, *Princeton* was still far from ready to take its place among the navy's frontline ships. But its crew was working hard. Down in the noisy space between two of the ship's four engines, Gas Turbine System Technician (Electrical) 3d Class Lawrence Nash was finishing up last-minute adjustments to a fuel preheater, a machine that warms the marine diesel fuel, leaching the water from it and making the engines burn more efficiently.

"I got three hours' sleep in two days, getting ready for workups," Nash said. "We gotta take care of what we gotta take care of. This ship can't do its job, we can't support the U.S. interests unless it can go."

Over the next three days, *Princeton*'s engineering crew would endure thirty to forty machinery casualty drills. Part of the standard training syllabus, the drills would be supervised by members of the Pacific surface fleet's Afloat Training Group. The stated mission of these experienced sailors is to help the ship's senior crew members train the junior ones. Ships' crews view them—at best—with deep ambivalence. "To a junior officer, an assist visit is just like an inspection," one lieutenant said after completing a sea tour. "We were fighting off training teams at the bow."

Standing at the center of the nine-deck ship, Lt. Cdr. Jim Morgan watched his watch team prep the engineering control room to begin the drills. As the ship's chief engineer, he "owned" this room. He also owned the job of keeping the ship powered up and ready to move. And making sure the air conditioners worked. And that fresh water flowed from the evaporators. And a hundred other machinery-related tasks.

Like every officer onboard, Morgan had the responsibility without the ability to do much of the work himself, which is why he was determined to get his crew trained right. Morgan pointed to a petty officer at a complex control board. "That guy's got a lot of power," said Morgan, an intensely focused yet affable man who was clearly proud of his troops. "He's got a nine-thousand-ton cruiser in his hands. That guy's only a second class petty officer. He was a third class a month ago."

A problem with a gas turbine control device held up the drills for half an hour. Finally Lt. (jg) Dave Zook signaled his readiness. "Ready to commence drills, aye," the engineering officer of the watch told Morgan. The chief engineer gave the trainers a nod.

For the next several hours, and on into the night, Zook and the rest of the engineering watch struggled with simulated malfunctions. The trainers manipulated the giant control board, causing it to show fuel valves springing open, clutches losing their grip, and gas turbines spinning out of control. Each casualty had a prescribed series of corrective steps laid out in the ship's manuals. Sometimes Zook and the rest consulted the books; sometimes they didn't need to. By deployment time, they would know the procedures cold.

While the engineers grappled with all types of disasters, other departments ran their own practice sessions. "We take every opportunity we can. The taxpayers spend a lot of money on us and we take it very seriously," Hill said.

San Diego was a dim glow to the east when Zach Bursnall arrived in the darkened pilothouse that evening. Ducking behind a blackout curtain, he watched a quartermaster review a chart. Pencil marks indicated the ship's position: circles for visual fixes, triangles for satellite fixes, squares for estimates.

Bursnall watched carefully. Like the ship's other signalmen, he was learning the navigation skills of the quartermasters. Although the navy's personnel bureau hadn't yet announced a merger of the two ratings, sailors aboard *Princeton* and many other ships were making a point of aggressive cross-training, just in case. "In two to three months, he ought to be able to be up here on his own," said Quartermaster 2d Class Kevin Kropp.

The next morning found Bursnall back on the bridge taking navigation lessons after a night of fitful sleep. Top-heavy with electronic gear, *Tico*s roll gently but steadily. "I thought someone was trying to wake me up," Bursnall said. "Well, at least I didn't puke." The foghorn cut loose again. "Oh, I hate that damn thing," the youthful sailor said.

By late morning, Zook and the rest of the engineering crew had completed more than a dozen drills under the watchful eyes of Morgan and the other engineers. It was time to get the whole ship involved.

Few things are more terrifying to sailors than a fire at sea. In a ship's iron chambers, fire fighting is literally a do-or-die proposition. Most ships train obsessively for damage control, but *Princeton*'s sailors have more reason than most. This cruiser is one of only a few ships in the fleet that have suffered combat damage. In 1991, it had to be towed into a Persian Gulf port after an Iraqi mine exploded nearby.

Murmuring into his walkie-talkie's headset microphone, Morgan passed the all-clear up to Moseman. Then the "Cheng"—surface navy slang for chief engineer—stepped back to watch.

At 11:09 P.M., an alarm buzzed in the engineering control center. A petty officer scanned his gauges. Fuel pressure was dropping fast in one of the ship's gas turbine engines. The tanks were full and the pumps were still running. That meant one thing: a leak.

Quickly, the watch standers moved to shut down the machinery—anything that might cause a spark—in the main engine space. But controlling the danger was going to take more than just the engineers. Zook pulled the general quarters alarm.

The ship's spaces filled with the *bong-bong-bong* of the alarm. A stream of sailors poured into the control space, which doubles in crisis as the damage control central. Most had already pulled socks over trouser cuffs. Now they nodded into olive drab "flash hoods," ski masks woven of nonflammable material, and slung orange plastic boxes—emergency breathing devices—over their shoulders.

Now equipped to survive, they turned to a locker and spread bulky damage control manuals across a table. Four minutes after the alarm went off, a voice boomed through the 1MC: "All repair lockers manned."

Nearby, the engineers punched buttons to flood the engine room with fire-fighting foam, then worked to drain the fuel into the scuppers at the bottom of the hull. Next, they obtained the skipper's permission—a sign of the new, more environmentally conscious navy—to pump the bilges into the sea.

Despite the precautions, the fuel ignited. There was a fire—simulated, of course—in Main Engineering Space Two.

In the control room, a siren whined. The lights dimmed. The 1MC sputtered guttural exclamations. The control panel indicated the failure of a fire pump. Slamming hatches, the firefighters drew an airtight seal around the engineering space, isolating it from the rest of the ship.

Red lights skittered across the control board. The crew's attempts to quench the blaze with extinguishers were failing. The damage control team prepared to release Halon, an inert gas that suffocates flames by displacing oxygen. A huge red evacuation lamp began to flash in Main Two. If this had been real, anybody left inside would have sixty seconds to get out—or die with the fire.

"Halon discharged in Main Two," someone reported in damage control central. Now there was nothing to do but wait. Outside the hatch that led down to the engine room, a dozen sailors in helmets and heavy olive coveralls wrestled with hoses. The scene leaders yelled muffled instructions through their flash hoods and masks.

A chief petty officer, attired like Morgan in a yellow "Damage Control Training Team" ball cap, gave a signal and the sailors yanked tabs on green flasks. Inside the canteen-sized containers, chemicals began to combine, filling their masks with an oxygen supply that would last half an hour.

Much of the drill was simulated, but the oxygen breathing apparatuses were real. "We've got so many new kids just out of boot camp, they need to actually light them off," the chief said. "It costs money, but life is much more than a dollar."

Ten minutes after the Halon injection, the damage control officer reported over the 1MC that the fire had been snuffed out by the laws of chemistry. The firefighters began a seven-minute countdown, waiting for the ventilators to clear the Halon and render the space habitable once again.

Waiting behind Main Two's dogged door, the training team flooded the space with special-effects smoke. Through the haze, Moseman exhorted a young officer to cut the sailors no slack. "It's a new team. No mistakes," the skipper told Lt. (jg) Brian Schultz. The ship's disbursing officer, Schultz had picked up the extra job of training officer. "If they screw up, slug 'em." His threat was no more real than the fire, but Moseman was serious about getting it right.

With such a green crew, the ship could ill afford bad habits. "There's real danger in a training situation when you let people do it wrong," said Schultz. "If a guy makes a wrong step, he'll do it two or three times."

Within minutes, the helmeted firefighters pulled open the door and began inching down the stairs. "Advance on one!" the first cried. "Advance on one, aye!" the next responded. The team took a step forward, dragging a heavy fire hose. Schultz admonished a sailor who failed to check a step for sturdiness. "Stomp on it!" he said. The sailor gave it a few kicks with a heavily insulated boot.

Schultz mused about the training role Moseman had given him. "My buddies on larger ships, they go to sleep during drills," he said. "Here, everybody plays."

In the crowded machinery space, the lead firefighter peered through an infrared camera. The big cylindrical scope would help him check for residual hot spots. The equipment is high-tech, but simulating hot spots isn't. The trainers microwaved a few onions, wrapped them in aluminum foil, and hid them among the machinery.

With a few clues from the training crew, the lead sailor recovered the tinfoil balls one by one. Through the mingled odors of smoke, lubrication, and insulation, the smell of roasted onions began to permeate the machinery space.

The drill ended at noon, and *Princeton* secured from general quarters.

When the alarm went off, Bursnall had headed to his GQ stations at the flag rack aft of the pilothouse. "This is the best place on the ship because it's outside. I don't like being down under the deck," he said. He gazed up at the antennae and dishes that sprouted all over the ship. "We haven't figured out what all that is."

Ranked third in his class of signalmen, Bursnall picked duty aboard *Princeton* and swung his bags aboard nine days before its 21 January departure. "It was real cool, until you realize you don't know anybody," he said. But armed with a friendly personality—and abetted by a common passion for Jerry Springer's talk show—he had already gotten to know many of his shipmates.

"When I was in boot camp, I thought I was in the navy. I wasn't in the navy; I was in boot camp. Then I was really excited when I got out of boot camp and I was going to 'A' school," he said. "Then you get here and you realize how much experience everyone has and how little you do."

Another lesson was not so pleasant: "Got my first command ball cap, went to take a shower, came back, and it was gone," he said. "Must've grown legs and walked away."

As a new crewman, Bursnall would soon be pulled off his signalman's watches and sent down to the mess deck for three months. The official name for the duty is "food service assistant," but everyone calls it "cranking." At any given time, eighteen junior enlisted sailors wash dishes, clean the mess deck, and generally help *Princeton*'s mess specialists serve up to fifteen hundred meals each day. "It doesn't sound like much fun, but I guess you have to start somewhere," he said.

All in all, Bursnall was rather pleased with his new career. "I haven't had any problems," he said. "A lot of people whine about it, but it's the funnest job I've ever had."

A school of dolphins was jumping around the ship's bow when the executive officer's voice boomed out from the 1MC. "The last time we had GQ was the first week of December, so we're a little dusty," Hill said. He noted that the crew was a bit slow manning the repair stations, and added a few reminders. "Dog the hatches behind your shipmates. Make sure you know where your gear is."

"Tomorrow," Hill said, "we'll run it again."

---

Aboard the USS *Vella Gulf* in the Baltic Sea, June 1998

A half year later and a hemisphere away, the cruiser *Vella Gulf* sailed across the Baltic Sea in pursuit of a Swedish submarine. Like *Princeton,* the cruiser was between deployments. But *Vella Gulf* was six months further along the training course and had been dispatched to Europe for a few weeks to fertilize international naval contacts.

Part of the same flotilla as the frigate *Halyburton, Vella Gulf* was playing the "mission-essential unit" in the BALTOPS antisubmarine exercises. Accustomed to protecting, the cruiser became the protected, at least for the duration of the two-week exercise.

*Vella Gulf*'s sonar techs weren't having any better luck than *Halyburton*'s in picking up the subs. "The water conditions are lousy," said the skipper, Capt. Brian Schires. "We got within two thousand yards and weren't able to get a fix."

"It's been unreal," said Lt. Phil Davis, the weapons officer. "A lot of times, visual is our best sensor."

And the Swedish sub used its home-field advantage. "It's kind of like playing hide-and-seek with a kid in his own backyard," Davis said. "I've never been on your block, and now we're in your backyard."

Like *Halyburton*'s skipper, Shires and Davis were discovering that the Balts played the antisub game by different rules. "In the U.S., we have the tendency to do standoff ASW, using helos or ASROCSS [antisubmarine rockets]," Schires said. "They're very comfortable getting very close and pounding on them."

Communications conundrums were par for the BALTOPS course. "We're having problems with the octopus," squawked the loudspeaker on the cruiser's bridge. Davis and another officer traded puzzled looks. Eventually, a sailor found the word in a NATO operating manual. "Octopus" is a maritime patrol aircraft term for a certain antisubmarine sensor.

The cruiser's air intercept controllers learned to speak slowly and think fast when directing Polish MiGs and Swedish Viggens around the cruiser's airspace. "The language barrier is a big thing. They have heavy accents and broken English," said Operations Specialist 2d Class (SW) Joseph D. Keehner.

His shipmates on the bridge had fewer problems. "Bumps in the road instead of roadblocks," Davis said. Of course, they were dealing with thirty-knot ships instead of fighter jets moving ten times as quickly. "I'm pleasantly surprised," he said. "Seamanship is universal. Taking station is universal."

For the American skippers, the exercise was a chance to inspect their counterparts' ship-handling skills. "You're always a bit nervous when there's a new ship on your beam," said Schires. "But by Friday, we'll know them really well."

The sailors were getting to know each other as well. Throughout the exercise, rubber boats and gigs carried a steady flow of visitors between ships of different navies. Fresh from a visit to the Lithuanian frigate *Aukstatis,* Electronics Warfare Technician 3d Class Martin Wood clambered back up *Vella Gulf*'s side. The Soviet-built ship's half-gray, half-black hull was still visible three hundred yards off the cruiser's starboard beam. Wood explained to curious shipmates that the unusual paint scheme covered a perennial smudge caused by hull-mounted diesel exhaust vents. He also outlined differences in operating procedures on the *Aukstatis.* Either the captain or the executive officer, he said, was required to be on the bridge at all times.

Engineman 2d Class (SW) Mike Lombardozzi reported that the ship's crew spaces were tiny, the technology was outdated, and water-making capacity—and shower stalls—completely absent. "Thank God

I'm in the U.S. Navy," he said, drawing lungfuls of fresh air.

Officers of various navies shared dinners afloat and ashore. Davis traded stories with *Aukstatis*'s skipper, a Lithuanian who had been the weapons officer on a Red Navy cruiser in the 1980s. After the Soviet breakup, he volunteered for duty with his new country's navy.

Davis found it deeply moving to sail with enemies-turned-friends. "I went over to a patrol boat, put my hand on a missile launcher, and said, 'OK, this was what I spent years learning to shoot down,'" he said.

The American admiral who ran BALTOPS 1998 maintained that getting to know the non-NATO countries was more important than working with America's NATO allies. But Rear Adm. William Copeland had harsh words for one missing player. Russia, the superpower-turned-superpauper, had declined an invitation to participate. "You build mutual trust and confidence at all levels, from the deck-plate sailor to the admirals," said the commander of Carrier Group Eight, the U.S. Navy unit in control of the BALTOPS flotilla. "I think Russia really missed the boat, big time."

---

Aboard the USS *Shiloh* in the Persian Gulf, July 1998

On yet another hot, steamy, muggy July day in the gulf, it was suddenly . . . Christmas . . . aboard the guided missile cruiser *Shiloh.* In the ship's darkened combat information center, sailors walked among a blizzard of paper snowflakes that dripped from overhead ducts and pipes and conduits. Dozens of electronic terminals, their faces aglow with air-search radar returns and navigational data, turned the scissored filigree faintly red and blue. A six-inch ersatz snowman sat atop a locked filing cabinet, a rotund form rolled from the tiny shreds of sensitive documents.

Up on the bridge, a quartermaster with a calligraphic touch had taped to the chart table a hand-lettered sign spelling out "Merry Christmas" in heavy Gothic strokes. Outside the sick bay, the ship's corpsmen had created a fake hearth, evoking the comforts of home with butcher paper and colored marker.

"It's just a little bit of fun," said *Shiloh*'s commander, Capt. Stephen Busch. "I got up on Saturday and said, 'Hey guys, it's Christmas in July in a few days. Get moving!' One young sailor—he's very clever—asked me for Christmas leave."

The skipper's whim conjured a hint of Americana in the Arabian Sea, an ironic response to the grinding heat outside the ship's skin, a day of levity in a deadly serious deployment. Six months earlier, the United States and Iraq had almost come to blows over the UN weapons inspection program. The situation had hardly improved in late June when *Shiloh* and the rest of the *Lincoln* carrier battle group pulled into the gulf. For the next few months, the cruiser was an American cop in a bad neighborhood.

Just weeks after the "holiday" celebration, *Shiloh* got a call to action, launching cruise missiles against a purported terrorist training camp in Afghanistan.

The twenty-ninth of July was not quite a typical workday, with *It's a Wonderful Life* playing nonstop on the ship's closed-circuit television and Christmas carols seeping tinnily from the 1MC. A few carolers made the rounds, participants in a not-exactly-voluntary sing-off between the ship's ensigns and its newly selected chief-petty-officers-to-be.

Much of the crew slept late, standard practice on reveille-free holidays. But the galley staff worked overtime to produce a savory feast of roast beef, turkey, and ham. Digging deep into secret caches, the mess specialists strewed hard candy across the salad bar, drawing gasps from more than one sailor.

The day even included a bona fide celebration. Three sailors had recently qualified to wear the silver ship-and-crossed-swords of the enlisted surface warfare specialist. Worn on the left breast, the pin marks a sailor who has studied the ship from keel to mast top, memorizing a wealth of technical data about the vessel's engineering, damage control, electricity, and more. Sailors rarely earn the pin in less than a year; most never earn it at all.

Chief Signalman (SW) John Norrell ran the qualifying process aboard *Shiloh,* a job he took very seriously. "If the man standing next to you is wearing an ESWS pin in the Persian Gulf and something goes down, the chances are that man is going to have a better idea what to do than someone who isn't," Norrell said.

As the lunchtime crowd ebbed from the cruiser's mess deck, several dozen more shipmates squeezed into the small room for the pinning ceremony. The three sailors—Hull Technician 3d Class (SW) Kenneth Woodard, Fire Controlman 2d Class (SW) Chad Crosby, and Signalman 2d Class (SW) Brian Brown—stood at attention. The skipper made a short congratulatory speech but deferred the actual pinning to another guest: Rear Adm. William Putnam, commander of the *Lincoln* battle group. Putnam added the silver insignia to each sailor's chest, then said a few words of his own. Afterward, the sailors talked about their feelings on attaining their long-held goal. In unison, Woodard and Crosby said, "Relieved."

The day wasn't all Christmas cheer and celebration. *Shiloh*'s adversaries in the Persian Gulf weren't taking the day off. And even if Saddam wasn't stirring, the endless summer heat beat on.

In a sweltering auxiliary space deep within *Shiloh*'s hull, Engineman 1st Class Terry Vaughn cocked an ear at one of the ship's four massive air conditioners. A rough whir told the fifteen-year veteran that his cooling machinery needed work. On a cruiser in the gulf, that's always a rush job.

"If we keep it down for more than three or four hours, you feel it and the equipment feels it," said Vaughn's shipmate, Gas Turbine System Technician (Mechanical) 1st Class (SW) Kirk Hood. "If we don't do our job and the SPY [radar] goes down, she's not performing our mission."

The cooling systems weren't the only machinery overtaxed by the weather. Even before *Shiloh* emerged from the Strait of Hormuz, the crew discovered that the ship's twin evaporators weren't built for the gulf's ninety-five-degree seawater. The evaporators were producing only about sixteen thousand gallons of potable water each day—about one-fifth less than usual.

Most of a ship's fresh water goes to rinse its exposed areas, an essential guard against the corrosion of salt spray. Faced with a choice between comfort and corrosion, Busch told the crew to cut back on showers and other nonessential uses. The crew responded like conservation champs.

"We went from thirty-five gallons [per sailor per day] to twenty-five gallons the next day, as soon as we made it obvious," said Master Chief

Machinist's Mate (SW/SS) Rodney A. Wells, *Shiloh's* command master chief.

The gulf's bathwater temperatures also kill off the Pacific Ocean mussels that live in the water intakes. Their dead bodies foul the grates, further reducing water flow. And the gulf ecosystem sends ships off with a parting gift: local underwater grasses that die in cooler climes, clogging the grates anew.

The July heat stress was affecting the sailors no less than their machines. On deck, the boatswain's mates cut their watches to tropical duration: two hours during daylight, the navy standard four hours after dark. Yet fleeing from the hot deck to a cool passageway proved hazardous as well. In a cruel irony, many crewmen caught colds simply by constantly crossing the air-conditioning boundaries.

In the ship's hangar, Damage Controlman 3d Class Robert Debruin sweated in thick protective coveralls. As he waited for the ship to launch a helicopter, the fireman tried to get comfortable in the narrow space between a hangar bulkhead and a helicopter's Plexiglas nose.

"You go from 116 degrees to 60 to 116 to 60—you get sick real quick," Debruin said.

Like many of his shipmates, Debruin took immense pride in *Shiloh*. "This ship just has higher standards than other ships." It shows, he said, in the awards that hang in a passageway by the mess deck. In five years, the ship won four battle efficiency awards, denoting the best cruiser on the West Coast. Its galley had recently picked up a Ney Award for the best meal service on a mid-sized Pacific warship. And nearly three quarters of its senior crew members wore the warfare specialist pins.

But the cruiser's enviable record couldn't immunize its crew against fleetwide manning shortages. Even on deployment, Shiloh was missing sailors in almost all of its specialties, spreading the workload on fewer backs. A dozen electronics technicians—essential personnel on modern warships—were doing the work of seventeen. Four of them had reported aboard just before deployment, missing months of preparation.

Especially galling in the rank-conscious navy, senior sailors found themselves doing jobs they thought they'd left behind. When a sea-man left his division for a few months of "cranking"—working as a food server or busboy on the mess deck—a third-class petty officer had to fill in, creating a ripple of job swapping that ended with chiefs taking on blueshirts' work.

The situation shortchanged everyone, ensigns and junior-grade lieutenants included. "The division officer doesn't get the time with his chief learning how to be a good officer," Wells said. One result was poor retention. "A lot of our best sailors are bailing," he said.

But overall, morale ran high throughout the ship's well-scrubbed spaces. "We do it right on *Shiloh,*" Hood said as he trod the engine room's steel grates. "The opportunities here are excellent. I'm qualled EOW," or engineering officer of the watch—unusual for a petty officer.

Having an important mission helps, Norrell said. "They still deal with the frustration and the manning, but there's a purpose in their step," he said. "This is the real navy here in the gulf. We're on station and ready to answer all bells."

---

Aboard the USS *Yorktown* in the Chesapeake Bay, September 1997

In an era of declining budgets, the arithmetic is simple. The navy won't be able to keep its fleet at anywhere near three hundred ships if it cannot drastically cut its operating expenses. In this brave new world, a *Tico* cruiser's Caribbean deployment pointed the way to the future.

A bold attempt to cut costs with new technology and new ways of doing business, the "Smart Ship" program put the cruiser *Yorktown* to sea with $8 million in new computers and communications equip-ment—and nearly 13 percent fewer crew members.

*Yorktown*'s performance was closely monitored during workups, but it took a real deployment to prove that a cruiser with just two bridge watch standers—instead of the normal eleven—could handle real missions. The crew got their chance in January 1997, when *Yorktown* left its Pascagoula, Mississippi, home port and headed south.

For five months of navy–coast guard operations, *Yorktown* served as the group's air warfare command post, helping to spot, shadow, and stop shipments of illegal drugs. Evaluation team after evaluation team delivered thumbs-up verdicts. The graders declared that *Yorktown* could safely cut forty-eight jobs from its normal complement of 350 crew members and twenty-six officers. The manpower savings would come to nearly $3 million per year.

The commander of the Atlantic surface fleet gave the high-tech, reduced-personnel experiment his stamp of approval. "Clearly, the Smart Ship initiative was a success and can provide a significant return on a modest investment," Vice Adm. Henry C. Giffin III wrote to CNO Adm. Jay Johnson in September.

By rethinking watch duty and maintenance chores, the crew had slashed their weekly workload by about 30 percent, or nine thousand person-hours. For example, frequent testing and better corrosion control techniques allowed a 15 percent reduction in preventive maintenance.

The crew set up a ten-section watch in port, meaning that sailors must show up for a twenty-four-hour watch only once in ten days. Most ships have three- and four-section duty. "There's no other ship in the fleet with ten sections," boasted Operations Specialist 3d Class Mike Wilkinson. The key is aggressive cross training. Ships must retain a certain number of qualified firefighters and other emergency personnel aboard at all times. On *Yorktown,* the crew spread the load by training many more people to fight fires.

That kind of change has made life better aboard ship, said Cdr. Eric Sweigard, lowering his voice as if telling a secret. "It's not even close to as hectic," said the ship's skipper.

Perhaps nowhere is the new thinking more evident than on the bridge. Lookouts, helmsmen, and coffee runners have been eliminated in favor of computers that allow just two watch standers to drive the ship, monitor its machinery, coordinate damage control, and track radar contacts—all from a single two-foot-wide color screen.

The technology is not glitch-free. The core systems are up 98 percent of the time, said Lt. Mark Mearig, *Yorktown*'s training officer. But 98 percent is not always enough.

In the wee hours of 20 September, the ship went dead in the water, reportedly after a computer attempted the mathematical impossibility of division by zero. *Yorktown* was out of commission for about an hour before it was able to get under way again, and the captain returned to port for repairs. Two days later, the ship steamed to Annapolis so Naval Academy midshipmen could see the future.

When the ship approached the academy on the Severn River, its sophisticated autopilot, working with digital charts on CD-ROM, brought *Yorktown* in with fully automated aplomb. "It was the easiest, most accurate anchorage I've ever done," Sweigard said.

Despite the nearly empty bridge, the new Windows NT–based computers have given Sweigard more combat capability than ever before. With an autopilot that takes direction from satellites in order to avoid shoals, eluding diesel subs in the littorals takes just a few mouse clicks. "I get over into shallow water with a great deal more ease than I used to," Sweigard said.

The navy can't afford to wait before putting the Smart Ship concept into action, said Rear Adm. James F. Amerault, the director of the fiscal management division of the navy's budget office. "We need it. From a budget perspective, I need to see those savings," he said.

By 1999, dozens of ships were slated to get the Smart Ship package, and the experiment was making waves throughout the fleet. Later that year, Giffin was encouraging Atlantic Fleet skippers to go ahead and adopt any of the reduced-personnel techniques that didn't need the new computer equipment. If the new methods continue to bear up under scrutiny, *Arleigh Burke*–class destroyers will follow, then carriers, frigates, amphibs, and the rest of the fleet.

---

Aboard the USS *Philippine Sea* in the Adriatic Sea, March 1999

The skipper's voice broke from loudspeakers across the ship. "I have some news. We have received tasking for one primary Tomahawk. We will launch in approximately five-zero minutes," said Capt. Ron Jenkins III.

There were two basic reactions from the 350 souls aboard the guided missile cruiser *Philippine Sea*. About one-third of the crew began the deliberate preparations for the missile launch. The rest mostly turned over in their racks and fell back asleep.

It was 12:27 P.M. local time, March 29. NATO's Operation Allied Force, which opened with a Tomahawk cruise missile blasting from the cruiser's forward tubes, was five days old. On station near the Yugoslav coast, the warship was hammering the Serb military in hopes of stopping attacks on Kosovo's ethnic Albanians.

This would be the *Phil Sea*'s fourteenth strike. Or perhaps its fifteenth. No one in charge was telling, and no one else seemed to be counting. "After awhile, it just goes away. It's just starting to be a normal thing now," said Engineman 1st Class (SW) Duane Clausen.

The first time had been different.

"We were all like, 'This is it. This is the moment,'" said Operations Specialist 2d Class (SW) Jeffrey Ingram. "It's what we are here to do."

When the first strike order arrived on March 25, Jenkins sent the crew to general quarters. In the combat information center, Chief Fire Controlman (SW) John Gibboney downloaded target data from a satellite into the missile's guidance computer. Gibboney had never fired a live missile until he pushed the launch button that night. "The ship performed flawlessly," he said later. "It's validation that the years of training have come to fruition."

When the missile tube erupted in flame and smoke, most of the crew was watching on little black-and-white monitors scattered through the ship. In a repair locker near the stern, Gas Turbine System Technician (Electrical) 3d Class (SW) John Rogers recalled a brief vibration, a gunpowdery smell, and the sounds of something taking off. "There was a boom and a whooshing," he said.

Navy Counselor 1st Class Victor Roman passed messages in the combat information center. "I thought I would be scared," said Roman. "But when it came down to it, I just did what I was trained to do."

That first launch pierced the bubble of excitement and stress. Certainly, the crew was proud of themselves—especially on learning that a photo of the ascending missile had played prominently in newspapers around the globe. But the act of war soon became routine. Most of the succeeding missile strikes were carried out by a regular watch team.

"It's not a whole lot different from the ordinary," said the ship's executive officer, Lt. Cdr. Tom Ransom. "Today, I did berthing and messing inspections." He gestured to wooden trays mounted above his stateroom desk. "These guys still load up my inbox."

The action didn't seem to affect anyone's appetite; *Philippine Sea*'s pantry was slowly emptying. Dashing to its station in the Adriatic, the cruiser skipped a port call where containers of food were to be picked up. Now the ship was running low on milk, fresh fruit and vegetables, even pancake syrup. "You start coming up with ingenious things to put on top of pancakes, like pie fillings," said one member of the cruiser's food service division.

Some crewmen turned their attention to the loved ones who flooded their e-mail boxes with concerned messages. "We get a lot of letters from home, and everybody's worried about us," said Fire Controlman 3d Class Daniel Morehead. But those worries didn't square with reality. "This is one of the most powerful ships ever put in the water."

Others used their new e-mail capacity to keep up with events. Sonar Technician (Surface) 2d Class (SW) Mark Roberts signed up for the daily digests delivered from CNN's Web site. "It's just like reading the daily newspaper, and it helps keep you focused on the mission," said Roberts.

Sometimes, *Philippine Sea* received notice of strikes a day in advance. On March 29, the crew had just an hour to prepare. Thirty minutes before launch, the cruiser's bridge was preternaturally dark and silent. A boatswain's mate drummed fingers on a metal housing. The executive officer cracked open a soda can. The noise split the darkness.

"Most of the sailors will just roll over and go back to sleep," Ransom said. "Frankly, I need them there, so that they'll be alert on watch."

As launch time neared, a siren rose and fell, once. The loudspeaker crackled with the voice of the ship's tactical action officer. "Two-minute standby for the aft launcher." Then, "Ten seconds."

It was a long ten seconds.

Then a pop, a roar, and a plume of smoke geysering beyond the radio masts. A tiny sun rose from the deck. There was a twenty-foot missile somewhere astride the blinding light, but naked eyes could not penetrate its cloak of smoke and fire. The ball tipped toward port, dropped a flaming booster rocket, and vanished into the night.

No one said a word. Lightning flashed on the horizon. The sailors on the bridge wing hustled back to the ship's warmth. "Launching a thousand pounds of high explosive over the beach is serious stuff, and they know it," Jenkins said later.

Down in central engineering control, Chief Gas Turbine Mechanic (SW) Mike Cetnarowski helped bring the gas turbines up for each launch. He firmly backed the strikes against Serb military forces, but the death and destruction on the other end stayed on his mind. "I think about it, and I know a lot of people do," said Cetnarowski. "I wouldn't want to be on the receiving end. It humbles you."

An hour passed. The sweet smell of cinnamon rolls wafted from the galley, drawing runners from the bridge and elsewhere.

The baker, who intended to serve the maple-drizzled pastries for breakfast, was reportedly growing frustrated at the pilferage. "He should've closed the vents," chuckled one chief.

# 5. THE HORNETS

Aboard the USS *Eisenhower* in the Adriatic Sea, July 1998

Even when you've got the navy's newest jets, maintenance takes as much attention, as much meticulous precision, as flying itself.

In *Ike*'s cavernous hangar bay, Aviation Electronics Technician 2d Class John Champion ran his hands slowly across a strike fighter's aluminum skin, using his fingers and a flashlight to find minuscule pits in the aircraft's gray finish. Behind him, the deep blue waters of the Adriatic Sea slid by, visible through the giant oval portal of the hangar door. Moving inch by inch, the aircraft maintainer marked the jet's painted body with white chalk, leaving circles around visible dings, slashes across possible ones. Later, other maintainers would repaint, reseal, or replace the nicked parts.

Nearly every day, one pilot or another flew this F/A-18C Hornet off the carrier's bow, across the Bosnian coastline, and back onto the flight deck. The aviators were training, protecting, preparing for battle. When they returned, smacking the aircraft at better than 150 mph onto the grimy flight deck, they turned the jet over to squadron maintainers.

Champion fought his own battle at the speed of rust. Corrosion can damage a combat jet as effectively as a bullet, although less dramatically. Infinitesimal, creeping rot starts with the mere act of flying. A zooming jet creates a heavy positive charge of static electricity, which attracts invisible airborne particles. At hundreds of miles an hour, wear and tear proceeds quickly. "When you hear the jet tearing through the air, that's not just the engine," another maintainer said. "That's the molecular structure tearing through the air."

A Hornet's steel-aluminum-composite body bears the seeds of its own deterioration. Where dissimilar metals touch, molecular breakdown can start. "Anywhere you have fasteners, you have the possibility of corrosion," said Champion's partner, Aviation Structural Mechanic (Structures) 2d Class Ralph Scott.

Scott and Champion were maintainers for the VFA-83 Rampagers, one of three squadrons of strike fighters aboard *Eisenhower*. On this deployment, the Rampagers had eighteen pilots, more than 150 enlisted crew members, and a dozen brand-new F/A-18C Hornets.

Along with the rest of the giant ship, they had sped through the Mediterranean Sea to be prepared for possible hostilities in the former Yugoslavia. Now, the squadron's pilots were flying a mission or two "over the beach" every day, practicing bombing runs and close air support of the United Nations troops below. "You just couldn't ask for better training," said Capt. Greg Brown, *Ike*'s skipper and a veteran attack pilot himself.

It was the best of times for VFA-83. For the pilots, there was lots of flying and a "real-world" mission. "I had a Belgian forward air controller walk me into three targets today," said Cdr. Pat Rainey, VFA-83's executive officer. "We're really into ground force protection. We're taking pictures of stuff to attack if things really go bad." For the enlisted maintainers, being on deployment meant access to spare parts and a chance to be on the tip of the spear. "The job satisfaction is getting out here to the Med and sending planes off the pointy end and having pilots come back safely," said Aviation Ordnanceman Airman Apprentice Jason Tagg. "This is the reward."

It was also the worst of times. Isolation from families, long chow lines, and the pressing hurly-burly of life in a steel hull stuffed with five thousand people all took their toll. The most junior Rampagers found themselves doing a three-month stint in *Ike*'s mess halls and galleys, providing manual labor to feed the enormous crew. And the recent frustrations of workups still rankled. Mechanics complained of a dangerous lack of spare parts ashore. Officers wondered why their administrative budgets were so tight that they had to do without copier toner.

But morale was running high. VFA-83's people boasted of being the best strike fighter squadron around. (And they acted as if they believed it, an attitude that didn't please everyone. "Eighty-three walks around like they're God's gift, and sometimes they don't get my last widget because of it," grumbled a maintainer from another Hornet squadron.)

Just doing our job, the Rampagers said.

A hangar full of new Hornets is a nice thing to have. VFA-83 was flying a dozen Hornets from production lots 19 and 20, the latest version to come rolling off the McDonnell Douglas (now Boeing) assembly lines in St. Louis, Missouri. The F/A-18C Hornet is the navy's marquee strike jet, a slim, sharp-edged aircraft that resembles its insect namesake. The strike fighter was born in the 1970s, a descendant of the losing plane in a two-way fly-off of prototypes. (The winner became the air force's F-16 Fighting Falcon.) The Hornet program costs had sprawled 50 percent beyond budget by the time the aircraft entered fleet service in 1981.

Still, the effort produced an agile strike aircraft with remarkably flexible digital avionics that can switch from dogfighter to bomber in seconds. And even if it doesn't have the payload or range of the F-14 Tomcat or the now-retired A-6 Intruder, it is cheaper to fly and better at adapting to new technology.

By the late 1990s, the navy had purchased more than thirteen hundred Hornets. A typical carrier air wing contained roughly three times as many Hornets as any other aircraft. Each new production lot brought improvements. VFA-83 received its new birds in 1997 and eagerly noted improvements over their last batch.

The plane's navigational system now includes a Global Positioning System unit that locks onto satellite signals. This gives the pilots a more accurate autopilot that makes it easier to find and hit targets. Hornets also have a variety of improved sensors to sniff ahead for enemies and targets: more accurate and reliable ground-mapping radar, air search radar, and forward-looking infrared pod, a helpful tool that can pick out hot targets against cooler backgrounds. The new birds also carry more low-tech tools to throw enemy missiles off track. Mounted near the rear of the plane are dispensers for chaff—long metal strips to confuse enemy radar—and hot-burning magnesium flares to distract heat-seeking missiles.

The squadron's parachute riggers—a venerable navy specialty now officially dubbed "aviation survival equipmentman"—were especially happy about the new oxygen-generating system that keeps the pilots supplied with breathable air at high altitudes. Older Hornets used canisters filled with liquid oxygen, one of the world's most flammable substances. Refilling the canisters after every flight or two was a hazardous, time-consuming task that the maintainers were thrilled to be without.

"Having the newest Hornets in the navy is pretty exciting," said VFA-83's commanding officer, Cdr. Thomas Cropper. He acknowledged that his crew was still working some bugs out of the planes. "Even with a new car, things are going to break."

Lt. Michael Tomelin, the squadron's maintenance materials control officer, had harsher words for the new planes, citing problems with landing gear and radios. "If I was a car buyer, I would have taken them back," he said. "You pay fifty-some million dollars for them, you want them to work."

The maintainers' work begins every time a plane touches down on the deck, and continues in cramped spaces scattered around *Ike*'s vast warren. Aviation Machinist's Mate Airman Greg Firth was a plane captain, the brown-shirted junior sailor responsible for making sure his Hornet was ready to fly. He spent a year training for the job on the flight line at Cecil Field, Florida, the Rampagers' home base.

Now the Tulsa native was part of the flight deck ballet, darting around his bird to ready it for flights sometimes just thirty minutes apart. He had memorized the checklist: clean the canopy, supervise the purple-shirted refuelers while they top off the tanks with JP-5 jet fuel, check the ejection seat, and perform a quick inspection. "It's easily done. It's just that you're sweating at the end of it," Firth said. His labors earned the airman the right to paint his name and hometown in white stencil near the nose landing gear.

When something breaks during a flight that requires more experience than a plane captain has—avionics, a hydraulic link—the call goes out for the squadron troubleshooter, an experienced maintenance person with a knack for quick work. Wearing distinctive white checkerboard jerseys, the troubleshooters are often the last to check the plane before it shoots off the bow and the first to try to fix its "gripes" when it returns. "Whiteshirts make the world go round," said one.

Hornets that require more work are pushed, pulled, towed, or driven onto one of *Ike's* four giant elevators. Moving planes is always a hairy maneuver, especially moving a plane onto one of the deck-edge elevators. There are no guardrails on a carrier deck, just a horizontal steel net that protrudes a few feet from the edge. The net is designed to catch careless people, not twenty-ton jets.

After they are lowered to the hangar level—the "basement" in carrier slang—the planes are towed inside by boxy little trucks. Finding space for them among the dozens of other aircraft that crowd the hangar bay is complicated, like a million-dollar version of the children's wooden games that have eight tiles sliding around a grid of nine spaces. Which planes are likely to be "down" for a few days? Which ones will return quickly to "the roof"? Guessing wrong can mean hours of extra plane shuffling for the mechanics.

The hangar bay can't compete with its upstairs neighbor for danger or noise, but it tries hard. Each aircraft is tied down with steel cables and chains that can trip the unwary. Electric extension cords crisscross the greasy nonskid deck. Even the canvas safety covers that protect fins, engines, and other parts of a resting plane are bound by cords that stretch across the few open spaces. It's easy to get hurt in the maze of fins and wires. One green-shirted technician sported an ugly wound, closed with stitches, across his eye, nose, and forehead. "I stepped under one plane, stood up, and ran into another," he said.

Unlike the other aircraft on today's flight decks, the Hornet was designed to make maintenance easier. Its electronic brains help mechanics with troubleshooting, and the plane itself was engineered to allow easy access to its innards. A handful of maintainers can pull an entire engine from the plane in less than an hour. Nevertheless, it is an incredibly complicated machine.

"There's this one box," said Aviation Structural Mechanic (Safety Equipment) 1st Class (AW) Ray McClintock. "Sometimes it seems that they stood this box on a table and built the rest of the aircraft around it." The Hornet has dozens of computers and hundreds of moving parts that are routinely subjected to blazing heat, numbing cold, and tight maneuvers that exert the force of six gravities. Things break.

Aviation Electronics Technician 2d Class William Russell sat in a Hornet's cockpit punching gray buttons on the instrument panel. Occasionally, he paused to suck water from a backpack canteen as he worked to get the plane's autopilot back in commission. "We're never below fifteen gripes," Russell said, using the aviation term for a plane's problems. "We get fuzzy displays, scratchy noises in the headsets."

Gripes come in two flavors: "up," which means the plane can still fly, and "down" which means the plane is either unable or unsafe to take off the ground. The line that divides the two types shifts. A training flight can generally go without chaff and flares, but jets don't fly into a potential combat zone if those survival systems are down. VFA-83's daily missions over Bosnia fell into the latter category, which meant that the aircraft had to be working almost perfectly before an aviator could take it "over the beach." That, in turn, meant long days and nights for Rampager maintainers. "We've been working our butts off over here," Russell said.

He paused for a moment, pondering the job that had pulled him away from his wife and three-year-old son in Florida. "I got out, then got back in for the medical benefits," said Russell, whose navy service totalled eight years. "It paid off. I got a lot more experience, made a lot more friends, bought a house. I don't mind the military. I just hate being away."

Just off the hangar bay, in a little angular space defined by the curve of the carrier's hull, a quartet of petty officers worked on VFA-83's ejection seats. Most modern tactical jets have them, for even in peacetime, military flying is a dangerous venture, practiced at the raw edge of capability. The rocket-propelled seats save a handful of American aviators every year.

A Hornet's ejection system has sixteen explosive charges, carefully engineered to blast the seat free of a plummeting aircraft without killing its occupant. When the pilot grabs the bumblebee-painted ejection handle, the canopy blows off, followed in split seconds by the seat itself. A few seconds later, the seat's parachute automatically deploys, lofting the aviator back to earth or sea or even the carrier deck. The explosion is powerful enough to boost a person to a safe altitude from an aircraft sitting on the ground.

There is a well-tended tradition in aviation: You parachute to safety, you buy a bottle for the people who packed your chute. "A few months ago, a guy went off the front end and punched out," said Aviation Structural Mechanic (Egress/Environmental) First Class (AW) Bob Munson. "He came down and started taking orders for Seagram's Seven and whatnot."

The Hornet's engines take as much care and feeding as its electronics. With parts that spin up to forty thousand revolutions per minute, tolerances are tiny and wiggle room doesn't exist. "People think of jet maintainers as grease mechanics, but we're not," said Ens. Joe Montes, a former enlisted maintainer who now helps run VFA-83's maintenance efforts. "We're high-tech, always checking things with micrometers."

A jet engine with a big problem might wind up in the jet engine shop, a largish space filled with braces and worktables and located in "Siberia," at the very tail end of the ship. This arrangement allows the jet repairmen to strap the fire-breathing engines into a massive cradle on the fantail and start them up.

Montes, who arrived in the United States as a teenager in 1982, started college a few years later but didn't finish his premed degree. "I was one of those kids who, if the tools were left out, when Dad came home the toaster was taken apart," he said. He joined the navy in the late 1980s and became a jet engine specialist. He earned a bachelor's degree in aeronautical science, then got out of the navy because, he said, "I had no life."

But after less than a year of civilian life as an inspector for a Miami charter aviation company, Montes signed back up. This time, he came in as a commissioned officer. He survived Officer Candidate School, the initial training for navy officers who don't graduate from the Naval Academy or take ROTC classes in college. "A lot tougher than boot camp," he said. By 1998 he was working toward a chance at gold pilot's wings. "There is still a slight hope that I will go to flight school, which is what I've been working for for ten years," he said.

Even with the carrier's cramped workspaces, spartan living conditions, and grinding schedule, the maintainers' jobs get easier in some ways when the air wing checks aboard "the boat." Parts and money, so hard for nondeployed units to scrounge, flow much more freely to those on deployment. A year prior to deployment, VFA-83 had only enough parts to keep four to six of its dozen planes flying. On the boat, the squadron was regularly achieving 100 percent aircraft availability, as the jargon goes. "The supply system is so much better out here than it is on the beach," said Aviation Electronics Mate 1st Class (AW) Anthony Riddick, taking a break in the squadron electronics shop.

There's also a mysterious phenomenon about aircraft that no one seems to be able to explain, although many maintainers swear to it. "They break more when you don't fly 'em," Riddick said. "You wouldn't think so, but it's true."

A wag once compared making an arrested landing aboard a carrier to throwing a brick across a room into a skillet. A plane that comes in a few feet too high will miss the cables, forcing the pilot to jam the throttles open and get the plane back in the air before it falls off the deck. Landing twenty feet left or right of the centerline—less than half a wingspan—risks collision with other aircraft parked on the crowded deck. Coming in low means fiery death in a crash with the carrier's blunt stern.

A good landing is only somewhat less violent. The airplane's tail hook grabs a cable, which hisses from the giant block and tackle mounted below the flight deck. For two long seconds, the rapid deceleration throws the aviators against their harnesses as the plane grinds to a halt more than three hundred feet down the deck.

This is the province of the naval aviator: a dangerous world where even coming home is life threatening. Tom Cropper had been there, done that, for nearly two decades, and now he was skipper of his own squadron. "I've had quite a few flights off a carrier, but I've never had a perfect flight," the commander said. "I guess I could walk away if I ever had a perfect flight. If the bombs all hit exactly on target, the light never left the ball." He didn't sound particularly convinced.

For Cropper, the flights over Bosnia offered both rewarding flying and a chance to knit his squadron into the tightest of teams. "There is real-world consequence. We have a mission, it's an important mission, and we're going to pull together and work around some of the petty things that come up," he said. "To be the best strike fighter squadron requires a constant sharpening of the sword."

It seemed to take a constant sharpening of the wits as well. There was steady joshing in VFA-83's ready room. Part fraternity house, part squadron office, the ready room was a living room–sized space where the aviators gathered for nightly movies as well as morning briefings. A photograph of the pilots' wives hung on the rear wall. A bon voyage gift, the picture showed the women lined up in front of a Hornet, clad in black tights and their husbands' uniform jackets.

Each aviator had a heavy chair with his name on it. All but one chair had blue vinyl headrest covers. The last was red—marking the poor unfortunate who last "boltered," missed all four wires in a landing. "Thick skin is required. Nobody gets up a peg without someone else yanking them down," Cropper said. "But when the brief starts, we're all business."

VFA-83's enlisted personnel had only the mess decks and the space around their bunks for their off time, but Cropper and Rainey had dipped into squadron funds to buy a big-screen TV for the cruise, an attempt to ease the bare-bones life aboard ship. "Without the troops, we're not going anywhere," the skipper said.

No amount of amenities can make a cruise bearable. It's the work itself that does that, the job satisfaction that comes with feeling part of an elite unit. "It's a sense of 'Do I own part of this?' It's people looking out for each other. That sense of belonging translates into good work," Cropper said. Sometimes, it's a lot of work for few rewards. "Your carelessness may scrub a mission that can make a difference in a campaign, but your professionalism may not have an immediate result," he said.

But together, the Rampagers helped give *Eisenhower*—and the navy—its striking punch. "The sheer flexibility of a carrier is that in two days, we could be off Libya," Cropper said. "We can do recon, we even train to do aerial mining. But we are not Mining Squadron Eighty-three. We are Strike Fighter Squadron Eighty-three. We fight our way in and fight our way out."

Call him the Angel who returned to earth. For three years, Lt. Cdr. Ryan "Doc" Scholl flew with the Blue Angels, the navy flight demonstration squadron that has wowed millions of spectators around the globe. Now he was flying dull gray F/A-18s off a carrier in the Adriatic Sea and cracking joke after joke about how hard it was to come back to the fleet. "I can walk out to the aircraft, start it up, and take off. After that, I'm kind of lost," said Scholl, the Rampagers' safety officer.

Scholl started his Blue Angel tour as the number seven pilot, the team's point man for public affairs. Before each air show, he served up a taste of navy flying to reporters and VIPs in the backseat of his polished blue-and-gold Hornet. During the shows themselves, Scholl stood ramrod straight between PA speakers and narrated as the other six Hornet pilots wheeled in perfect formation above. After a year, he moved into one of the "solo" positions and learned to fly with his wings just inches from the next plane. Over two years, he flew scores of air shows with the elite group.

Scholl's tour ended in 1997, and he checked into VFA-83 a few months before its deployment. All joking aside, turning himself back into a tactical aviator proved tricky after years of performing precision aerobatics to a big dashboard stopwatch.

"Flying with the Blues was like you were on a highway all by yourself but at superhigh speed," Scholl said. "Now a car approaches you and you're going to make a knife-edge pass. It takes a lot of focus and is very intense."

Flying missions from the carrier, he said, is more like the Los Angeles rush hour—right down to the guns. "'Uh-oh, I'm in this guy's lane, and I've pissed him off and he's going to shoot me.' You've got to focus, but you've also got to widen your view."

Scholl, whose last pre-Blues deployment was also with *Eisenhower,* found life aboard the carrier a bit different with e-mail on the computers and the oak leaves of a lieutenant commander on his shoulders.

He was also flying in relative anonymity after three seasons as one of the navy's most public faces.

"It showed you emotions you didn't know you had," said Scholl, who was constantly surprised at the feelings the Blue Angels evoked. "You'd go to a school, and kids would be hugging you and telling you how cool you were because they saw your air show, and you say to yourself, 'All I did was fly.'"

Scholl gave the author a thrilling half-hour ride in the back of his Hornet during his first year as a Blue Angel. He loosened up considerably after he traded the Angels' blue-and-gold flight suit for a standard green one.

"Yeah, I curse a lot more now that I'm back in the fleet," he said.

---

Naval Air Station Lemoore, California, January 1999

One week after navy officials breathed new life into Strike Fighter Squadron 122, the vast hangar at the end of flight line stood empty. An F/A-18E Super Hornet—borrowed for the ceremony—had been returned to a testing facility hundreds of miles away.

But behind the freshly painted rear wall, a small group of pilots, maintainers, and support staff labored in its absence. As members of the first Super Hornet "fleet replacement squadron," they would soon train aviators to fly the navy's newest strike fighter. They had just sixteen months to draw up a curriculum.

The establishment of a training squadron was a big step for the Super Hornet. The aircraft had flown through a Sturm und Drang of controversy to make it that far.

In development for nearly a decade, the F/A-18E/F will become naval aviation's bridge to the twenty-first century, the strike fighter that will bridge the gap between the F/A-18Cs and F-14 Tomcats and the stealthy planes of the new millennium. The idea is simple: take an existing strike fighter, expand it slightly in every dimension, and get a big improvement at a small price.

Officials lauded the plane's greater range, payload, "survivability," room for growth, and ability to land on a carrier with bombs still hanging from the wings. By February, navy officials had ordered 62 Super

Hornets at a cost of nearly $6 billion. If the jet passes operational eval-
uation in summer 1999, officials plan to order at least 486 more over
the next ten years. The total program cost will come to roughly $47
billion, and the plane is scheduled to enter fleet service in 2001.

But disturbing details have leaked about the 1998 flight tests; performance indicators hint that the $54 million plane isn't as good as
hoped. The program's opponents gained further ammunition in February when a defense industry newsletter claimed that a classified navy
report cited twenty-nine "major deficiencies" in the plane that make it
only slightly better than the aircraft it will replace. One frustrated sen-
ator introduced a bill to kill the program outright.

The navy's previous aviation program—the stealthy A-12 Avenger
attack jet—was a costly debacle that underscored the soaring expense
of tactical aviation. When Pentagon officials pulled the plug on the
drawing-board Avenger in 1991, the navy faced a dismaying choice in
the new century: drastically reduce fighter jet operations—a key mission and source of deep pride for the navy—or make deep cuts in the
rest of the fleet. Or perhaps they could just build a cheaper plane.

The F/A-18E/F became the anti-Avenger, the inexpensive alterna-
tive that will fill carrier air wings until the next-generation Joint Strike
Fighter arrives around 2010. By altering an existing design, navy officials proposed saving several years and billions of dollars.

The Hornet's fuselage would grow a yard longer, providing seventeen cubic feet of space to accommodate anticipated innovations.
New engines would boost thrust by one-third. Its wings would be substantially redesigned to carry more fuel and two additional bomb
racks. A wingtip twist would be removed, the leading edges pulled forward, the wings themselves made thicker and broader.

For all these changes, navy officials predicted an easy gestation for
the E/F. In 1992, planners decided to skip the usual construction of a
wind tunnel prototype. But within weeks of the plane's first flight in
1996, test pilot Cdr. Rob Niewoehner discovered the plane's disturbing
tendency to roll unpredictably in climbing turns at near-supersonic
speeds. The airflow problem, called "wing drop," affected maneuvers
commonly used in dogfights. After a year of testing, the test team
marked it as a "part double-star-one" deficiency in February 1997.

Uncorrected, the problem would make the aircraft unsuitable for navy use.

One month later, Secretary of Defense William Cohen approved the navy's request to purchase its first dozen Super Hornets. Eight more months went by before Cohen learned of the potential show-stopping problem through press reports. (Chief of Naval Operations Adm. Jay Johnson apparently learned about the problem in a November memo from the navy assistant secretary for acquisitions.)

Critics cried foul, saying that this was just another version of the old Pentagon game that pushes flawed weapons programs forward. Super Hornet program officials retorted that they did not stress wing drop in briefings to higher-ups because they expected to fix the problems without degrading aircraft performance below acceptable standards.

Cohen threatened to withhold money for the second batch of Super Hornets until the test team demonstrated a solution. And in early 1998, they did: a perforated fairing about three quarters of the way out from the fuselage. Cohen pronounced himself satisfied.

Initial versions of the fix caused a buffeting that one navy memo compared to riding on a "gravel road." The shaking was eventually reduced significantly. Testing continued in 1999 to determine what effect it would have on the plane's range, speed, and handling.

The episode did not reassure fleet aviators. As word got around that the Super Hornet is not going to fly circles around the older model, program review officials called for a dose of hard information to forestall grumbling. The navy should pursue "aggressive indoctrination of operational community to help them match expectation to reality of F/A-18 E and F," a 1998 memo said.

A few months later, an article by Niewoehner appeared in a naval aviators' magazine. Entitled "Super Hornet: A Test Pilot Dispels the Myths," the article notes that the program specifications emphasized more fuel, better range, higher payload, and survivability—not increased maneuverability. Nevertheless, the pilot wrote, "In the subsonic regime, the E/F performs as good as or better than a C/D in almost every respect." And he praised the Super Hornet's performance in "high-alpha" maneuvers—those used to line up weapons on air and ground targets.

To Cdr. Mark Fox, skipper of the VFA-122 Flying Eagles, the Super Hornet's advantages are as plentiful as they are obvious. Fox knows something about the Hornet. In Operation Desert Storm, his strike fighter was the first naval aircraft to shoot down an Iraqi MiG——and he flew on to bomb his assigned target several minutes later.

Fox's office has a view of the Lemoore runway and the vast flatness of California's Central Valley, which stretches away for miles. Leaning back behind a conference table, Fox ticked off the "Super Hornet Mantra": range, payload, growth, survivability, bringback. "This is going to be an incredibly effective and lethal weapon," the pilot said. "It'll keep naval aviation relevant as the sharpest tool in the military toolbox."

Indeed, he said, the heftier payload and racks for new smart weapons are spawning an entirely new capacity for strike warfare. To destroy four targets, it might take eight Hornets, but only two Super Hornets. "In the seventies and eighties, we always thought, 'How many sorties will it take to kill the target?' Now we're thinking, 'How many targets can we kill per sortie?' It's a completely different mind-set."

Fox has heard all the counterarguments——he spent a previous tour dispelling them in the navy's legislative affairs office on Capitol Hill. The navy can't simply upgrade the C/D version to include the powerful new radar and helmet-mounted gunsight now in development, he said. "We reached a point in the 'legacy' Hornet where we have to take stuff out to upgrade," Fox said. Nor can the fleet wait for the Joint Strike Fighter. "I say it would be wrong for my son, who's sixteen, to be flying the same airplane I flew in Desert Storm," he said.

Besides, when was the last time a weapons program arrived on schedule? "If JSF comes in and it meets all of its cost goals and performance goals, then great," Fox said. "If it doesn't, then we still have a viable airplane."

Actually, the F/A-18E/F program has run on time and on budget, a rarity in weapons procurement. Since 1992, the program has stuck to its $4.88 billion development cap and has never slid past a deadline, program manager Capt. J. B. Godwin said.

And maintainers say the Super Hornet is going to be even easier—read "cheaper"——to keep flying than its predecessor. It has 33 percent fewer parts; the jet engine uses only four moving parts to control fuel flow. Its maintenance system downloads its "gripes" to a squadron computer. "Troubleshooting is going to be a dream for most people," said Chief Aviation Machinist's Mate (AW) Jon DeWees, a VFA-122 member who helped develop the Super Hornet.

Fox said that he isn't looking at the aircraft through rose-colored flight goggles. "People attack the plane and say it was a compromise, and they're absolutely right," he said. "It is a compromise-design airplane—and the compromises were made intelligently." Still, the pilot can't help wanting it all. "I would like it to be faster in acceleration, you know, but we made the wing thicker for more stores."

The Flying Eagles will throw open their classroom doors in June 2000. Officials said the speedy schedule will save money by getting the Super Hornet to the fleet as quickly as possible. Fox called it "juggling crystal." Not the least of his challenges: aircraft won't arrive at Naval Air Station Lemoore until October 2000. But that doesn't mean his team won't be flying. In an innovative timesaver, VFA-122 aviators and maintainers plan to travel to Naval Weapons Station China Lake, California, in May 2000. They are slated to help other test pilots with the Super Hornet's operational evaluation—while acquiring valuable hands-on experience in its cockpit.

Because the Super Hornet comes in two varieties—the single-seat E model and the two-seater F—the squadron will train pilots and weapons-controlling naval flight officers. The plane's two models created a dilemma: Should all pilots be trained to work with a backseater? The training team studied similar aircraft—current Hornets, F-14 Tomcats, even air force F-15 Eagles—and decided no. Some pilots will learn to fly alone in the E. Others, the F pilots, will learn to rely on their weapons systems operator, or "wizzo," a term borrowed from the air force. "They'll be a crew from the first day they walk into the [fleet replacement squadron]," Fox said.

Given aviators' intensely competitive nature, the situation seems ripe for rivalry between E and F pilots. Fox and his executive officer, Lt. Cdr. Hal Murdock, are determined to stress "community unity" and squelch the notion that one group can outfly the other.

Fox doesn't think it will take E/F pilots longer to get ready for the fleet than those who fly the older F/A-18C. Like the C model, the E and

F training programs will aim to send aviators through in thirty-eight weeks. The Super Hornet curriculum will make much use of computer instruction and simulator work. Boeing, the plane's manufacturer, is producing software that can incorporate cockpit video into PC-based training programs. Students can safely find out what a stall looks like, for example. And because the Super Hornet can carry so many different kinds of weapons, students may use simulators to experience the configurations they can't try out in the cockpit.

VFA-122 will blaze a trail for the strike fighter community in other ways as well. Its ready rooms will have projection screens hooked up to a local-area computer network. Briefers will be able to use this to display the airfield's meteorological Web page instead of printing out, photocopying, and distributing a weather report.

"It's a brave new world in strike warfare," Murdock said.

## 6. THE AMPHIBS

Aboard the USS *Wasp* in the Adriatic Sea, June 1998

The amphibious assault ship *Wasp* was anchored off Turkey's southern coast when the call came in from Sixth Fleet headquarters. We're going to do something about Kosovo, the message said. Get your ship to the Adriatic Sea—now.

*Wasp* itself could be ready to go in an hour. One oil-fired steam boiler had been simmering since the ship pulled into the port of Antalya a few days ago, and the enginemen were already lighting off the other one. But there was another problem: most of *Wasp*'s sailors and marines had gone ashore.

Located on the rocky southern coast of Turkey, Antalya is a sun-drenched city whose lively bazaars make it a favorite port call. More than four months into their deployment, *Wasp*'s sailors and marines had earned their precious liberty hours. Few had passed up the opportunity to tour an exotic port of call, one of the naval life's great perks.

Like the sailors under his direction, the commander of Amphibious Squadron Six Capt. Lee Mahoney was taking advantage of the port call that day. When the urgent messages began arriving in the ship's communications center around noon, the commander of Amphibious Squadron Six had just returned from a carpet-shopping jaunt. Mahoney acknowledged the order and set departure for 4:30 P.M.

There was one difference between the commodore and the crew.

Finding Mahoney was easy. Rounding up more than a thousand American servicemen on liberty in a foreign city was a lot tougher. The word went out around 1:00 P.M.: the ship was leaving in three and one-half hours. Two teams of sailors fanned out across the waterfront, checking for shipmates in restaurants, bars, hotels. Others phoned the tour bus companies that ran day trips to nearby historical sites.

The dragnet proved as effective as it was impromptu. When the amphibious assault ship weighed anchor, all but forty-one sailors and marines had been located and hustled back to the ship. In a day or so, the rest would be picked up by the dock landing ship *Portland* and reunited with their shipmates in the Adriatic Sea.

Under way at twenty-two knots, *Wasp* prepared for action.

For nearly four months, Serbian forces had skirmished with separatists in rump Yugoslavia's southernmost province. Hundreds of ethnic Albanians died when government forces shelled and burned Kosovar villages. Thousands more fled their homes. The architect of the violent crackdown, Serbian president Slobodan Milosevic, had rebuffed diplomatic pleas and admonitions. Leaders in Washington and other NATO capitals were frustrated. Speaking softly had failed. Maybe it would help to wave a big stick.

Spurred by a growing flood of media reports from the beleaguered area, NATO officials assembled a plan in several days. The alacrity amazed several American naval officers, who said they were accustomed to seeing the organization grind its gears for weeks or more. The plan was conceptually simple, an Air Age update of gunboat diplomacy. An airborne parade of fighters, bombers, and attack planes would skirt Kosovo's southern border, staying within Serbian earshot but out of Yugoslav airspace. The message, NATO leaders hoped, would be clear: Stop the killing or else.

The planners secured the participation of a dozen nations and about sixty aircraft for the exercise, which they dubbed "Determined Falcon." Most of the planes would fly from bases in Italy.

No carrier-based aircraft would participate in the exercise. The nearest flattop, *Eisenhower,* had just deployed from Norfolk and was still in transit west of Gibraltar. But naval forces weren't going to be left out. *Wasp* was just a day's steaming away, and its 844-foot hull carried a remarkable mix of forces.

At a glance, *Wasp* resembles the World War II aircraft carriers whose name it bears. The forty-thousand-ton warship sports a single superstructure, an island on the starboard side of a rectangular, two-acre flight deck. A hangar just below provides room for aircraft storage and maintenance. But the modern *Wasp* has capabilities far beyond its wartime namesake.

Commissioned in 1989, *Wasp* is a "big-deck gator," the first of a class of the largest amphibious ships in the world. Like the rest of the navy's "amphibs," *Wasp* was built to transport and support marines in amphibious operations. The ship's thousand-person crew provides troopship services for nineteen hundred marines and their equipment. The capacious holds accommodate three hovercraft, plus amphibious personnel carriers, supplies, ammunition, and other equipment. The ship can disgorge the troops, their vehicles, and their gear through giant doors in its squared-off fantail. Ballast tanks in the hull enable the stern to sink as much as ten feet, flooding the lowest cargo hold and easing the exit for amphibious assault vehicles, which plop off the steel deck into deep water.

On the flight deck and in its hangar bay, *Wasp* was carrying a formidable mix of marine aircraft: four AV-8B Harrier vertical-takeoff attack jets, four AH-1W Super Cobra helicopter gunships, four CH-53E Super Stallion heavy-lift helos, two UH-1N Iroquois utility helos, and a dozen troop-carrying CH-46E Sea Knight helos.

The big-deck gator generally sails with a pair of smaller amphibs: one amphibious transport dock and one dock landing ship. These "gator freighters" have big, blocky superstructures forward, two-hundred-foot helicopter flight decks aft, and squared-off sterns. The three-ship squadron can hold an entire marine expeditionary unit (special operations capable): some twenty-one hundred troops plus their weapons, vehicles, supplies, and aircraft. Together, the navy and marine forces make up the force called an amphibious ready group.

The ARGs have become the nation's "911 force" for a growing list of missions. When air force captain Scott O'Grady was shot down over Bosnia in 1995, the marine rescue team flew from the *Wasp*-class ship

**Keeping a safe distance.** Standing on the bridge wing of the guided missile frigate *Halyburton,* the skipper, Cdr. Kevin Morrissey, issues a maneuvering order. A hundred yards to starboard, the German destroyer *Moelders* looms in the Baltic Sea's early morning fog. Rob Curtis, *Navy Times*

**Hunting the killer tomato.** Aboard the guided missile frigate *Kauffman,* Sonar Technician (Surface) 2d Class (SW) Joe Stump fires a twenty-five-millimeter Bushmaster deck cannon at a gunnery target floating in the Black Sea. Bradley Peniston, *Navy Times*

**Shoot 'em up, shoot 'em up!** An F-14 Tomcat waits as an F/A-18 Hornet is catapulted from the bow of the aircraft carrier *Abraham Lincoln* during exercises off San Diego. Already, the deck crew is preparing for the next launch.
Steve Elfers, *Navy Times*

**The last trap.** An E-2 Hawkeye early warning aircraft catches the three wire on the aircraft carrier *Independence*. This was the final arrested landing on the last day of flight operations in *Indy*'s thirty-nine-year career. The next day, the carrier dropped off hundreds of crew members in Pearl Harbor, Hawaii, and headed for eventual decommissioning in Bremerton, Washington.
Jud McCrehin, *Navy Times*

**Eye in the sky.** Aboard a P-3 Orion over Bosnia, Chief Aviation Warfare Systems Operator (AW/AC) Rich Kowalczyk, *right,* operates the maritime patrol aircraft's video surveillance system. Aviation Warfare Systems Operator 2d Class Phillip Moss, *left,* notes traffic patterns of interest on the ground thousands of feet below. Rob Curtis, *Navy Times*

**Double-check.** Chief Sonar Technician (Surface) (SW) Mark Roehm confirms movement orders in the combat information center of the guided missile cruiser *Vella Gulf.* Over his shoulder, a video screen displays the surrounding Baltic Sea. Rob Curtis, *Navy Times*

**Think your garage is crowded?** After pilots return from missions over Bosnia, maintainers from the VFA-83 Rampagers and other squadrons work on their F/A-18 Hornets in the hangar bay of the carrier *Eisenhower.* Rob Curtis, *Navy Times*

**Preparing to land.** Belted in for safety, an aircrewman examines the amphibious transport dock *Trenton* from the side door of an SH-60 Seahawk helicopter above the Black Sea. Rob Curtis, *Navy Times*

**Medevac practice.** U.S. Navy corpsmen from *Trenton* and a French soldier, *center,* perform triage after a simulated bus accident on a Black Sea beach near Constanta, Romania. Rob Curtis, *Navy Times*

**Rattling sabers.** A pair of Marine Corps AV-8B Harrier attack jets return to the amphibious assault ship *Wasp* after participating in Determined Falcon. The June 1998 NATO exercise sent some sixty jets zooming by southern Serbia in an effort to persuade Serb leaders to stop the violence in the province of Kosovo. Rob Curtis, *Navy Times*

**Danger zone.** A flight deck crewman watches as an F-14 Tomcat catches the one-wire aboard *Lincoln*. The carrier was in the Persian Gulf to enforce the no-fly zone over southern Iraq. Jud McCrehin, *Navy Times*

**Coming alongside.** Electrician's Mate 3d Class Ilcias Vargas heaves a line from the torpedo retrieval boat *Harrier* to crewmen aboard the ballistic missile submarine *Florida* in the Pearl Harbor channel. The torpedo retrievers do a lot more than their job description; here, *Harrier* prepares to ferry some guests of the boomer's captain back to shore. Jud McCrehin, *Navy Times*

**The navy's fastest craft?** Quartermaster 1st Class (CC) Joe Riffey, *center,* and other members of Special Boat Unit Twelve show off their new eleven-meter rigid-hull inflatable boat in San Diego Harbor. Riffey's unit uses the forty-seven-knot boats to deliver SEAL commandos and perform special warfare missions of their own. Steve Elfers, *Navy Times*

**Weighty decisions.** As Cdr. Mark Vaughan's crew prepares to offload cargo at Naval Air Station Souda Bay, Crete, the skipper of the VR-57 Conquistadors ponders the final leg of the day, which will take his C-9 Skytrain back home to Naval Air Station Sigonella on Sicily. Rob Curtis, *Navy Times*

**Train like you fight.** Master Chief Personnelman Pablo Custodil calls for help in the damage control trainer at the American naval base in Yokosuka, Japan. Part of the crew of the amphibious command ship *Blue Ridge* was practicing flooding control.
Jud McCrehin, *Navy Times*

*Kearsarge.* When regional unrest forces Americans to evacuate foreign soil—in Somalia in 1991, in Sierra Leone and Albania in 1997—amphibious naval forces get the job. "The challenge for us at present is to train for everything from humanitarian aid to downed pilots to war," said Capt. T. J. Anderson, *Wasp*'s skipper.

Amphibs don't get the glamour accorded aircraft carriers and their escorts. Yet they go in harm's way as much or more. Their province is shallow water, in deadly proximity to minefields and shore-based guns and antiship missiles. When America calls in the Marines, the Gator Navy weighs anchor and sets sail.

Determined Falcon was a case in point. In thirty-eight hours, *Wasp* steamed more than nine hundred miles to arrive on station early on 14 June. The exercise was set for the next morning. Thirty miles off the Albanian coast, the sailors and marines readied their equipment for combat. Riflemen fired from the flight deck, creating a thunderous racket and littering the nonskid surface with brass cartridges. The twin smells of gunpowder and oil momentarily obliterated the salty sea tang. Sailors loaded the Phalanx antimissile gun with live ammunition, supervised by Lt. Homer Denius, *Wasp*'s fire control officer. Like his sailors, Denius wore a bulletproof vest when handling the live ordnance. "We've been doing exercises for five months, and suddenly we get this unscheduled evolution," he said. "There's a heightened sense of readiness."

Four of the marines' Harrier jets would fly with the NATO formation. Intelligence officers briefed the pilots on the Yugoslavian air defense network. The Serbs had Soviet antiaircraft missiles and MiG-21 and -27 fighter jets. The NATO planes would carry dummy bombs and live air-to-air missiles. Nobody knew how the Serbs would react.

*Wasp* had another vital job in the exercise: combat search and rescue. The gator would be the closest NATO ship to the operation. If an aircraft ditched in the Adriatic, the ship would send a helicopter to retrieve the aircrew. If a plane went down over land, the marines would send troops and gunships after it, just as they had for Scott O'Grady.

As day turned to late afternoon, the rescue team donned their gear and ran preflight inspections on their aircraft. They would round out their preparations with a practice rescue from the flight deck. They were waiting, however, for a few spectators.

For *Wasp* had a third role to play in Determined Falcon: photogenic front for the entire exercise. If tomorrow's events went as planned, the aircraft formation would trace the Serb border without incident. Serb radar operators would see the airborne flotilla, and some troops might hear the roar of jet engines. But the NATO planners wanted a more visceral way to draw Milosevic's attention. The solution: get the exercise on CNN; the method: put the news network's cameras on *Wasp.*

Two days before the mission, the Sixth Fleet's public affairs staff had telephoned newsrooms across Italy. Meet us in Bari if you want a front-row seat, they said, naming an Adriatic port near the country's boot heel. More than twenty reporters, photographers, and television crews showed up on 14 June; they represented CNN, ABC, National Public Radio, Reuters news service, *Navy Times,* several Italian news organizations, and more. The civilians crowded aboard a pair of navy and marine helicopters and flew out to the ship.

The marines call the act of rescuing a downed aviator a TRAP, the acronym for "tactical recovery of aircraft personnel." No amphibious ready group deploys without extensive practice in a rescue operation's careful choreography. With the cameras rolling, the troops of the Twenty-sixth Marine Expeditionary Unit (MEU) were ready to demonstrate their expertise.

In a crescendo of rotor noise, a brace of helicopters lifted off from the broad flight deck: Cobra gunships and Sea Stallion and Sea Knight airborne troopships. They would return momentarily. The flight deck represented the "hostile territory" from which they would extract the downed pilot.

The Cobras took up station a half mile to port, ready to swoop in with covering fire. The twin-rotor Sea Knights reapproached the flight deck, flared out, and landed. Flak-suited marines sprinted down the rear cargo ramps. Bearing rifles and machine guns, they fanned out into a broad half circle and then flopped down onto the rough, greasy deck. The Sea Stallion roared in next, its seven-bladed rotor churning the air.

As the huge helicopter dropped to the deck, its tremendous downdraft buffeted troops and media alike. The wind whipped the sunglasses from a reporter's face and sent them spinning over the side. As she turned instinctively to go after them, a sailor pounced and held her still, lest she follow her shades into the drink.

The "pilot" was hustled into the Sea Stallion, which lifted off quickly. The marines retreated to their troopships and followed them into the sky. They had not been on deck more than a few minutes.

The rest of the day was given over to interviews. *Wasp*'s crew had set up a makeshift press center high above the flight deck in "debark control." Located aft of the bridge atop the island, the room is normally used to supervise the loading and unloading of troops and equipment. "We're going to make a lot of noise and show the Albanians we're here," said Maj. Mike Butters, the Marine Corps aviator who would lead the Harrier flight in the morning. "But mainly, we'll show the Serbs we're here."

Mahoney noted that this wasn't *Wasp*'s first experience with saber rattling on this cruise. Two months ago, the ship had participated in a multicountry amphibious landing in Bosnia-Herzegovina. Like Determined Falcon, Dynamic Response was meant to send a warning to local warring factions. "To muster this amount of force in this amount of time—that is a bigger signal than Dynamic Response," Mahoney said.

The senior marine aboard was Col. Emerson Gardner, the commander of the marines embarked aboard the three ships of the *Wasp* ARG. "This is just the air part. What they have to understand is that we've got Tomahawks, ground forces, the whole gamut," he said.

On the mess deck below, sailors contemplated the upcoming action with a thousand shades of emotion. "We practice this stuff all the time. It's really cool to know that our training is going to pay off," said Photographer's Mate 3d Class Aaron Englund. "It's kind of sad that this is happening, but this is what I signed up to do. My parents are worried, but we're doing important stuff out here."

Not everyone was so pumped. Some sailors said Determined Falcon wouldn't compare with Dynamic Response. "Been here, done Bosnia. This is no big deal," said Data Processing Technician 3d Class Todd Cohrer. "If we get sent in, then it's going to be exciting."

Around 3:00 A.M., Lt. Greg Geisen took to a cot in debark control, hoping to catch a few hours of rest before sunrise. The Sixth Fleet public affairs officer had slept little in two days. There were too many helicopters and interviews and communications to arrange. But Geisen was exultant. His job was central to a major military operation. "And they say we're not operators," the public affairs officer crowed just before he dropped off to sleep.

With a roar meant for the ears of Slobodan Milosevic, four attack jets lifted off *Wasp*'s flight deck and headed for Balkan skies. It was 9:30 A.M. on 15 June. One by one, the Harriers taxied to the middle of the deck. Four movable exhaust ports allow the AV-8B to lift off vertically, but short rolling takeoffs save fuel and extend range. So each pilot set his engine nozzles for horizontal thrust, cranked his engines past "loud" to "screaming," and released the brakes. The aircraft headed for the flight deck's forward end, gathering speed along the way. At the bow, the pilots rotated the nozzles, adding vertical thrust to the lift generated by their wings. The jets leapt from the deck—not a typical curving ascent but a rather sharper line, as if they were driving up a ramp.

The Harriers shrank and vanished, leaving their whirring lifeguard, a CH-46 helo, hovering alone in the sky. At altitude, the attack jets joined dozens of fighters, bombers, radar-jamming planes, and aerial tankers that had taken off earlier from bases across Italy. Together, they funneled through Albanian airspace, headed for an old Warsaw Pact bombing range in the former Yugoslav republic of Macedonia. Located just south of Kosovo, the range was judged by planners to be an ideal location for a noisy practice session.

As the aircraft sped off, Mahoney and dozens of others gathered several decks below the flight deck in a darkened, air-conditioned control center jammed with computers. The commodore monitored the aircraft on a trio of projection televisions. Like most navy ships, *Wasp* can combine the data from its own sensors with the radar returns from other ships, aircraft, and ground stations. With a word to an enlisted operator, Mahoney could see air or surface traffic across the globe.

Today, the screen showed the area from western Greece to Italy's southeastern coast. The land masses were outlined in white. Scores of multicolored symbols—military as well as commercial aircraft—moved across the black background. The NATO planes were easy to spot: thick blots of radar contacts moving through a pair of yellow lines. Superimposed on the map, the lines defined the airborne flotilla's flight path like highway stripes.

Over the next hour, the commodore watched the planes navigate the winding course, flying within ten miles of the Yugoslav border. Some dropped dummy bombs on the range. "We're sending the message but being gosh-darned careful that we're not provocative," Mahoney said.

Sailors carefully monitored the Serbian air defense network, ready to warn the planes of imminent danger. There were flickers of reaction—here an antiair missile radar, there a heightened alert at an air base. But no overtly hostile acts were detected. The planes began to pull away from the border.

The commodore waved a red laser pointer at Tirana, Albania's capital. The aircraft were beginning to fly over the municipal stadium at two thousand feet and 450 knots. "This is the only place I'd rather be than at that soccer field, watching sixty-five high-performance jets fly over," Mahoney mused.

Two hours after they left, the Harriers reappeared in the sky around *Wasp*. The first one pulled up next to the flight deck and hung there, some ten stories above the dark blue water. It looked like a magic trick, except for the bone-rattling roar of the jet engines. The Harrier drifted sideways until it was directly over the painted star that marked the landing zone. Then Major Butters, the pilot, lowered his raging beast to the deck on a cone of thin black smoke.

Butters climbed from the cockpit and was instantly mobbed by reporters. He said the mission had gone well and described the flight over the stadium. "You could see people waving at us," he said.

The exercise ended without incident. The violence, sadly, did not. Eight months later, in March 1999, NATO launched its first strikes against Serbia. American cruisers, destroyers, and submarines launched cruise missiles. An aircraft carrier sent strike fighters to bomb Yugoslav targets. An amphibious ready group stood ready for action.

---

Aboard the USS *Kearsarge* off North Carolina, January 1999

By the time an amphibious ready group deploys, its marines have learned to perform amphibious landings, civilian evacuations, pilot rescues, humanitarian aid, and a whole lot else. They've also learned not to trip over watertight doors.

In December 1998, *Kearsarge* steamed down to the U.S. Marines Corps's Camp Lejeune in North Carolina to pick up elements of the Twenty-sixth MEU, the unit that had landed in Bosnia and flown near Kosovo earlier that year. The Twenty-sixth had returned in July, and its members were already months into their interdeployment training cycle. In April 1999 they would embark aboard *Kearsarge* for their next "float."

The old hands would find this amphib quite similar to *Wasp*. Launched in 1992, *Kearsarge* is the third of its class. But the Twenty-sixth MEU was not the same experienced group that had sailed with the older ship. Like ships' crews, marine expeditionary units endure lots of personnel turnover after a deployment. New troops flood in from boot camp. Senior ones move on to other assignments. Of the troops that boarded the *Kearsarge* in December, nearly 80 percent had never been on deployment. So the sailors and marines would have to learn to work, live, and fight together in their steel-hulled home. The process includes a little culture shock and a lot of hard work.

A week aboard ship introduced the marines to the basics of shipboard life. There were safety lectures. One tip: don't step on "knee-knockers"—the raised jambs of the ubiquitous watertight doors lest you bump your head. There were drills aplenty: man overboard, general quarters, damage control, abandon ship. The junior marines who drove amphibious assault vehicles and Humvees got the chance to practice on the ships' steep loading ramps.

The sailors and marines searched out their counterparts and teammates in their specialties. "You learn who to talk to and how to talk to them. So much is founded on people getting together," said Lt. Col. Daniel E. Cushing, who commanded Marine Medium Helicopter Squadron 365.

Shipboard life itself was a shock for the newcomers, and it started the moment the marines drove their windowless amphibious assault vehicles onto the ship and parked them in a cavernous hold. "When that AAV hatch opens up, they get out and say, 'What the heck?'" said 2d Lt. Donnie Hasseltine.

The marines learned to stuff their gear into a narrow space under their mattress. "You can't sit up in the racks. You'll hit your head. They're like coffins," said Cpl. Frederich Mancuso, a radioman who was on his first deployment.

They learned through painful practice the safe negotiation of hatches and steep ladders. "For some reason, they are clumsier. They're always falling," said Hospitalman 3d Class Tim Goehle. On deployment, Goehle and his fellow corpsmen generally give stitches each week to one or two shipmates who stumble and bang into things. In the same week, their marine counterparts will account for half a dozen shipboard injuries.

Meanwhile, *Kearsarge's* crew learned to live with their newly crowded ship and long lines on the mess decks. They taught their new teammates about shipboard life, and in return got a bunch of gung-ho colleagues. "Marines infect the whole shop with a get-it-done attitude," said Aviation Ordnanceman 1st Class (SW) Harvey Bradford. "You only have to tell a marine once or maybe twice to do something. A sailor you might have to tell two or three times. Not to make our sailors look bad, but that's the way it is."

There can be friction between the "blue" and "green" sides. Sailors resent the crowds. Marines have been known to look down on the "taxi drivers" who wait offshore while they hit the beach.

Little of this was evident on *Kearsarge,* with sailors like Fire Controlman 1st Class Don Millman on attitude patrol. "I get really mad when I hear people talking bad about the marines. They see them eat, sleep, and exercise, and that's all they see," Millman said. "I tell the junior sailors, 'Yeah, they take up space, but then they hit the beach, and then who gets shot at?'"

Marine Hasseltine put it into perspective. "We're like cargo on this ship, quite honestly. We're kind of a novelty for them, as they are for us," he said. "But we still talk the same way: 'head, overhead.' And we're trained to be part of a team."

The week ended with some challenging nighttime recovery and launch operations. A quartet of Harriers took off in the waning daylight, then returned after dark to scream down onto the barely lighted deck. The maneuver completed the pilots' night landing qualifications, allowing them to proceed to more complicated combat training. Navy and Marine Corps helicopters hovering a few hundred yards away followed the jets onto the flight deck. In the dim red light of *Kearsarge's* hold, a trio of air-cushion landing craft growled as the rear door opened. Rising smoothly, the hovercraft backed out of the well deck and headed for the North Carolina coast. Up in the ship's control tower, the commander of the embarked marine air combat element shook his head. "LCACs, Harriers, helos," Cushing marveled. "Let's see if there's anything else we can throw out there."

The idea of spending a solid week on the basics is only a few years old, but the commander of Amphibious Squadron Two views it as indispensable. "If you don't have the basic building blocks, there's no way you're going to be able to react as fast as we need to," said navy captain Jim Bolgar.

This is as true for the officers as the enlisted personnel. The first time the MEU and ARG commanders got together to plan a noncombatant evacuation in September, it took them two days. By the time they deploy, that time will be down to six hours or less.

---

Aboard the USS *Duluth* off California, April 1998

As dusk drew a hazy curtain across the California coast, the pace picked up aboard a thirty-three-year-old gray-hull floating off San Clemente Island. H hour—showtime for amphibious transport dock ships like *Duluth*—was set for 4:00 A.M.

This landing was part of *Duluth's* predeployment "final exam," one of the centerpieces of a two-week joint task force exercise that brought together the *Essex* amphibious ready group and the *Abraham Lincoln* battle group. In just a few weeks, the ships and marines would sail for the western Pacific and the Persian Gulf.

For more than a week, *Duluth* had dodged simulated threats while sending small troop detachments on short-duration missions. Now the ship's 350 sailors and 550 marines were wrapping up preparations for a predawn landing. *Duluth* would soon lay off the jabs and deliver its roundhouse punch.

If all went according to plan, about forty minutes before H hour, a dozen amphibious assault vehicles packed with marines would drop from *Duluth's* well deck and wallow several thousand yards to Camp Pendleton's Green Beach. A few miles away, the amphibious assault ship *Essex* and the amphibious landing dock *Anchorage* would be launching their own marines. All three groups would meet on the beach. Protected by their Cobras and Harriers, the marines would move inland. Their mission: protect a U.S. embassy from warring local factions.

Displacing 9,128 tons empty and 16,900 tons fully loaded, and capable of carrying nearly one thousand marines, *Duluth* and the other *Austin*-class amphibious transport docks were designed for these kinds of large-scale landings. The backbone of the Gator Navy, the LPDs make up the biggest chunk of the fleet's thirty-eight amphibs. Launched between 1964 and 1970, all remain in service. One of them, *Coronado,* was redesignated AGF-11 and transformed into the Third Fleet's amphibious command ship in 1980.

*Coronado* was pampered. The rest of the *Austin* class, now going on their third decade of globetrotting and salt spray, are showing their age. In the mid-1980s, navy officials planned a service life extension program that would fix them up and keep them steaming for another ten or fifteen years. When Congress scuttled the proposal in 1987, the navy kept the LPDs steaming anyway.

*Duluth* and its sisters will likely serve into the new millennium, until the new LPD-17 amphibious transport dock *San Antonio* and its sister ships begin arriving in force. It's likely the fleet won't say farewell to the last of the class until 2015, some four decades after they entered service, although, says naval historian Samuel Loring Morison, "if the *San Antonio* class hadn't come along, they'd probably all have lasted into the second decade of the new century."

In the meantime, nothing exempts *Duluth* and its sisters from the changing times. In the shrinking, multimission navy of the 1990s, old gators have to learn new tricks. "A naval ship like the LPD can't just do 'LPD stuff' anymore. It has to earn its keep," Morison says.

This means learning to operate away from the other ships in the amphibious ready group—in gator lingo, doing "split-ARG ops." It means experimenting with unmanned aerial vehicles and other new gear. It means deploying special warfare teams: SEAL commandos and special-boat operators. "This is the workhorse of the ARG," said Ens. Bob Willingham, the officer in charge of *Duluth*'s special-boat squad.

With eight hours until H hour, it was time for the amphib to ante up for a little insurance. From 8:00 P.M. until dawn, Willingham and his team would take their black boats up and down the landing zones, watching for enemy minelayers and other troublemakers.

*Duluth* slowed to five knots. Some twenty boatswain's mates in coveralls and baby blue hardhats surrounded a pair of thirty-foot rigid-hull inflatable boats squeezed into the forward corners of the flight deck. Unlashing them from their mounts, the sailors readied the boats for launch.

Willingham, clad in olive drab flame-retardant coveralls nearly identical with an aviator's flight suit, watched *Duluth*'s crane lift a boat from its trailer. The sailors guided the craft to the ship's starboard rail and held it there, allowing four men in waterproof suits and helmets to board. With hoarse shouts, they lowered the craft thirty feet to the darkening water below.

The process was repeated on the port side, with Willingham joining his men in the black boat. Once in the water, the eight men of Special Boat Unit Twelve's RHIB Detachment Delta sped off into the twilight.

In this and a dozen other ways, the special-boat crews and their swift craft extend the amphibs' reach. The gators enforce maritime embargoes, snap photos for the intelligence analysts, patrol coastlines and rivers, and more. Their craft reach speeds of forty knots and have ranges of seventy-five miles, allowing the special-boat teams to transport SEALS and Force Recon marines farther and faster than the commandos' own boats. A few nights before the landing, the boat crews ferried a raiding party from *Duluth* to San Clemente Island. The marines mopped up a pocket of "enemy" troops and snuck back to their ship.

Once the exception, these kinds of focused, short-duration operations are becoming the rule in the messy post–cold war world. Rarely are *Duluth* and its sister ships called on to conduct the massive beach assaults that inspired their design. Instead, the 1990s have seen the embarked MEUs take on special operations missions such as raids, evacuations, and relief work.

"The operations are less traditional but more frenetic. Take the NEO [noncombatant evacuation operation]. There are a lot of moving parts," said Terry McKearney, a naval analyst who once commanded the Pacific fleet's utility landing craft.

Pulling off these operations requires more flexibility than the three-ship ARG can offer—at least while sailing as a single unit. Instead, the commodore may detach the amphibious transport dock and dispatch it over the horizon on missions of mayhem or mercy. Or both.

Urban warfare's quicksilver nature means that gators must be nimble, for a morning firefight can dissolve into an afternoon of food distribution. "They'll send an LPD ahead to take some objective with a SEAL team or a raid," McKearney said. But in the event of an evacuation, "they've also got to be prepared to take care of pregnant women."

For *Duluth*'s commander, the new missions mean more independence—backed up with a lot more communications gear. "In the old days, I'd spend a lot of time flying across to the big deck," said Cdr. Paul Cruz, who took command of the amphib in December. Like the rest of the navy these days, he and his crew rely more and more on encrypted e-mail and the navy's secret Internet. Much of this technology relies on line-of-sight, ultra-high-frequency radio waves to pipe data between the ships. They're still working on ways to keep the data flowing when *Duluth* sails over the horizon, Cruz said.

If the boat squads are the gator's new arms and the commo boxes its new ears, a four-foot flying fiberglass triangle may be its new eyes. It's called the Dragon Drone unmanned aerial vehicle.

Invented in the 1980s and used by special-operations forces during the Gulf War, the drone has more accessories than a GI Joe action figure. Its telephoto cameras shoot with either visible or infrared light, beaming live images to the ship. It can carry a laser range finder for accurate battlefield reconnaissance. It even has bomb bays of sorts. The marines are reluctant to talk about its ability to drop ordnance, but they'll list any number of nonlethal loadouts, including pepper spray, propaganda leaflets, acoustic sensors, and antivehicle caltrops (like toy jacks with four sharp points).

Aboard *Duluth,* marines and industry contractors were working to prep the drone for shipboard service. A new pneumatic launcher can propel the ninety-pound drone into the air from an LPD's flight deck, eliminating the need for a runway. The drone has a combat endurance of about three hours, during which time its operators can scrutinize hostile territory from the safety of the ship.

For recovery, the drone crew erects a loose net the size of a garage door. Its operators, bunkered in a cargo container on an upper deck, fly the drone straight into the net. The "landing" almost invariably snaps its wooden propeller, but the drone lands otherwise unharmed.

The drone's price tag puts it into the "expendable" category. "Even $100,000 is cheap, compared to getting an F/A-18 shot down," said marine captain Marc Halyard. Best of all, say the rough-and-ready marines, it's easy to fix. "If worse comes to worst, we'll just duct tape it," said S.Sgt. David Francis, one of the drone's operators.

In the belly of the gator, more than duct tape is needed to keep the six-hundred-pounds-per-square-inch boilers up and running. *Duluth* is one of a dwindling number of navy ships powered by steam. Its two boilers generate twenty-six thousand horsepower through twin propeller shafts, moving the ship along at twenty-one knots. Compared with modern ships with highly automated internal combustion plants, *Duluth* relies heavily on humans to control its high-pressure systems.

The boilermen have a daunting commute to work: down endless

ladders through heavy watertight hatches. Should the ship strike a mine or take a torpedo, the hatches might save the ship—but they seal off escape for the engineers. "These guys are down here for the long haul," said Lt. (jg) Doug Munz, heading for the ship's lowest deck.

The ship's boiler room is hotter than the Tropics, more cramped than a submarine, and more demanding than a two-year-old. It's also dangerous. The boilermen live with one eye on the pressure gauge and another on the smoke pumping out of the ship's stack, an early warning sign of problems.

But there's pride in this sweaty work. The ship doesn't move without the boiler room. Amid the noise and the heat, an off-duty boiler technician carefully daubed paint onto a bulkhead. Perspiration dotting his shaven head, he filled in the crimson outlines of a demon who held in his talons the double-venting black circle of the BT rating.

"When I got here, I was nervous because it was a 'stick-shift' plant," said Cruz, who took command in December. "Now I don't even worry about it. Last night I went from two-thirds bells to two-thirds backing bells and it never even crossed my mind that I wouldn't be able to do it."

It's not something to take for granted. Stationed before a wall full of quivering gauges, Machinist's Mate 1st Class Jorge Santana, the fire room supervisor, noted the changing pressures on a clipboard, then turned toward a periscope to get a glimpse of the smokestack one hundred feet above. "If the smoke's black, there's too much fuel and not enough air. If the smoke's white, that's even worse," he said. White puffs indicate that fuel vapor has emerged unburned—and explosively volatile—from the engine room. "We're taking a chance of it blowing up," Santana said.

The job of adjusting the air-fuel mixture belonged that day to Machinist's Mate 3d Class Isidoro Madrigal. Santana called Madrigal, who had four years of service, his best boilerman. As the bridge indicator moved from ahead standard to ahead one-third, the Santa Clara, California, native twisted a red-handled dial to keep the steam pressure at 650 pounds per square inch.

"If I don't know what I'm doing, I'll kill everybody," he said.

Madrigal received some of the navy's finest technical training, but he wasn't supposed to use it in the belly of an amphib. A bit more than a year ago, the petty officer was a nuclear-qualified machinist's mate helping to run the eight reactors aboard the aircraft carrier *Enterprise.* But when Madrigal—who was then not yet twenty-one—was caught drinking ashore, the nuclear-propulsion community booted him out of their ranks.

"I was doing so good, but I wanted to have fun. I got caught," said Madrigal, now twenty-two. "It was a mistake, and I regret it." Aboard *Enterprise,* he had fifteen hours off after a five-hour watch. Now he found himself pulling six-hours-on, six-hours-off shifts on an undermanned ship.

The longer hours weren't just a matter of nuclear power versus conventional steam. Like the rest of the fleet, *Duluth* was short of sailors. The skipper shrugged ruefully when asked about it. "We're getting the job done," Cruz said. "We're just being creative about it."

As H hour approached, so did a thick predawn layer of fog that delayed the planned landing almost twelve hours. It wasn't until 3:00 P.M. that the call "Land the landing force!" finally came.

A dozen amphibious assault vehicles waded off the well deck and churned their way toward land. Unopposed at the beach, the marines moved inland to protect friendly "diplomats and civilians," the object of the exercise.

Back on the amphib, the skipper contemplated his three-decade-old ship and the new uses to which it was being put. "The LPD, in my opinion," Cruz said, "is the most versatile ship in the ARG."

---

With the USS *Trenton* in the Black Sea, June 1998

As the Romanian rescue helicopter swooped in, the volunteers playing bus accident victims worried briefly that they would soon require real medical attention. Flaring to a halt over a grassy landing zone near the Danube River's mouth, the helo passed barely overhead, giving the "victims" a disturbing view of the landing gear's tire treads.

The idea was to land a squad of U.S. Navy corpsmen on the accident scene. The pilots did that with speed and precision. Nine corpsmen and officers—attached to elements of the Twenty-sixth MEU aboard the dock landing ship *Trenton* charged out to minister to the "injured."

Running toward a prone figure, Hospitalman Jon Mau pulled out a stethoscope. A paper tag attached to the Romanian's striped shirt listed his "injuries," but the flak-jacketed Mau questioned him anyway.

"Tell me what hurts. Your arm? Can you move it at all?" Mau asked. Tucking the stethoscope away, he signaled to two French corpsmen wearing fatigues and red-cross armbands. They sprinted over, placed the victim in a litter, and loaded him aboard a marine CH-46 helicopter.

In fifteen whirlwind minutes, the victims were bandaged, splinted, and "medevacced out" to a French mobile hospital a few hundred yards away. It was the first time American, Bulgarian, and Romanian helicopters had operated together, officials said.

Held along Romania's Black Sea coast in June, Exercise Cooperative Partner 1998 was yet another Partnership for Peace event. This one stressed Bosnia-style peace enforcement operations. Besides the Americans, French, Bulgarians, and Romanians, units from Greece, Turkey, Italy, Georgia, and NATO's Mediterranean Sea standing naval force also joined in.

As ever, U.S. sailors and marines often struggled to communicate with their international confreres. "The pilots are really professional in the aviation aspects, but the language barrier is the big problem," said marine captain James Dupont, a forward air controller.

The same was true for the medical crew, a team of U.S., Romanian, and French personnel. "The problem is not one of spirit. Everybody wants to show what they can do," said French navy lieutenant Gregoire de Boiseheury, who boasted that the only surgery his parachuting medical crew couldn't perform was bringing someone back from the dead. "The problem is one of language. Most of the Romanians also speak French, or German. When we don't know a word, we take a piece of paper and draw the word."

The visiting American troops found Romania resurgent. The clean streets, bustling restaurants, and new glass-and-steel airport terminal in Bucharest seemed remarkable for a land only a decade removed from Nicolae Ceaușescu's communist dictatorship. Romania is the first

Eastern bloc country to sign on to the Partnership exercises, and the Romanians have already begun holding their briefs in English. In 1998, some of their helicopter pilots learned to land aboard *Trenton,* which would have been unheard of just a few years ago. "They want to be in NATO so bad," one navy officer said.

Their neighbors may have been similarly inclined, but their economies were definitely not yet up to speed, officials whispered. The Ukrainian and Bulgarian troops managed to join the exercise only with grants of American food and fuel.

During the mass-casualty exercise, *Trenton* rode at anchor just a few miles offshore, not far from Romania's largest oil refinery. Afterward, Hospitalman Seaman Apprentice Anthony Eisenhardt led Romanian and Bulgarian corpsmen on a tour of his ship's medical facilities. "They came down to sick bay and hung out, watching to see how we did things," the corpsman said. "They were just so thankful to be there."

But *Trenton* may one day attract attention from U.S. Navy officials as well, and not for its medical facilities. The amphibious transport dock is pioneering the art of waste disposal at sea.

The crew started rethinking trash in 1997, when a shipboard compactor was installed to turn plastic waste into colorful hubcap-sized disks. That bright idea inspired a flood of innovations. Over the course of an entire Sixth Fleet deployment, the crew dumped only food tins and ungrindable waste into the deep. "If you can grind it, or you can burn it, or you can process it, it has not gone over our side," said Lt. Cdr. John Lape, the ship's executive officer.

The biggest waste saver is the ship's confidential-documents burner, which does double duty as a general-purpose incinerator. The paper is collected in waist-high paper bags scattered through the ship and is burned in a furnace the size of a hotel refrigerator. "It's like eating an elephant bit by bit," said Lt. (jg) José L. Feliz, the ship's waste control officer.

The job takes two sailors eight hours a day, and it rotates around the crew. The ship's electrical division had the trash-burning duty on 24 June. Electrician's Mate 3d Class Clifford Gaines ferried the bags from a passageway stuffed with them. His partner, Electrician's Mate 3d Class Avtar Singh, fed tissue boxes and food cartons to a blazing fire.

Clad in a facemask, fireproof apron, and gloves, Singh picked pieces of charred metal from the glowing coals. Someone had been careless. "Each bag is marked with the compartment, so if somebody has some unseparated waste, we can call them on this phone, get their butts down here, and say, 'Hey, we're not going to do this for you,'" said Chief Electrician's Mate Juan Marpuri, who was supervising the fiery work.

The next target: aluminum soda cans. Sailors and marines aboard the ship consume twenty-four hundred cans of soda each day. But instead of sending them over the side, the new strategy is crush, stow, and recycle, using six hand-operated can smashers purchased at Kmart. *Trenton*'s first-class petty officers accumulated metal enough to earn several hundred dollars during a port call at Souda Bay, Crete.

The crew has even rethought the unrecyclable aspects of trash: bones, eggshells, food cans. The tops and bottoms of steel food tins are removed to make them crush smaller. "Wet" food trash is separated from "dry" to keep things from rotting. "Keep it wet, and that's when it starts to get nasty," Feliz said. Not so coincidentally, Feliz is also in charge of the ship's food services. With the packaging, peelings, and uneaten food they produce, the galleys are the biggest contributors to the ship's waste stream.

The new trash procedures mean a bit more work for the crew, and it isn't always done to perfection the first time around. The news of an upcoming visit from Romania's president sent *Trenton* into a cleaning frenzy. But when it came time to dump the trash, the handlers found that it had been poorly separated. Some two dozen petty officers hauled it up to the flight deck and went through it piece by piece.

Still, waste control officer Feliz is convinced that the effort is well spent: "It's a cleaner ship, which leads to cleaner morale and better living conditions."

And on an amphib—where thousands of sailors and marines live cheek to camouflaged cheek for six months at a stretch—a little cleanliness goes a long way.

# 7. THE TOMCATS

Nobody flies anywhere in an F-14 Tomcat until they've been through Fighter Squadron 101.

Each year, the instructors at VF-101 turn dozens of new aviators into Tomcat drivers and radar intercept officers, or RIOs. Experienced pilots coming off shore duty also brush up at the unit, located at Oceana Naval Air Station in Virginia Beach. The enlisted sailors who tend the navy's Mach 2, swing-wing strike fighter jets receive instruction in line shacks and hangars, learning to fix, fuel, and maintain the twenty-ton warbirds under the watchful eyes of petty officers.

The navy calls units like VF-101 "fleet replacement squadrons," and there is at least one for each type of aircraft in the naval inventory. The FRS is often the largest squadron in a community. At twelve hundred people, VF-101 is nearly five times the size of a fleet unit. Most people in the F-14 community refer to VF-101 by an older moniker: "the RAG," which stands for "replacement air group."

By any name, it is a busy place, and the day's work stretches well into the night. "The RAG is a factory that can never slow down," said Cdr. Brad Goetsch, the squadron skipper. "It has the reputation of being the real meat grinder of the fleet."

The metaphor can be horrifyingly apt. Just weeks earlier, VF-101 pilot Lt. Cdr. Logan A. Allen III had been killed when he ejected over an Atlantic Ocean flight range.

Death grants the training unit no immunity, and the RAG offers no shelter from the winds that buffet the Tomcat community. Parts shortages bedevil the flight line. The rising pace of operations strain crews and airframes alike. Pilots debate their career options: USN or TWA? The aging fighter jet itself is scheduled to retire by 2007, for navy planners want to fill carrier flight decks with F/A-18E/F Super Hornet strike fighters and Joint Strike Fighters.

But the plane's partisans, who say the fleet will need the F-14 longer than the planners think, refuse to accept orders to oblivion. They stalwartly argue the Tomcat's superiority over existing versions of the Hornet, citing the F-14D's acceleration and top speed of sixteen hundred miles per hour, its 13,700-pound carrying capacity, and its unrefueled range of one thousand miles.

Tomcat drivers like to tell stories of Hornets struggling to perform a classic photo-op maneuver: buzzing an aircraft carrier while punching through the sound barrier. In the F-14, they say, you can go supersonic just thinking about it.

More to the point, new equipment such as the LANTIRN bombsight and digital photo pods have turned the air intercept fighter into a fine aircraft for strike and reconnaissance missions. New tactics and techniques are debated, developed, and taught in the cinder-block halls of VF-101. "It's the home of the community, the wealth of information, the home base. You want to know about an F-14 issue, you come here," said Lt. Steve McShea, the squadron's program officer.

Out on the flight line, rows of brawny Tomcats wait to chase bogeys through the sound barrier. The squadron's nickname is the Grim Reapers, but it might as well be Tomcat Central.

An October morning found aviators in olive flight suits downing rivers of coffee in the squadron's ready room. Some studied flight plans, perching their mugs on the lap desks of the heavy chairs that are standard issue in navy ready rooms everywhere. Other aviators leaned around a magazine-strewn coffee table trading stories and sharing advice. Behind the duty desk, a huge message board spelled out the day's flight schedule: thirteen training exercises involving dozens of people and planes.

Strolling in at 7:30 A.M., Lt. (jg) Garrett V. Krause checked the whiteboard for his morning flight: a series of touch-and-go landings. Like the RAG's other green pilots, the twenty-five-year-old ROTC graduate had already completed initial flight training. Krause's logbook recorded about 275 hours in the cockpits of the jet-powered T-45B Goshawks. And the wings of gold on his uniform commemorated his passing grade on one of the world's toughest final exams: repeated landings on the empty flight deck of an aircraft carrier in workups. Indeed, he had excelled, earning a prestigious assignment as a fighter pilot.

Krause arrived at the RAG without so much as five minutes in the Tomcat's cockpit. This morning's touch-and-go hop was part of the standard familiarization process for newly winged aviators. Dubbed "fams," the month of plain vanilla flights—takeoffs, landings, basic maneuvers, instrument flying—gives pilots and RIOs alike a chance to get used to their powerful twin-engine steed.

His first flight in the fighter jet was enough to tell Krause he was riding a different beast. With more systems and a heavier stick, the Tomcat was a big change from the lightweight Goshawk. Maneuvers that took a nudge in the T-45, Krause found, required a good deal of muscle in the Tomcat. "You get a little electrical help, but it's not fly by wire," he said.

The aircraft's designers added a measure of resistance in the system to give the pilots a bit of "feel" for the flight surfaces, but some Tomcat drivers say they could do with a bit less. Experienced pilots learn to lift weights between missions to prepare for the grueling in-flight workouts, and to take a two-handed grip on the stick for airborne twists and turns.

After fams, the students move on to tactics. Here, they learn to shoot things out of the sky, blow them up on the ground, and stay alive in the process. It's the glamorous side of military flying, the right stuff that powered the movie *Top Gun,* and the raison d'être of naval aviation. Learning how to do it is a lot of work. Classroom lectures on strike and air-to-air warfare beget endless hours of study, followed by the chance to air it out in the cockpit. Every flight is followed by a half-hour debrief—longer when the students head out on their two cross-country field trips.

For two weeks of bombing practice on the desert ranges of Naval Air Station Fallon, Nevada, and several weeks of air combat maneuvers—dogfighting—off Key West, Florida, the new Tomcatters endure hours of postflight attention. The aviators' efforts are picked apart by instructors, every tiny mistake painfully reconstructed. Pain now will keep you alive later, the instructors say. Classes, flights, and evaluations stretch the workday from 7:00 A.M. to late at night. VF-101 instructor Lt. Mike "Bart" Bartelloni unknowingly echoed his skipper's metaphor when he said, "The op tempo is so crazy. We put students through a meat grinder."

New equipment and missions have made the courses increasingly rigorous. Veteran aviators say today's students go through training that is tougher than the elite Navy Fighter Weapons School used to be. "Fifteen years ago, [the RAG's syllabus] was almost a rudimentary course, not a lot on paper," said Goetsch, whose command tour marked his fourth time at the RAG. "Now, the course is higher in technology and knowledge than the Top Gun course of 1984."

In all, new Tomcat aviators log 123 hours in the cockpit and about 400 in the classroom before they leave for the fleet. Lt. Mark Garrison, one of the squadrons' naval flight officer instructors, called the program surprisingly effective. "It's like coming back to college," said Garrison, whose radio call sign, "Beaker," refers to his Muppet-like cowlick. "You're actually ready to do your job when you hit the fleet."

It can take awhile. On paper, the program requires thirty-six weeks, but it's not unusual for aviators to spend up to a year at the RAG, their progress slowed by bad weather, a paucity of working aircraft, and the fleet's personnel needs.

Garrett Krause's October morning was not unusual. After a ready room briefing, the student made his way out to the flight line, climbed into a fighter, taxied, and took off. Three more aircraft followed him into the darkening sky, but it was already too late. An opaque layer of clouds clamped a thousand-foot ceiling over the Virginia airfield, canceling the touch-and-goes. Krause and his twenty-three classmates fell another day behind schedule.

No less than the students, the RAG's instructors endure a hectic, demanding pace. Some fifty experienced pilots and RIOS—often called backseaters—share responsibility for about eighty students at any given time. In 1997, VF-101 sent seventy-six new pilots and eighty new RIOS on to the fleet.

The instructors spend hours prepping their students, green and seasoned, for operational flying. Then they plan and fly more than sixty, often nerve-wracking, training sorties a day. There are no "driver's ed" versions of the two-seat F-14; when a new pilot lifts wheels from runway, the instructor in the backseat has nothing but an intercom to get the aircraft down safely.

The instructors are an elite within aviation's elite. No one teaches at the RAG without placing first or second in a fleet squadron evaluation. Many of the lieutenants wear Top Gun patches, and some of the commanders have been instructors at the famous dogfighting school.

The exacting guardians of the operating squadrons, the instructors make sure no one leaves land who is not prepared for war at sea. "Would you be willing to fly with this guy at night? Because that's the standard we have to hold ourselves to," Garrison said.

Their awesome workload and responsibility are complicated by the RAG's status. As a nondeploying unit, VF-101 is low on the navy's pecking order for bodies and parts, making long workdays longer and exacerbating the shortage of instructors. When a fleet squadron needs a body immediately, they often pull a RAG instructor. In late 1997, the squadron "owned" twenty-five pilots and twenty-seven RIOS. It was supposed to have forty-one of each.

In the operations office across the hall from the ready room, Lt. Cdr. Bill "Hack" McMasters was on the phone, juggling VF-101's planes and people. Working a continent-sized jigsaw puzzle, he arranged the deployment of five training detachments to the West Coast and three to Key West, each taking about 150 people, twelve jets, and an eighteen-wheeler packed with suitcases. That was on top of the many daily flights around Virginia. The routine adds up to an annual total of 8,300 sorties and eleven thousand flight hours that burn $11 million in fuel. The operations officer loves his work.

"There's no better job in the navy than ops O of the RAG," said McMasters, a former Top Gun instructor. "It's pure operations and flying, and you're running the community for a year and a half."

McMasters was dealing with the navy's 1997 decision to shrink fleet squadrons by retiring older F-14As. The move was designed to help fleet maintainers keep aircraft flying during a parts shortage. It also caused a student backup at the RAG.

McMasters traced the shifting personnel patterns with colored markers on an erasable white board. Fleet pilots trained on the relatively underpowered F-14A were returning to the RAG for lessons on the more powerful D model of the aircraft. More senior pilots pre-empted slots slated for recent flight school graduates. Between late January and July 1998, no green aviators became Tomcat-qualified pilots.

From the fleet's perspective, this was no big deal. The shrinking squadrons had no urgent need for new bodies. But any young aviator who had dreamed of flying Tomcats was out of luck if he or she happened to earn gold wings at that particular time. By such winds of fortune are careers determined.

Over at Lt. Cdr. Paul "Butkus" Haas's desk, things were more immediately dire. When clouds scrubbed Krause's flight, VF-101's training officer began to rework the class timetables—again. Foul weather slows things down, but when occasional parts shortages ground the unit's jets, Haas's real problems start. "We start looking at hard choices: Do we stop this class to finish that one?" he said.

As elsewhere in the navy, the training squadron's funding has declined while the tempo of operations has risen. But it is the shortage of parts that has really created problems. "We have more ops money than we have parts," skipper Goetsch said. "It's the worst now it's ever been throughout the fleet."

That's most of the reason why the navy took its older F-14As out of service: to rob them of scarce parts, get the others flying, and ease the fleet's maintenance burden. The Grim Reapers, who began 1997 with almost sixty airplanes, finished 1998 with thirty-seven.

Many unit maintainers were glad to see them go. No less than the officers, the RAG's enlisted maintainers face jam-packed workdays. Each hour-long training flight may require fifty hours of groundwork.

Even with eight hundred enlisted machinists, electricians, ordnance specialists, and other maintenance personnel in the squadron, there is more than enough work to go around.

Trimming VF-101's own roster, in fact, merely put a dent in the Grim Reapers' maintenance burden. If the squadron is the crossroads for the people and ideas of the F-14 community, it also sees most of the aircraft. In a typical year, other squadrons send about one hundred Tomcats to Oceana for repairs and upgrades. Usually, it is because shipboard crews lack the time or space for complicated fixes, but even jets that are flying well come to VF-101 for the latest modifications.

Most of the maintenance departments work three shifts to take care of all the planes—and train the junior enlisted sailors who will one day take care of F-14s aboard carriers. Out on the tarmac, a battered, grimy line shack serves as toolshed, administrative headquarters, and pit stop for fifty-two airmen—the plane captains and their trainees. Over the three- to five-month training period, the junior maintainers earn full responsibility for an aircraft's well-being. "They bust their butts. They're the beginning and the end of what happens out here on the flight line," said line shack supervisor Stacey Dain, an aviation structural mechanic (safety equipment) 1st class.

Between washing the aircraft, changing the lubricants, and looking for problems, the maintainers spend an awful lot of time scrounging or improvising airplane components.

"Spare parts? What spare parts?" said Dain, a seventeen-year navy veteran. Getting planes in the air, he said, takes "patching and bubble gum and tape." Especially scarce lately had been a piece that keeps several fuselage panels from coming off. "I don't understand why it's so hard to get common parts: screws and fasteners," he said.

Plane captains check out their aircraft thoroughly before turning them over to the aviators, but the very last preflight inspections belong to the ordnance crews. VF-101's "ordies" work next door to the line shack, learning to load the planes with weapons, both simulated and real. Much of Ordnanceman 3d Class Michelle Nicolle's work was installing "blue tubes." Dummy missiles with real seeker heads, they allow aircrews to practice locking Sidewinder heat-seekers or Phoenix radar-guided weapons onto enemy aircraft.

Nicolle also handled the Tomcat's defensive ordnance. On the morning of Krause's abbreviated flight, she pulled open a gray panel just forward of a Tomcat's elevators and carefully loaded flares into a compartment. In a dogfight, the pilot could pump out the burning flares to distract enemy heat-seekers. On the ground, they're nothing but dangerous. "If one of those things goes off, you're toast. It'll kill you," said Nicolle.

Airman Jenny Mitchell, one of Nicolle's protégés, called her job the best one in the navy. "It's a little more pressure, but it's fun," Mitchell said. "I get to fix a multimillion-dollar aircraft. We could probably blow up Virginia Beach."

Actually, some pilots and maintainers probably would consider that idea if it meant they could move back to sunny California. The congressional decisions to close military bases gave Miramar Naval Air Station in California back to the Marine Corps in 1997. It also forced the navy to evacuate the airfield, the former home of the Top Gun school and long known as "Fightertown, USA." In 1996, the six fighter squadrons from Miramar began moving to share space with Oceana's seven units.

Consolidating the navy's F-14s at the sprawling Virginia Beach complex may have saved money, but it was not a popular decision with the aviators and airmen who loved the weather at Naval Air Station Miramar.

"Look outside," one pilot growled as mid-October clouds descended on the airfield, scotching the morning's touch-and-goes. Autumn in Virginia Beach is a blunt meteorological contrast to San Diego's near-perfect weather. Besides the clouds, the Virginia skies have rain and snow—unheard of at the West Coast base and the cause of many a grinding headache in the East.

"It's a crime that we left Miramar," said Aircraft Electrician's Mate 2d Class H. T. Johnson. "It's corroding the planes away."

But the weather is not the only factor that annoys the aircrews. Oceana's gunnery and dogfight ranges over the Atlantic Ocean are smaller, farther offshore, and less flexible than the ones near Miramar. The extra distance means less time spent training—and in case of a mishap, more difficult rescues. As the line goes, nobody ever drowned ejecting over the desert. "Two hundred miles off the coast is not where you want to be," said program officer McShea.

Worst of all are the long "commutes" to West Coast training exercises that can keep crews away from home for months—and this is on shore duty. For example, if an F-14 squadron needs two weeks of workups with its San Diego–based aircraft carrier, then waits ten days to start its three-week strike training at Fallon Naval Air Station in Nevada, the squadron might be out West for two full months. Miramar squadrons flew in each day and went home to their families at night.

"We are stressing these people beyond belief serving both coasts," said Johnson, who has seventeen years in the navy. "It affects manpower and manpower attitude."

Navy brass believe that the arrangement will save hundreds of millions of dollars, balancing out the complaints and the millions spent on enlarging and improving the Oceana flight line. In a Pentagon office decorated with airplane pictures and models, Rear Adm. John M. Johnson, the head of the navy's aviation plans and requirements, explained the reasoning. Much of the savings would come from consolidating repair and maintenance facilities, he said, while putting all twelve Tomcat squadrons in a single row of hangars would concentrate a body of expertise on a single flight line.

But some experienced aircraft mechanics switched communities rather than come to Virginia. "We lose our best maintenance guys because they want to work on F/A-18s or helos in Florida," McShea said. Not all of the "mech flight" can be blamed on the Virginia weather. Some career-minded maintainers don't want to be experts on a platform that's slated to leave the navy before they do.

Career-minded pilots around VF-101 were having similar doubts for different reasons. In offices and Officers' Club alike, talk turned often to a topic heard round the fleet: Should I stay or should I go? Flight hours were down, time away from home was up, and airlines were hiring.

"I have until March 1998 to resign. Unless things start to improve, I'll probably be getting out," said Lt. Michael Anderson, a pilot instructor.

He wouldn't be the first. One airline-bound pilot said the only button he was going to be pushing next year was the one that called the flight attendant for coffee. Of the VF-101 aviators who would fulfill their service requirements in the next year, Goetsch said, one-third had already handed in their resignations.

It's not the conditions at the RAG, the Grim Reapers hastened to say. It's a fleet thing. In their view, a higher op tempo and long training trips are keeping them away from home, while actual cockpit time is declining. Goetsch disagrees. Flight hours are about the same today as what he got fifteen years ago, but that itself is a problem, he said. "It's the same dissatisfiers, and people are saying, 'It was the same ten to fifteen years ago.'"

Fighter-jock camaraderie used to compensate for a lot, the skipper said, but the spirit has eroded since the 1991 Tailhook scandal rocked the service and tarred many careers. No officer above the rank of commander attended the 1997 version of the Norfolk "Fighter Fling," the often-rowdy gathering of the F-14 community, he said. Things like that make junior officers feel that the admirals aren't supporting them. "That's what killed a lot of the fraternity and esprit de corps that made us as great as we've been," said Goetsch. "We need to recognize that it's OK to have fun and recognize leadership." A soft-spoken man, Goetsch has been bending ears in Washington, trying to bring attention to the reasons his junior officers are leaving. Improvements in junior officer retention can't happen just at VF-101, even if it is the crossroads for the fighter community, he added. "That's got to be a navywide decision."

One servicewide decision that sent shock waves through the community is the navy's plan to retire the F-14 in less than a decade. The bottom line: the F-14's 1970s technology and design are too expensive to maintain and upgrade.

But that hasn't stopped the navy from retrofitting new technology onto the aging fighter. Even as planners prepare the death certificate, the Tomcat is proving to have several lives: strike aircraft, tactical reconnaissance platform, night bomber. "The Tomcat will be alive and well long beyond 2010—I'd bet my life on it," said McShea.

With years of experience concentrated in one squadron, VF-101's instructors are part of the reason for the plane's continued vitality.

When flight simulator technicians at Atlantic Fleet Strike Headquarters wanted to produce a training device that replicated the fire-breathing F-14D, they turned to the RAG, located less than a mile down the road. The instructors obligingly wrung the engineers' first effort out in simulated flight, and sent them back to their computer terminals with advice. "We'll say, 'The engine doesn't feel like that,'" said McShea. "We have to take a brand-new piece of gear and make it feel like a twenty-year-old F-14."

When the navy began pushing night-vision goggles, the RAG was right there to advise the Atlantic fighter wing on tactics and cockpit modifications. These days, the devices are used on just about every tactical nighttime mission, allowing navy attack pilots to swoop in while peering through devices that amplify moonlight, starlight, even streetlights. Tomcats first deployed with the devices in the summer of 1996, and more than two hundred F-14s are now being modified for them. The modifications consist primarily of dimmer switches for the instrument lights, to prevent the glow from washing out the aviators' vision.

VF-101 also helped adapt the Tomcat to carry the new Digital Tactical Air Reconnaissance Pod System. Slung under a wing, the digital camera transforms the F-14 into a flexible platform for gathering battlefield intelligence.

But the biggest change by far has been the navy's decision to add a strike capability to the fighter. With the fresh experience of Desert Storm and the looming retirement of the A-6 Intruder, the navy brass demanded more strike capability from carrier flight decks than Hornets alone could provide. The solution: mount bombs on the Tomcat's missile stations and sling a targeting pod under the fuselage.

The Tomcat first drew blood on the ground in 1995, when F-14s from the carrier *Theodore Roosevelt* dropped two-thousand-pound bombs on Serb positions in Bosnia. But the fighter became a precision strike weapon a year later when the aircraft started carrying the air force's LANTIRN targeting pod. The hybrid has been a tremendous success, and Tomcat aviators have begun adding "Bombcat" patches to their flight suits.

Atlantic Fleet strike planners say LANTIRN actually gives F-14 crews better views than the F/A-18's Nite Hawk targeting system. With these systems added to the Tomcat's longer range and heavier bomb load, the plane's fans are wont to wonder aloud why the navy bothers with those wimpy Hornets.

It's the money, of course. Putting a Tomcat in the air for an hour takes roughly twice as much maintenance time and money as flying a Hornet for the same time. And the Hornet's digital cockpit can be updated as better software and hardware come along.

There are plans to retrofit a few later Tomcats with a similar suite of instrumentation, but planners say there's no way to refit the entire fleet. "To bring [the Tomcat] into the twenty-first century with the all-digital control systems would have been too expensive," Rear Adm. Johnson said.

So the Tomcat's new life as a bomber is an interim solution until the Super Hornets appear. The F-14A variant, which constitutes nearly 90 percent of the production run, will be gone by 2003, a move hastened by the navy's decision to trim its Tomcat squadrons.

By 2015, navy planners hope to see carriers with only four types of aircraft: the Super Hornet, the SH-60R helicopter, the Joint Strike Fighter, and the Common Support Aircraft. Indeed, the push for newer stealthy aircraft sealed the Tomcat's fate. "Can DOD afford these things? They couldn't afford them if we continued to have twenty-five different kinds of airplanes," Johnson said.

"The Tomcat is still a great airplane, and it will be a great airplane the day we put it away. But naval aviation as a whole will not be any lesser," he said. "The airplane was designed around a threat that existed from the Soviet Union. That threat's no longer there."

But even the admiral admitted to a few second thoughts. "You say, holy cow, am I doing the right thing? It's working just the way it's supposed to be advertised," Johnson said. "Will we miss some of the conveniences that we had with the flexibility of having a whole bunch of specialized airplanes? Probably."

# 8. THE SUBMARINES

Aboard the USS *Houston* off San Diego, February 1999

When the harbor tug sailed into the channel, the submarine was already waiting, a venomous black slit in the water between North Island's naval airfield and the antenna-studded hills of Point Loma. Only a narrow slice of the attack sub's hull rode above the restless surface of San Diego Harbor. Most of the 360-foot steel tube lay below, invisible even up close.

Nearly a dozen men stood atop the sub's humped back, like storybook mariners astride some great steel leviathan. Most wore deflated life preservers over their blue coveralls. They also wore yachtsmen's deck shoes, for the rounded hull, some thirty-three feet in diameter, offered little traction for topside riders. Two safety divers waited in wetsuits against the possibility that someone might slip. The sailors transferred boxes of strawberries and lettuce and baby carrots from the tug to the sub, then handed them down a three-foot hatch to their shipmates below.

The sub's sail rose a bit aft, a narrow, teardrop-shaped tower supporting a small forest of periscopes and antennas. Two broad horizontal fins, the diving planes, sprouted from its sides. The diving planes control a sub's motion underwater as an aircraft's elevators do through the air.

An improbable number of sailors packed the flying bridge atop the sail. Most wore the ubiquitous life preservers, but one stood out in a jacket of international safety orange and a ball cap with command laurels stitched in gold thread—Cdr. Mike Zieser, the commanding officer of the attack submarine *Houston*. A thick cigar smoked in his fingers.

*Houston* is a windowless wonder built to shadow Soviet subs by their sounds alone. Nuclear propelled, able to draw potable water and air from the raw ingredient of seawater, the sub can stay submerged indefinitely. Endurance is limited only by the amount of food aboard: a three-month supply packed into its tight living spaces.

When *Houston* dives beneath the waves, she is all but undetectable—by friend as well as foe. Zieser believes the danger and isolation of submarine operations link his crew to a naval tradition that existed before computer networks, before radio. Like the warships of old, no one knows where a sub goes once it disappears from sight.

"We're the last group of sailors like John Paul Jones. We're not connected. They just assume we're okay," the skipper said.

But even Zieser and his fellow submariners have been caught up in the churning currents of the post–cold war world. The submariners' main mission—preparing to destroy Soviet ballistic missile subs in the event of nuclear war—all but evaporated as the rusty Russian fleet fell into disrepair. In the decade after the dissolution of the Soviet Union, nearly fifty boats—half the American sub fleet—were decommissioned. *Houston* itself would make only one more cruise before heading to the scrapyard.

Yet the submariners who remain are busier than they used to be, and they have always done more than has been widely advertised. Subs' stealthy nature makes them perfect for any number of covert missions. In one of the most secret operations of the cold war, they dispatched teams of divers to tap the Soviets' undersea communications cables. They have long delivered navy SEALs and other special forces to foreign shores in the dark of night. They can lurk off coastlines with a single periscope eye poking above the waters, snapping digital photos and plucking radio signals from the ether. "We're the original stealth platform," Zieser said.

These days, there are new missions afoot. The *Los Angeles*–class attack subs can shoot Tomahawk cruise missiles—and did, several times, in 1998. One of them fired the first shot in Operation Desert Fox. Regional commanders value the stealthy subs as missile platforms. They can strike with true surprise, and they are impervious to ship-killing missiles tipped with conventional, chemical, or biological warheads.

*Houston* can launch its missiles only through four bow-mounted torpedo tubes, which is one of the reasons this sub is slated for decommissioning. The twenty-three "improved" members of the sixty-two-boat class have a dozen vertical launch tubes—submersible versions of the weapons found on cruisers and destroyers.

Like the surface ships, today's subs find themselves playing escort to the aircraft carriers. Carrier groups routinely deploy with one or two silent bodyguards, which often dash ahead of the battle group to sniff out hidden threats in a role called "battle-space preparation."

Nine years after the fall of the Berlin Wall, subs were spending twice as many days on missions as before it. The load heaped on the dwindling submarine fleet became so great in mid-1998 that its leaders took the unusual step of asking their superiors to ease up.

Uncertainties lay ahead. By 1999 the navy planned to complete three superquiet, superexpensive *Seawolf*-class boats, then move on to design an even more capable group called the *Virginia* class. But there were not enough new boats on the drawing board to maintain a fleet of more than forty subs.

The questions—What should subs do in the post–cold war world? and how many would it take?—remained unanswered as Zieser conned *Houston* out of the harbor for a few days of predeployment shakedown.

Clear of land, a dozen miles from the hilly California coastline, the sub prepared to dive. There were several things to accomplish over the next few days. A team of civilian experts had embarked to pin down the source of a mysterious noise that occurred when the sub's diving planes moved. And the crew was still testing the boat after a repair period in the shipyard. If something wasn't working, best to find out about it in the shallow water of the continental shelf.

Zieser and more than a dozen shipmates filled the control center, crowding the bedroom-sized space with bodies in navy-standard blue coveralls. Only the blue and khaki web belts distinguished the junior enlisted personnel from the chiefs and officers. From the ankles down, it was anybody's guess. Everyone wore a different brand of athletic shoe.

"Subs are different," explained Storekeeper Seaman (SS) Andre Taylor, a four-year veteran of underwater warfare. Sailing beneath the sea takes a special kind of sailor: one who's especially smart, focused, and disciplined. Everything in a nuclear sub goes by the book. Yet this rigorous professionalism often breeds a relaxed camaraderie, and the riotous variety of footwear on *Houston* was just one example. Besides, Nikes and Reeboks offer a quality of paramount value on subs: silence. Soft soles muffle noisy footfalls.

Located just below the sail, the control center was the sub's operational hub, the combined equivalent of a surface ship's bridge and combat information center. The low-ceilinged space was about twenty-five feet square, but seemed smaller. A low riser in the center supported the quartermasters' chart tables and the twin periscope columns. The walls were packed with dials and display screens. A suite of electronic navigational instruments occupied the port bulkhead. To starboard, four petty officers manned a row of fire control computers.

"Less computing power there than in my desktop calculator," Zieser said. The skipper may have been exaggerating, but he had a point. *Houston*'s keel was laid in 1979, and the sub was filled with computer equipment almost that old. The equipment had been calculating firing solutions on Soviet subs for a decade before anyone coined the term *Pentium.*

The forward port corner of the room was occupied by the quartet of enlisted sailors—two senior, two junior—who controlled the ship's movements. The helmsman steered the sub, moving the massive rudder with small movements of an oval wheel. He also controlled the diving planes. A healthy push on the wheel would send the sub downward; pulling back would bring it toward the surface.

To his left sat the planesman, whose own wheel moved another set of planes mounted aft near the rudder and screw. The rear planes set the tilt of the sub's hull. The man in the next seat over—the chief of the watch—faced a complex instrument board. He controlled the sub's buoyancy by regulating the flow of seawater and air into a warren of ballast tanks. Flooding the tanks would sink the sub beneath the waves. "Blowing them" with stores of compressed air would bring it to the surface. Between these extremes, the chief would keep the sub trimmed for slight positive buoyancy. Trimming a sub is a tricky process; everything from changing water temperatures to dropping garbage capsules can affect its weight in water.

Looking over their shoulders was their supervisor. The diving officer is usually a chief petty officer with years of submarine experience. All four men wore seat belts, testament to the sub's maneuverability.

The mustachioed skipper and his youthful officer of the deck, Lt. Adam Plumpton, moved out from behind the periscopes.

"Quartermaster, sounding on periscope?" Plumpton asked.

"Fifty fathoms," came the response.

Three hundred feet of water below the keel—plenty of room for a sub.

"Prepare to dive," Zieser said.

An electronic klaxon filled the ship: *"Aooga, aooga, aooga."* "Dive, dive," the 1MC announced.

Plumpton gave the order to take the sub down.

"After venting," he said.

"All vents open, sir," responded the chief of the watch. Seawater rumbled into tanks mounted beneath the hull.

"Make your depth thirty feet," the lieutenant said.

"Thirty feet, aye," replied the diving officer. He relayed the order to the helmsman and planesman, who pushed their heavy controls a few inches forward.

To an outsider, the lack of a windshield was disconcerting. The submariners concentrated on their gauges instead: depth, heading, dive angle, and more. Dive angle was critical as the sub moved away from the surface. If the propeller came free of the water, it would quickly accelerate until something broke.

Suddenly, there was seawater in the room. It dribbled down the side of the periscope, then flowed into a growing puddle in the middle of the control room. A few civilian and military visitors exchanged looks. Was this supposed to be happening? None of the submariners batted an eye.

"Speed eight knots," Plumpton told the diving officer. Then the blond lieutenant called for a grease gun and some rags. In an eye blink, two sailors were mopping the deck while another was pumping lubricant into a valve hidden among the ceiling pipes. The skipper grabbed a metal flashlight and peered up the column. Plumpton rotated the scope, spreading the lubricant around the metal tube and resealing it against the sea. The dripping water slowed and stopped.

"The periscope had recently been removed, refurbished, and reinstalled," someone explained. "Sometimes, the grease seal takes a little work."

That solved that problem. Next up: "angles and dangles." These maneuvers would swing the sub back and forth, heel the hull over, and slant the boat up and down to make sure everything in the sub was secured. In underwater warfare, a noisy boat is a dead boat. *Houston*'s engineers had built the sub to run silent. Each piece of machinery rested on rubber feet that stood on a platform with rubber feet. The pipes were clamped with vibration-reducing fittings. Every precaution had been taken to keep noise from reaching the hull and leaving audible footprints in the water. But all of this expensive muffling couldn't stem the force of gravity. If something fell to *Houston*'s metal deck while the sub was stalking another sub, the hunter could quickly become the prey. "What kills a submarine is transients: a toolbox comes loose, a box falls off a shelf," said Chief Machinists' Mate (SS) Jeff Davidson.

Everything on *Houston* was supposed to be stowed securely enough to withstand a fifteen-degree angle in any direction. But people can get careless while the sub is being repaired in port. *Houston* had returned from a deployment in October and undergone several months of repairs afterward. It was a good idea to shake things up.

"General quarters," Zieser said. Getting everyone to their battle stations, the skipper reasoned, prevented injuries that might occur if the aggressive maneuvers took the crew by surprise. Besides, you can never train too much.

Once again, an electronic alarm resounded through the ship, the *bong-bong-bong* of general quarters. The control center soon became twice as crowded as sailors rushed in, rolling down their sleeves and tucking pants into socks.

Senior Chief Missile Technician (SS) Rick LaFave slid into the diving officer's seat. *Houston*'s battle station watch bill generally put the most experienced sailors in the top slots. LaFave was the senior enlisted man aboard, the chief of the boat.

"Make your depth five hundred feet," Plumpton said. "Five-zero-zero, aye," LaFave replied.

The *Houston* headed down. The deck tilted twenty degrees. Everyone leaned backward. "Yeeha," someone said from the back of the room.

"Passing three hundred feet," LaFave said.

"Very well," Plumpton responded.

"Officer of the deck, you have one hour at the present course and speed," called a quartermaster.

"Very well."

"Four hundred feet, coming to five hundred feet," the COB said.

The water pressure mounted around the hull, squeezing it slightly and compressing the air within. Ears popped.

Two minutes after the dive began, the hull leveled out, fifty stories below the surface. New orders: make depth 250 feet, twenty degrees up angle.

"Two-five-zero, twenty up, aye," the COB said.

As the deck tilted again, there was a rustling behind the periscopes. A microphone fell from a ceiling rack. Zieser caught the mike by its springy cord and stowed it.

From the sonar room came news of a nearby ship, a "contact" in military parlance. In a cramped space forward of the control center, a sonar technician leaned over his monochrome computer screen. Like his headphones, the screen was filled with the static of underwater noise. The ocean is filled with sounds, especially in shallow water: rumbling ships, lowing whales, keening brine shrimp. The sensitive microphones embedded in the hull and towed from the rudder could even pick up aircraft if they flew close enough. Once in a long while, they even sniffed out a Soviet missile sub in the vast darkness.

*Houston*'s sonar techs were trained to recognize patterns and anomalies in the crackling underwater ether, so pegging this one was no great feat.

"Bearing seventy-seven degrees, a four-bladed screw doing 120 rpm. Probably a merchant ship doing four or five knots. About twenty-five thousand yards away," announced the executive officer, Lt. Cdr. Paul Marconi.

The heavy maneuvering continued. Under Plumpton's command, the sub rolled left and right, dove to 650 feet, came back up to 500. Satisfied, the skipper turned his attention to the merchant ship. An old submariners' homily divides the seafaring world into two classes: subs and targets. The merchant ship was about to fall into the second category.

Zieser's sub would not fire on the other vessel, of course. Indeed, the civilians would never even suspect they were being shadowed. But playing cat and mouse is always good training for the crew of an attack submarine. Plus, it's a lot of fun.

"Let's take a look at him," Zieser said. "Come right and close track."

Someone called out, "Closest point of approach in nine minutes, nine thousand yards."

The captain directed another course change to allow his sonar operators to triangulate on the merchant. The fire controlmen began setting up an attack trajectory; in naval parlance, a "solution." A passenger asked whether the merchant's captain had any idea that he was being hunted by a submarine.

"Zero," Zieser said. "Our own surface warfare ships don't have any idea we're here unless I do something stupid."

The crew prepared to move to periscope depth. The sub rose to 150 feet, high enough for a good listen, deeper than any ship's draft. "Everybody's concentrating when we come to periscope depth because you don't want to knock anybody over or come crashing into a ship," a sailor explained.

Another sonar contact appeared on the sparkling green screen. It had a five-bladed screw like a warship, but no telltale military noises. "Possible warship," the exec told the skipper, who was bending toward the periscope. The skipper decided to ignore the second contact in order to go after the merchant vessel.

"Come to periscope depth," Zieser said.

LaFave read decreasing numbers from the digital depth gauge. Zieser swung the scope in a circle, crab-walking around its column.

"One-zero-zero, nine-zero, eight-five feet," the COB intoned.

Someone punched a television screen that hung amid the overhead clutter. The watery "periviz" image appeared, showing the captain's view through the periscope. The water's surface rippled above the camera, silvery and enchanting, then fell toward the camera, broke around the lens, and receded below. The California coastline came into view.

The sub leveled out. Only the periscope's tiny eye showed above the waves.

"No close contacts, no air contacts," Zieser said. "How's your depth?"

"Five eight, sir," LaFave replied.

For five minutes, Zieser and his crew maneuvered carefully for a simulated torpedo shot at the ship, now ten miles to the east. Two decks below the packed control center, torpedomen carefully drew water into one of *Houston's* four tubes. They opened the outer door. The fire control team double-checked its data. "Firing solution," the XO told the skipper.

"Merchant, zero seven eight, twenty-two. Firing procedures," Zieser announced.

"Ship ready," Plumpton said. He grabbed the periscope and helped his skipper line it up again. "Weapons ready."

"Weapons stand by. Shoot," Zieser said.

Compressed air blew the seawater from the torpedo tube, simulating the launch of a nineteen-foot torpedo armed with 650 pounds of high explosive. The boat shuddered. Ears popped again.

In a real mission, this is the moment of truth—and not just for the target. The act of firing rips away the attack sub's protective cloak of silence. A sub that shoots betrays its existence, if not its exact position, to enemy sonar operators. "When you do that, the finger of God points right at you," an officer said later.

As if on cue, a loudspeaker began humming intermittently. The periscope-mounted radar detector was picking up signals. The low tones meant a civilian navigation radar—no threat there. But other tones—faster and more dangerous—could indicate that someone was trying to find the sub by bouncing radar energy off the scope's narrow stalk.

The tones grew more urgent, a quick staccato squawking that indicated the probing radar of a sub-hunting plane. Even among friends, that was enough for the submariners.

"All right, let's go deep," the skipper said.

"Emergency deep," Plumpton told the COB.

By nature and design, the U.S. Navy's submarines dive to depths that would crush an unprotected human. And they carry a nuclear reactor amidships, its radioactive pile glowing for decades on end. So what do submariners fear most? Fire.

"The reactor's very safe. We can always blow ballast if we get a [seawater] leak," Zieser said. "But there's nowhere to vent our fumes if something catches fire."

Not that he was much worried about it, the captain said. He slapped the cabinets in the small wardroom. All metal sheathed in Formica, he said; not very flammable. Most of the threat came from sparks in the aging electronic equipment. New sensors were being installed to shut things down at the smallest spark.

For all that, Zieser still ran his crew through three hours of drills a day: fire, flood, reactor shutdowns. Senior Chief Electronics Technician (SS) Bruce Talbot said he spent half his time just keeping track of them. But it was a job he enjoyed immensely. The crew called him the "master of disaster."

Sometime after the skipper called off the general quarters, Talbot gathered up his props and set up for a fire drill. In the machinery space just forward of the reactor, he threaded a cord of blinking lights around one of the carbon-dioxide scrubbers that keeps the ship's air fresh. A sign behind him read "Radiation Area. 12 Hours A Day Maximum. No Bunking."

"This is going to spread to the ceiling," Talbot declared. "It'll be a class-alpha fire: multiple things on fire, different types of materials."

Then he began waving a gray rag and called in an alarm.

In seconds, the 1MC began bonging. "Secure power to number one scrubber," someone ordered, acting quickly to keep the flames from melting live wires together.

Two sailors appeared immediately, pointing the black cones of extinguishers at the waving cloth. Talbot added a bigger gray rag and a red rag. "Fire!" they cried, backing away.

At the alarm, Electronics Technician 3d Class (SS) Jason Valentine had leapt from his repair station behind the control center. Grabbing a breathing mask and gloves, he slid down a ladder and popped into place behind the extinguisher men. He threw the mask over his head and took a short breath, sucking the rubber seal tight around his face. ("It's a claustrophobic feeling," he said later.) Then he plugged his air hose into a nearby vent.

Every bunk on the boat had a similar mask, designed to plug into emergency breathing spigots placed throughout the hull, marked on the deck below with rough stickers. In a major conflagration, sailors might have to crawl through black smoke, feeling blindly for a lifesaving flow of untainted oxygen.

Valentine grabbed a fire hose and shoved himself into the space. Talbot met the firefighter at the door and added another prop to the petty officer's ensemble: a floppy blue surgical cap that covered his mask and simulated the reduced visibility of heavy smoke. Valentine squatted to avoid heat and fumes and repeatedly mimed the motions of spraying the blaze.

Implacable, Talbot kept waving, both hands full of cloth now. A sailor in full fire-fighting gear slapped Valentine on the shoulder. Time to retreat. Clad in a heavy olive-colored flame-retardant suit, gloves, and boots, the sailor wore a self-contained breathing apparatus on his chest—twenty pounds of gear in all. A Darth Vader noise emanated from the device. The sailor dragged his hose closer to the flames. "Firehose team three is fighting the fire in the machine room," the 1MC announced.

A teammate in similar gear poked the barrel nose of a heat-seeking camera into the space and directed the flow of water toward the string of lights. Talbot dropped one red rag, then the other.

"Fire's out!" someone yelled.

In time, a pair of chief petty officers arrived to determine the extent and cause of the damage. "I think it was electrical," the machinist's mate said. "I think it must have been mechanical," the electronics technician retorted, concealing a smile.

Later, Valentine talked about the dangers of his job. "You don't think about it," the four-year submariner said. "You just concentrate on your job and pray that everyone else does too."

Submariners are often described as the fleet's elite. This observation is usually followed by the sentiment that one has to be a little different to live in a cramped 367-foot tube for months at a time. Submariners cheerfully admit it's so. "Pretty much it's culture shock when you come down for the first time," Andre Taylor said.

It takes some adjustment to get used to living in a space so small. There were no brooms or mops on *Houston*—too much wasted space. Instead, the crew got by with sponges and dust brooms. The most junior enlisted men—the navy does not permit women in sub duty—did not get a bunk of their own. Of *Houston*'s roughly 140 crewmen, 30 were "hot-racking," tumbling onto a mattress someone else had recently vacated.

Likewise, every space did double or triple duty. The torpedo room also held a dozen or more sleeping racks—plus the overflow from the chow line. And when general quarters sounded, the corpsman scooped up his laptop computer and headed for the wardroom, which became the surgical ward. His office, meanwhile, was occupied by sailors whose job it was to feed decoys and other countermeasures into the water.

Long showers are frowned on in most navy ships, but submarine bathroom etiquette is even more restrictive, thanks to the limited ability to create fresh water. "You got to use water like it's your best friend," said Taylor. "You rinse up the major areas, soap, and you're out of there."

On *Houston,* the close quarters bred a tight crew, as eager to brag about shipmates as they were to play practical jokes on them. Electronics Technician 3d Class (SS) Philip Warren fell prey to a common prank in the weeks after he first came aboard. Someone was slipping three-pound disks—used to sink the sub's trash—under his mattress. Each day, it grew a bit harder to lift the bed to get at the six-inch "coffin locker" that held his clothes.

"Even after I figured it out, I didn't do anything about it," Warren said. "I wanted to see how far they would take it. But after it to grew to thirty-five weights, I said forget it."

The rewards of the submarine life are many. For Warren, they included his wife, Claudia. A native of Uruguay, she met her future husband while he was on a port visit to Punta del Este. "She stuck her tongue out at me. I chased her for two blocks. We had a great time," Warren said. They exchanged phone calls and letters for months. In May, she came up to San Diego for two weeks. The two were married on the last day of the month. "There have been rough spots, but that's just been due to culture shock on both our parts," he said.

More conventionally, there's the food. Submarines get a larger galley budget than their surface counterparts, a small compensation for the isolated life. Late one night in the messroom, Warren noshed on pizza dripping with cheese and chunks of vegetables. "This is what I like about being a submariner," he said.

Most of all, there's the professional pride shared by those who wear the dolphin pins. Unlike their brethren on ships or aircraft, submariners must qualify for their warfare specialty pins within a year or be booted out to another branch of the sea service. To earn his silver dolphins, Andre Taylor studied his sub's systems two hours a day for nine months. Most of the curriculum concerned damage control. "I couldn't tell you how to put it together, but I know how to turn it off," he said.

Those who survive the process earn the rights and responsibilities of a superior sailor.

"We expect every man on this ship to be able make a decision and do the right thing," Zieser said over dinner in the wardroom. "You say, 'He's a nineteen-year-old.' But if he's a dolphin-wearing nineteen-year-old I expect him to know what valve to shut."

The process itself builds community, Zieser said. "Yeah, it sucks. I know it sucks; I've been there. I'll help you through it," he said.

More than most, *Houston*'s skipper made a ritual of pinning on gold and silver dolphin pins, paying tribute to the submariners who have perished in the Silent Service. It was usually a command performance. "If there's a dolphin-pinning ceremony, you go," said Lt. Cdr. Brian Reed, the ship's engineer.

After topping off a lasagna dinner with Boston cream pie, the skipper pushed back his heavy chair and indulged in a little bragging about his ship. *Houston,* it turns out, played the part of the USS *Dallas* in the movie version of *The Hunt for Red October.* A blown-up still from the film is framed on one wardroom wall. It shows *Houston*'s nose and sail bursting from the water in a full-bore emergency surfacing. Zieser was even prouder of his crew.

"We have some of the finest people in the nation. We're blessed. Everyone wants to be here," the skipper said. He had particular words of praise for the junior officer who had conned the boat earlier in the day. "Adam Plumpton is one of the finest junior officers I've ever worked with," he said.

The wardroom door burst open, and the wardroom attendant, Mess Specialist 2d Class (SS) Ronald Sturtz, entered with a pitcher of water. The skipper continued.

"He's smart. He graduated second in his class from the Naval Academy. He's thoughtful and patient. The crew loves him."

"Lieutenant Adam Plumpton," said Sturtz, guessing correctly.

But a few hours later, as midnight passed into memory in the artificially lit wardroom, the weary lieutenant fell into a chair and declared that he planned to resign from the navy.

Plumpton grew up in the small town of Lafayette, New York, and applied to the Naval Academy for fairly standard reasons: he wanted to travel and he wanted financial independence from his parents. The midshipman graduated in 1993, the top naval architect in his class, and signed up for submarines. His first assignment was disastrous, a constant series of personality clashes with the skipper.

"My first two years on the boat was utter hell. I would have given my last two years' pay to get out of it," he said. "I don't want to have another experience like that and not be able to walk away."

Life aboard *Houston* had been completely different, Plumpton said.

Zieser encouraged his junior officers to make decisions, but was patient when they came to him for help. "It's hard to explain the relationship to a civilian," the lieutenant said. "He's part The Man, part father figure, part teacher."

The main reason Plumpton was getting out: a desire for a family life that didn't involve six-month deployments. He was getting married in San Francisco in early 1999.

"We've been dating five years. I've been in different parts of the country for four years of it. I've been underwater for maybe two of it," he said. "I want to coach Little League, do that kind of stuff."

Besides, Plumpton said, he didn't like the trends he saw in the sub service. More missions and fewer boats meant hard times ahead. "I think we're hurting. I don't see how we're going to do it. We're going to hit forty subs if we're lucky," he said. "The military is never going to say, 'We can't do it.'"

Plumpton saw the sub force suffering as officers and enlisted men left for more lucrative civilian jobs. It's a peacetime navy, he said. We stand inspections and do paperwork. Even the missions aren't as exciting anymore. And the travel he joined the navy to get? In two six-month deployments to the western Pacific, Plumpton said his liberty —excluding ports with U.S. naval bases—totaled nine days.

"A lot you give up and the rewards aren't there. It's not money. . . . If they gave us more sailors per ship and more ships per squadron and more support, it would be nice," he said, resignedly.

Plumpton said he had learned much during his years in the navy —especially those aboard *Houston.* "I felt good up there. I felt confident," he said of the day's maneuvering watch. "Eight years ago, I didn't have the confidence to stand in a room and shout out orders to people who are mostly older than me. And to take command of the situation."

Zieser had entered the wardroom a few minutes earlier, taking up station in his chair at the head of the table. The skipper's appearance caused Plumpton to halt a moment, almost guiltily, but Zieser bade him continue. He and his young lieutenant had discussed it all long ago. No one likes to see the profession downsized, Zieser had said.

The lieutenant said he would miss parts of the naval life, such as the camaraderie. He had invited all of *Houston's* officers to his wedding. Other parts he wouldn't miss. "Today started at 1:00 A.M. Tomorrow starts at 3:00 A.M. All right," he said, rising and heading for the door. "Let's fix that periscope."

*Houston's* skipper didn't share his lieutenant's bleak outlook. He placed his faith instead with the navy's leaders. The sub force was taking on more work but at some point would be compensated for it, he believed.

"I think we are doing the right things," Zieser said. "It's the right thing for the national security. I'm sure it is. You have to trust the leadership."

## 9. BIG SHIP, LITTLE BOATS

The navy is not just aircraft carriers and fighter jets and submarines. But most of the sea service gets considerably less press. Consider the torpedo recovery boats of Naval Station Pearl Harbor. When subs go out to hone their hunting skills, someone has to pick up after them. In Hawaii, that someone is often the sixty-foot *Harrier* and its tiny crew.

Or take the navy's dwindling ranks of submarine tenders. When deployed subs develop broken periscopes, empty larders, or a hundred other symptoms, tenders in Guam and the Med supply experts, food, and repair workers.

And while the subs give plenty of rides to SEALs on surreptitious missions, so do the navy's special-boat squadrons.

---

Coronado, California, April 1998

The frigate *Jarrett* glided through San Diego Harbor, its hull barely raising a ripple as the ship headed south past the waterfront's hotels and high-rises. Sailors leaned on the rail, idly surveying the familiar water. The harbor was still as slate, the April skies cloudy.

Heads perked up. A rugged military powerboat ripped past the ship, doing maybe fifty knots. The frigate's crowded forecastle came alive with waves and whistles.

Wedged behind the little boat's controls, a trio of men grinned. They knew the feeling. Like most of the men of Special Boat Unit

Twelve, they had signed up for their jobs after watching someone else
tear up the ocean in a floating pocket rocket. They did not, however,
wave back. They were too busy holding on. When the speeding craft
hit the frigate's mild wake, its fiberglass hull reared, then plunged back
down with a bone-rattling splash. Undeterred, the driver steered for
the mouth of San Diego Harbor.

"Everybody wants to be a 'boat guy' on a calm day in the harbor,"
Quartermaster 1st Class (CC) Joe Riffey said.

But few know where they go after dark.

"The best special ops mission is the one nobody ever knows about,"
said Gunner's Mate 2d Class (SW/CC) Ryan Renner. Like Riffey, the
gunner's mate belonged to Special Boat Squadron Twelve, a particularly obscure corner of the hidden world of naval special warfare.

Today's special-boat squadrons trace their lineage to the PT boats of
World War II, the "mosquito fleet" that raided Japanese shipping in
seventy-foot torpedo boats made of plywood. John F. Kennedy skip-
pered a PT during World War II. So did Lt. John Bulkeley, who won a
Medal of Honor for evacuating Gen. Douglas MacArthur from the
besieged Philippine peninsula of Bataan. During the Vietnam War, the
navy resurrected the idea of small-boat units for brown-water operations on rivers, in deltas, and along coasts. After the war, most of the
squadrons were dismantled.

A few survived. The navy's SEALs—special warfare commandos,
themselves descendants of World War II's frogmen—found the boat
operators eminently useful for covert operations. The "boat guys," as
they called themselves, became experts at sneaking up to a coastline,
dropping off the SEALs, and returning to collect them after their shad-
owy tasks were completed. As the Naval Special Warfare Command
evolved, it created four special-boat squadrons to assist its SEALs.

In the post–cold war world, military leaders have turned to special
warfare forces with increasing frequency. In the mid-1990s, the six
hundred special warfare combatant crewmen began to carve out their
own special-ops niche. With their shallow-draft craft, the boat crews
can get within feet of a beach or riverbank to gather intelligence with
high-speed cameras. Patrol missions—watching for enemy minelayers
before an assault, for example, as Willingham and his troops did from

*Duluth*—are performed closer to shore and with more stealth than any ship. The boat crews also enforce maritime embargoes, in the Persian Gulf and elsewhere.

With new missions in the littoral zones and a nine-week school that combined the physical rigors of SEAL training with a crash course in small-boat operations, the four small-boat units were busier and more useful than ever. In 1997, the navy changed its personnel rules to allow sailors to stay in the small-boat units, husbanding their hard-won skills. "Before, they were considered special forces support," said Lt. Andrew Yenchko, SBU 12's operations officer and a SEAL officer himself. "Actually, these guys *are* special forces. They're not a taxi service for anyone."

Like the SEALs, the boat teams are designed to go anywhere in the world, and quickly. A phone call from a regional military commander can summon a detachment within forty-eight hours. Even the largest of their boats, the eighty-two-foot Mark V Special Operations Craft, fits—barely—into an air force C-5 Galaxy cargo jet. SBU 20, based at Virginia's Little Creek Naval Amphibious Base, is learning to airdrop smaller boats, fully loaded and crewed, from C-130 Hercules aircraft.

The teams are trained to work ashore with their passengers—usually SEALs, Force Recon marines, or army Special Forces soldiers—in case they lose their boats on a delivery mission. "You learn to work on the beach, but you never want to be there," said Chief Boatswain's Mate (SW/CC) Jim Gordon. "It's going to be a bad day if you're swimming."

As special forces, the boat crews are often sent to train members of foreign militaries. Riffey, who joined the boat unit in 1993, has worked with forces from Qatar, Jordan, Egypt, and Kuwait. His teammates have instructed small-boat sailors in Latin America. The training runs from the basic—how do you get passengers aboard in a storm?—to the complicated doctrine of riverine warfare.

These missions can look an awful lot like combat. Several sailors said they had faced hostile fire in the Persian Gulf and off the coast of North Korea—mostly small-arms potshots. The impacts, one crewman said, looked like rocks hitting the water. Riffey shrugged. "That's the thing about working with other countries. Generally, they're always fighting with somebody."

When the boat crews go in harm's way, they ride aboard an assortment of powerful and nimble craft. Most of them are rigid-hull inflatables, souped-up versions of the boats used by the frigate boarding crews. Ringed with neoprene pontoons to make them stable in high seas, the craft are capable of operating at forty knots amid ten-foot swells. The boats generally carry a machine-gun mount or two, but just about everything outguns these lightly armed craft. "Once they start shooting at us, we're pretty much going to run," said Renner.

In 1998, the crews were operating boats in three lengths of fiberglass-composite hulls. But the commercially available twenty-four- and thirty-foot versions were being phased out in favor of a thirty-six-footer with features designed especially for the demands of special warfare. Passengers in the older boats propped themselves against smooth, if padded, backboards. The new boats have hip-level panels —to make it easier to stay put during high-speed maneuvers—and a cab-forward design that puts the eight SEALs behind the three boat drivers. "The platoon always gets in the way," said Chief Gunner's Mate (SW/CC) Tim S. McCurry, whose detachment drives the smaller boats. "We're always telling them to sit down."

The new design keeps the SEALs out of the way. It also keeps them moving. Powered by a pair of turbocharged 473-horsepower water jets, the newest RHIB is rated—conservatively—for forty-seven knots. "I've had it way over that," said Riffey, grinning.

The quartermaster and the rest of SBU 12 work out of the navy's amphibious base in Coronado, California, in view of the San Diego skyline across the harbor. On a cloudy day in April 1998, he and the rest of his three-man crew took their thirty-six-foot RHIB out for a spin.

In green coveralls, water survival gear, and high-tech helmets with earphones and microphones, the three men could have passed for fighter pilots. Riffey swung himself aboard the RHIB, goosed the twin throttles, and accelerated away from the pier. Within seconds, the boat was skimming the harbor at nearly fifty knots. The speed turned the glassy water into something more menacing, like pavement.

Zooming across *Jarrett*'s wake, the little boat nearly took flight, then slammed back into the water. Riffey threw the helm full over, and the craft wheeled through a high-speed half turn in less than two boat lengths. The deck tilted forty-five degrees. The passengers tightened their grips on the railings, longing for seat belts. The driver just hung onto the steering wheel. "You get a lot of blisters," Riffey said later.

The boats are equipped with "buckets," scoops that can redirect the water jets forward. They give the RHIB the best brakes to be found on land or sea. Riffey chopped the throttles, punched a button to redirect the water jets forward, and held on as the boat nosed down to a stop —in two lengths of its hull. Anyone who wasn't alert would have left tooth marks in the dashboard. Back at the Coronado pier, Riffey rotated the boat as if on a spindle and moved straight sideways into a pier-side parking space.

If the eleven-meter RHIB is the MG of naval craft, the Mark V is its Lexus. A sleek seventy-five-ton boat built from the keel up for special warfare, the Mark V is designed to tote larger loads longer distances.

After the RHIB ride—which seemed at times life-threatening—the Mark V seemed more civilized. Although the larger boat is capable of slightly higher speeds and the same tight turns and "crashback" stops, a pilothouse protects the five-man crew and sixteen passengers from the elements. "If you're doing a night operation in an open boat, you're going to get cold, wet, and miserable real fast," said Lt. (jg) Vaughn Williams, who commands one of SBU 12's Mark V detachments.

The harbor ride merely hinted at the brutality of a fifty-mile, high-speed transit in heavy seas. It also explained why boat guys are physical conditioning nuts. "These boats will take their toll on you if you don't have the muscles," Gordon said. "This boat will eat you alive."

Equipped with restraining harnesses, the Mark V's bigger seats provide a bit more security during violent maneuvers than the smaller RHIB. But when the big boat goes airborne, the impact is every bit as jarring to the spine. "You brace for the shock. That's all you can do," said Boatswain's Mate 1st Class (SW/CC) Anthony Smith. "Then you spend a little time at the chiropractor."

Capable as the boats are, it's the boat guys' training, not their equipment, that makes them so effective. Take RHIB Detachment Delta, the eight-man team that was embarked aboard *Duluth* during its 1998 cruise. The unit's two boats were operated by six petty officers, a chief, and a SEAL ensign. Most of them could do every job on the boat. "You have at least five people who can take command in a heartbeat. We're just like the [SEAL] platoons: cross-trained," said Chief Gunner's Mate (SW/CC) Tim S. McCurry.

For enlisted men—like the SEALs, the special-boat ranks are closed to women—the journey into the special-boat units starts with the Special Warfare Combat Crewman course. Created in 1993 and expanded in 1995 to nine weeks, the curriculum offers a grueling mix of physical conditioning, classroom instruction, and hands-on experience with engines, radios, and guns. How tough is it? Even surviving the legendary sixth week of SEAL training won't guarantee you graduate, said Engineman 1st Class (CC) David McClain. "We've had guys get through Hell Week and then not get through swcc," the instructor said. The course turns navy sailors into small-boat specialists— extremely fit small-boat specialists. In the first three weeks, prospective combat crewmen endure grueling physical conditioning designed to prepare them to survive hazardous missions. Like the SEAL trainees across the street, they run miles, swim in boots and uniforms. They learn to row—and hate—the small Combat Rubber Raiding Craft, more commonly called Zodiacs. "I thought I was ready. I was swimming. I was running," said Boatswain's Mate 2d Class Mike Caldwell, who graduated from swcc in April 1998. He should have been lifting weights as well. "Day one was the toughest. You hit the beach and start pushing [push-ups] out."

The school is meant to imbue students with enough knowledge to perform in the boat units, but it also teaches them to exceed their limits. "I honestly never thought I could do so many push-ups and run as fast as I did," said Caldwell.

Classroom work starts the first week. McClain and the other seven instructors introduce their charges to small-boat fuel and water systems. They teach them to keep engineering logs—all part of the cross training that allows the small teams to function in combat. "As soon as someone takes a hit, you have to jump right in," said quartermaster Riffey.

The runs get longer and the swims move out into San Diego Bay. To simulate a water rescue, students swim 250 yards in their boots, uniforms, and gear—while towing training partners. More and more hours are spent in classroom lectures and aboard small craft. The students learn to drive, navigate, repair, and maintain their boats. For most, it's the first taste of working outside their navy specialties.

Two months into the course, the boat training moves to the open ocean, where students battle the sea from 7:00 A.M. until midnight. Back on land, lectures introduce the students to mission planning and the various techniques of coastal and riverine patrol.

The two-week "final exam" takes the students to San Clemente Island, the navy's special warfare preserve off the California coast. The SWCC students learn to fire and maintain a variety of small arms. They work on mission planning by day and conduct operations by night, often until 5:00 A.M. Caldwell's graduation exercise took his team fifty miles to their objective in seas that swelled to ten feet.

About one quarter of those who enter the school don't make it through. Of Caldwell's twenty-four classmates, nineteen graduated. Most washed out during the grueling swim training. "If people knew there were water skills needed, our attrition rate would be 2 or 3 percent," said Chief Boatswain's Mate (SW/CC) Mario Echeverria, the school's course manager.

And although four of the recent graduates came to SWCC after enduring weeks of SEAL training, the school's officials insist the course is no "recycling bin." No one is accepted from the SEALs program unless he survived Hell Week, its toughest part.

By completing the course, graduates earn assignment to one of the four special-boat units. But they don't have the right to stay there unless they keep learning. In nine months, they must earn their combat crewman qualification. The process is similar to sailors on ships, subs, or aircraft earning warfare pins: they must demonstrate advanced knowledge of their craft from stem to stern.

If they qualify as chief engineer or petty officer in charge during their four-year tour, they are eligible for permanent attachment to the special-boat service.

The training regimen has helped the special-boat community take a step away from the SEALS' shadow. "The school brought us a lot of respect," Renner said. So did a 1997 decision by the navy's personnel bureau. Frustrated by the loss of trained combat crewmen to the gray-hull fleet, officials created three hundred billets for combatant crewmen who wish to remain in the units indefinitely.

Officers, however, are still rotated through, and they don't get the special training. "There's talk of a warrant officer program, and that sooner or later they're going to start putting officers through SWCC," said Gordon, the chief boatswain. "I hope so."

Despite the punishing rides and frequent deployments, many boat guys wouldn't trade their jobs for anything. "It's a good opportunity to be something special. This is for people who come and excel," Gordon said. "You get an opportunity to do a job that not everybody can do."

Enlisted men can become petty officers in charge—essentially skippers of their small craft, with weapons-release authority and all. "We're not going to be holding their hands," Yenchko said.

For officers, too, special boats can mean more responsibility. "This is the best job an SWO [surface warfare officer] can have. I was a lieutenant in charge of two craft overseas," said Lt. Ron Walton, a former commander of a Mark V detachment. "When I was an engineer on a ship, all I had was 'I have to make my evaporators run today.'"

As the in-theater commanders of special operations units, the junior officers are bigger players in high-level planning. "You get more into the strategic game than as an SWO lieutenant on a ship," Walton said.

Plus, there's the fun of turning heads when you pull up to a pier. "It's just like a Corvette," Williams said. "Everybody wants a ride."

---

Aboard the USS *Simon Lake* near La Maddalena, Italy, June 1998

Few contingencies could pry the submarine tender *Simon Lake* from its pier at the tiny Mediterranean island of Santo Stefano. For seven years, the 20,515-ton repair ship had helped keep the Sixth Fleet in fighting trim. Generally, subs and ships in need of repairs came to *Simon Lake*—or made do with the lumbering tender's traveling teams of specialists.

But the navy's Persian Gulf buildup in April 1998—the result of the dispute over Iraqi weapons inspections—threatened to overwhelm the area's limited maintenance facilities. The call went out for the tender and its thirteen hundred crew members. "We're expensive, but vital, and there's no cheaper way to do forward-deployed maintenance," said *Lake*'s skipper, Capt. David A. Duffie.

So, like a traveling tinker for the Nuclear Age, *Simon Lake* packed up its formidable repair facilities and headed out to fix the fleet. Within five days of arriving on the scene, the crew had performed some fifteen hundred repairs. During its seven-week sojourn, the massive vessel serviced twenty-six vessels. "They loved *Simon Lake*. We'd build them a locker, or fix a prop that hadn't worked in four months," Duffie said.

For their efforts, *Simon Lake*'s crew received a letter of commendation from Adm. Jay Johnson. "I told my crew, 'This is not just another attaboy. This is from the Big Kahuna in the Sky who controls the destiny of the navy,'" Duffie said.

But the Big Kahuna didn't save *Simon Lake* from sailing into the sunset. The thirty-four-year-old vessel and another tender, *McKee,* were slated for decommissioning in 1999.

Once considered an invaluable supporter of the forward-deployed fleet, *Simon Lake* was part of a tender network that stretched from Guam to Holy Loch, Scotland. For decades navy officials held tightly to their seagoing jacks-of-all-trades. The fleet still had tenders of World War II vintage in 1993.

But the expense is now too much for post–cold war budgets. Navy officials say each tender costs about $65 million per year more than comparable shore facilities. Since the early 1990s, the navy has sent some two dozen destroyer and submarine tenders to the ship graveyards.

When *Lake* and *McKee* are gone, shore-based facilities will shoulder all stateside repair work. The fleet will keep one pair of forward-based repair ships: *Frank Cable* will remain in Guam, while *Emory S. Land* was slated to sail from Norfolk in spring 1999 to become the Med's repair ship.

*Simon Lake* returned from its gulf deployment in early June. The journey took the ship fourteen days at eighteen knots. But there was little chance for *Lake*'s crew to rest after returning home. Soon after the tender docked, the converted ballistic missile submarine *James K. Polk* snuggled up for maintenance and replenishment. A missile sub no more, *Polk* humped a pair of giant cylinders aft of the sail. These "garages" were built to carry SEAL Delivery Vehicles, a sort of underwater scooter that the commandos use to pull themselves toward the beach.

*Simon Lake*'s crew could repair these and thousands of more common items: bookshelves, locks, computers, deep fat fryers, gyros, intercoms, periscopes, optics, prosthetics, refrigerators, fiberglass hulls, air conditioners, clocks, torpedoes, fire control systems, and nuclear propulsion plants. With a crew of four hundred and thirty shops, the repair division had seven main divisions: welding and ship fitting, machine shop, electronics, divers, nuclear propulsion, quality assurance, and administration.

Even on the rare days when there wasn't much in the way of repair work, there were parts and stores to hoist aboard with the ship's six cranes or reel in by helicopter. More than just a repair ship, the tender was a replenishment vessel. *Lake*'s vast holds carried food, fresh water, distilled battery water, fuel oil, lubricants, oxygen, nitrogen, pyrotechnics, antisubmarine weapons—and fifty-two thousand spare parts.

The biggest replacement parts aboard were the Tomahawk missiles, which hung in a huge magazine four decks high. The spaces were painted white, and access was tightly controlled. The space was designed to carry cargo of terribly greater lethality: the nuclear-tipped Tridents of the navy's ballistic missile subs.

The supply department's 240 sailors divided their tasks into seven units: food service, barbershops, disbursing, quality assurance, a really big ship's store, and a post office that handled half a ton of mail a day.

The tender even had a small flotilla of its own. A small tugboat, two utility boats, the captain's gig, and a few others were scattered around the broad topside spaces.

The July schedule was so busy that Duffie began interrupting work for an hour every Thursday morning at eight. This gave his sailors a chance to study for the tests that help determine advancement in pay grade, or to work toward surface warfare pins. So many enlisted sailors earned the pins—175 in the first half of 1998—that their names filled a passageway dubbed "ESWS Alley." "Ninety percent of the crew is really into getting it done," said Hull Technician 3d Class Mike Salyards. "Everybody wants it; the command pushes it."

When *Simon Lake* was at its Italian pier, it was part of Naval Support Activity La Maddalena. After arriving in 1992, the tender welcomed more than its share of distinguished visitors: fleet commanders, CNOs, ambassadors. *Lake*'s popularity was partly due to the fact that the tender was a hardworking ship with a distinguished record of forward-deployed service. But there were at least three other reasons: location, location, location.

Like crumbs broken from Sardinia's northern coast, the islands of La Maddalena, Santo Stefano, and a few smaller isles form a tiny archipelago just offshore. The landscapes are breathtaking, with lush Mediterranean vegetation and rocky coasts leading to cobalt blue water. La Maddalena has a village of close-packed, tan-and-orange villas, apartments, stores, and restaurants. It's a resort town of some fifteen thousand souls. The population triples in summertime. Smitten, many senior sailors volunteer for shore duty here after their sea tours expire. Many more extend their tours for a few years.

The village and the naval facility are quite remote. Cargo and passengers arrive at the airport or ferry landing in Olbia, a Sardinian city some two hours away by car and ferry. Serious medical cases must be medevacced across the Tyrrhenian Sea to Naples. "It's like a farm, a small rural community in the navy," said Master Chief Ship's Serviceman (SW/SCW) Ralph Rao. Consequently, attracting younger sailors to this island archipelago is tough. "They think it's the Third World," Duffie said. "The younger ones we had to sell on Italy. They live on malls and video games."

Some, of course, have little choice. *Simon Lake* got a high proportion of the fleet's incoming general detail sailors, largely because the ship's vastness made it easy to segregate berthing spaces for men and women. That was just fine with Duffie. "Females are better workers because they're more focused. Give me a female every time," he said, noting that women made up only 30 percent of the crew but held most of the surface warfare qualifications onboard.

The sedentary *Simon Lake* didn't offer the typical sailor's lifestyle, but most sailors seemed to enjoy life aboard the tender—even if it took a slightly twisted appreciation for teamwork. "By the end of the day you're worn out, but it's the best day. It's fun because it sucks, everybody knows it sucks, so it's fun," Yeoman Seaman Amanda Land said earnestly.

---

Naval Complex Pearl Harbor, Hawaii, July 1998

On the other side of the world, sixty-seven sailors in five boats support the submarine fleet with a different kind of service. When Hawaii-based subs head to the open ocean for weapons practice, these shiny little craft tag along to retrieve the expensive dummy torpedoes.

Officially, they comprise the Naval Station Pearl Harbor Torpedo Recovery Division, but the unit has as many unofficial names as the giant naval base has uses for it; "water taxi central," for instance, or "the photo boats." Boatswain's Mate 3d Class Walter Bernaquez offered "heaven on earth."

The weather was doing its part to back up the petty officer's contention. A tropical sun and light breeze surrounded Bernaquez on the deck of the recovery boat *Harrier* as it made its way down the harbor channel. A sixty-seven-foot slip of a vessel, *Harrier* is pretty much a hull, a pilothouse, and a canted rear deck lined with rollers for hauling torpedoes aboard.

Bernaquez's shipmates included a craftsmaster, chief engineer, electrician, fireman, and deck seaman; his own title was deck leading petty officer. The cramped space below the deck held the engine room and little else: a few racks, the craftsmaster's stateroom, and a refrigerator jammed with canned soda. "Fifty cents apiece," Bernaquez said. "For our own little MWR fund."

On this July day, Bernaquez and *Harrier* were to rendezvous with the ballistic missile sub *Florida*. The sub had departed the base early in the morning, shoving off from a long concrete pier with its crew and a few passengers. The party included a local politician or two, some teachers, and a quartet of college students—engineering majors whom the navy would love to commission and train as nuclear officers.

*Florida* had used the day as a coastal shakedown before heading for deeper waters, and was returning only briefly to drop off the passengers. By meeting the sub in mid-channel, *Harrier* would save the submariners several hours.

"Heaven on earth," repeated Bernaquez, and then laid out the evidence. Some was obvious. Set among volcanic ridges that glisten green with tropical flora, Pearl Harbor offers an unparalleled ambiance that's part physical, part historical, part professional. The ghosts of the 1941 Japanese surprise attack still walk the base. As the little boat chugged toward the sea, the battleship *Missouri* loomed just up the channel. The giant battlewagon, destined to become a museum, had been towed to an anchorage next to Ford Island earlier in the year. Dwarfed by the ship's vast bulk, the bone-white USS *Arizona* Memorial peeked out from behind its bow.

Some of the selling points were not immediately apparent. "This is an aluminum boat, which means rust-free, which is very important to a boatswain's mate," he said. Bernaquez and his deck seaman were generally responsible for keeping the craft shipshape. The uncorroding aluminum hull made things a lot easier for them. Often dispatched to ferry VIPs around Pearl's waterways, the boats are kept in pristine condition. "We're always bringing on captains, full birds, admirals. We always gotta look our best," Bernaquez said.

He lives off base—escaping the barracks for the privacy of an apartment, something not always possible on a petty officer third class's salary. His squadron works in eight duty sections, which means he has a full week between twenty-four-hour watches. Five-, four-, even three-section watches are common elsewhere.

Although his boat never leaves port for more than a few days at a time, Bernaquez gets credit for a sea tour, which means more money and better options should he ever decide to change duty stations. Plus, the petty officer third class was drawing close to earning the right to pilot the craft—unusual anywhere.

If he qualifies as craftsmaster, he'll be able to find a shore-duty job on base after his sea tour ends. "You never have to leave," Bernaquez said.

In the channel, *Harrier* rocked with sudden violence as a bigger harbor tug passed by. "This is what we call being waked out," said Bernaquez.

If a wake can rock the boat so, what of the giant trade-wind swells between the Hawaiian Islands? Chief Boatswain's Mate (SW) Simon Nash insisted that the boat is perfectly safe. "It equates to a roller coaster," Nash said. "She's built to take it."

It took the boat an hour to reach the rendezvous point, not far from the shore where the battleship *Nevada,* under way but under fierce Japanese attack, had beached itself to prevent blocking the channel. Soon, the massive, locomotive-black boomer appeared around a beachhead and glided into the channel. Its six-hundred-foot hull dwarfed the smaller boat. Quickly, *Harrier's* crew rigged a brow and took the passengers aboard. The brow came down, and the boat peeled away from the giant sub. "Once those screws start turning, we have to be out of here," Bernaquez said. "We get caught in that wake, we're done with."

*Harrier* adroitly evaded the swells and headed back to the pier. Up on the pilothouse, Chief Quartermaster (SW) Robert Golden steered the boat with the touch of long expertise. A radiant look animated his grizzled face. "This is a great life; you gotta love it," the twenty-one year veteran said. "Best duty station there is."

# 10. THE VR NAVY

Most sailors never meet the airborne couriers who help connect North American supply lines with the fleet. If warships are the navy's muscles, the logistics squadrons are its sinews.

But in 1999, the aircraft that carry the fleet's parts and mail were aging. The jetliners averaged a quarter century old, and with each passing year it became more expensive to keep them flying. In the fight for the navy's tight pool of money for new airplanes, the men and women of the Fleet Logistics Support Wing feared that they had two strikes against them: they were reservists, and their planes didn't have tail hooks.

Olbia, Sardinia, Italy, June 1998

Clad in the olive coveralls of a navy flight crewman, Aviation Structural Mechanic (Hydraulics) 2d Class (AW) Kenneth Jay strode through the air terminal. All glass and steel and terrazzo flooring, the modern-looking facility could have served just about anywhere. It was, in fact, several hilly miles from downtown Olbia, an ancient city on the northeast coast of Sardinia. Between the city and the airport, gas stations and strip malls mixed with farmland.

The lanky airman rounded up a dozen passengers, mostly *Simon Lake* sailors seeking a plane ride to the mainland, or at least to a busier airport. A few were traveling on official orders. The rest were taking advantage of "space-available travel," the military version of hitchhiking. The idea is simple. A plane comes in. If there's space, you travel. If not, you wait for the next one.

Outside the terminal, the morning sun was warming the air into a full-fledged summer day. Most of the other members of Jay's aircrew —part of the VR-57 Conquistadors logistics squadron—were wearing sunglasses as they ran preflight checks on their C-9B Skytrain. The crew chief attached a thick hose to one wing. Kerosene flowed from a fuel truck, replacing the hundreds of gallons burned in the morning's flight from Sicily.

The twin-jet Skytrain is a close cousin to the DC-9, the jetliner that was once the backbone of many civilian airlines. In the military version, passengers travel in utilitarian comfort. The cabin is slightly less plush than the average coach class, but its ninety seats offer substantially more room from knee to seatback. Only the rear of the fuselage is given over to humans. In the forward half, the beige paneling is stripped away, the carpeting replaced by reinforced flooring topped with roller bearings. A massive door in the side of the fuselage facilitates the loading of cargo. Webbing as thick as fire hoses protects the cockpit should the cargo shake itself loose.

The C-9 is the navy's fastest logistics aircraft, capable of lifting five tons nearly three thousand miles in six hours. But more cargo means less range, so its commanders frequently close the manifest to space-available passengers long before the seats fill up. The aircrew often has empty rows of seats to stretch out on, and a long trip and a heavy load might mean no extra riders at all.

The itinerary of 18 June was relatively short and uncomplicated: a triangular journey between various Mediterranean islands. Jay and the rest of the crew began the day at Sicily's busy Sigonella Naval Air Station, where they rolled pallets of engine parts and lubricants through the plane's yawning cargo door. After the Olbia stopover, they would head east to Souda Bay, Crete, drop off their cargo, and then fly back to Sigonella. The whole circuit would take about seven hours.

Aloft and bound for Crete, Cdr. Mark Vaughan spread out air route charts, puzzling over an Italian air controller's order to divert from his planned flight path. The maps, opened like newspapers across the cramped cockpit, revealed the Med's invisible web of airborne high-ways, intersections, and road signs.

"Always wondered what the pilots were doing up here, right?" the aviator said, looking up from his chart. The Athens and Rome author-ities, it appeared, had different ideas about where they wanted the navy jet. "One of the joys of working in Europe," the pilot said good-naturedly. "They just kind of say, 'Do this,' and you have to figure out what it means." Vaughan punched a five-letter code into the aircraft autopilot, aiming the plane toward an invisible point in the sky. The airliner banked right and headed toward the Peloponnesian peninsula.

For Vaughan, Jay, and the rest of the crew, it was just another day at the office. "We're here to move the fleet sailor, and that's what we do, plus his stuff, plus his ship's stuff, plus the mail," the airman said.

In a nutshell, that is the mission of the Fleet Logistics Support Wing. Its fourteen squadrons handle most of the fleet's medium-range trans-port needs. Generally speaking, they fill the gap between a theater's major supply centers and its smaller airfields. People and cargo arrive at the former aboard navy cargo ships or air force planes; helicopters and carrier-bound C-2 Greyhound turboprops hop to nearby warships from the latter.

In 1998, the VR Navy—named for the transport squadron designa-tor—operated some fifty aircraft. Seven squadrons flew Skytrains, two operated the C-130T Hercules, a massive cargo turboprop; and two flew the C-20 Gulfstream, a small, corporate-type jet.

The forty-five hundred aviators and airmen of the VR wing rack up about sixty-two thousand flight hours annually, and the wing flies everyone from Chief of Naval Operations Adm. Jay Johnson to the navy's mine-hunting dolphins. When there is an aircraft carrier near-by, supplying its battle group becomes Job One. Skytrains are occa-sionally dispatched to the States from Europe or Asia for a critical spare. And when a flattop comes home to Norfolk or San Diego or Jack-sonville or Seattle, a swarm of C-9s descends on the local airport. Because a carrier's squadrons are not necessarily homeported near their ship, hundreds of maintainers catch rides home on VR planes.

The logistics squadrons are different in one respect from most of the units they serve: they are part of the U.S. Naval Air Reserve. About three hundred of the pilots and crew in the San Diego–based Con-quistadors are reservists with full-time civilian jobs. Some of these "selected reservists" show up for the minimum service commitment: one weekend a month, plus an annual two-week stint. Others, lured by money or patriotism or the thrill of travel, volunteer much more often.

The balance of the squadron's members—about one hundred offi-cers and enlisted people—are active-duty sailors permanently as-signed to the reserve unit. Navy personnel argot labels them "TARs," for "training and administration of the reserves." Vaughan, VR-57's skip-per, put it this way: "We've got active-duty folks who keep us running paperwork-wise, and reserve airline pilots who come in and fly four or five days a month."

A TAR himself, Vaughan earned his helicopter wings after gradu-ating from the Naval Academy in 1980. He flew six-month deploy-ments until 1986 and was planning to get out of the navy—too much time away from his family—when he found out about the TARs. Now he flies a handful of deployments each year—none longer than four weeks—and goes home to his family during the months in between. For a military aviator, it's a schedule that's hard to beat.

That's not to say that an airline pilot's paycheck isn't alluring. For many, it proves irresistible. "There's not a pilot in the TARs who doesn't think about getting out," said Lt. John Decker, an aviator with the Jacksonville-based VR-58 Sunseekers. He was nearing the end of his first tour as a TAR and was mulling a career decision. "If I take [another set of] orders, I'm going to commit to twenty years in," he said, piloting his Skytrain across Caribbean skies toward Panama. "If I don't, I'd bet-ter cut the umbilical cord and start building up seniority" at an airline, he said.

Still, "getting out" doesn't mean "lost to the navy forever." If he quit, Decker said, he'd apply to become one of VR-58's selected reservists.

That's what Cdr. Dave Delancey did. He resigned from the active navy to fly for TWA, but found himself returning to beg for VR flights at Willow Grove Naval Air Station–Joint Reserve Base near Philadelphia. By 1998, Delancey was commanding two-week missions for the VR-52 Taskmasters. "I like this better," said Delancey. "They give you the mission and say, 'Do it and don't screw it up.' At TWA, they give you your route and you're just . . . an employee."

Philadelphia to Honolulu, July 1998

You know you're not just an employee when your promotion ceremony involves two sets of coveralls, a swat from a sword, and a contender for the World's Largest American Flag.

One of VR-52's crews was gearing up for detachment to the western Pacific. For two weeks, a dozen pilots, maintainers, and cabin crew would shepherd the Seventh Fleet's people and cargo between Asian ports of call. Outside on the tarmac, a handful of enlisted reservists were struggling to fix the C-9's nose landing gear. Another handful of active-duty "mechs" hovered nearby, itching to do it themselves but holding back to allow the weekenders to practice their trade.

In the hangar, the detachment's officer in charge hurried to attend to one last detail: pinning on the silver oak leaves of a full commander. It was not quite the textbook ceremony—Cdr. Bob Muro was clad in his flight suit rather than a dress uniform—but the reservist was determined to take off for the western Pacific as a full commander.

So the squadron's officers mustered on a Saturday afternoon to see one of their own trade in his gold oak leaves—the insignia of a lieutenant commander—for silver ones. They came to attention in khaki and white and green before an enormous American flag hung across the hangar. Muro raised his right hand, and VR-52's commanding officer, Cdr. Bill Morrill, readministered the commissioning vows of a naval officer. Things got very unorthodox shortly thereafter.

Muro knelt and received a touch of his commanding officer's sword to his left shoulder. Gravely, Morrill declared him initiated into the "knighthood of full commander."

Muro stood, unzipped his flight suit, and stepped out of it. Underneath, he wore another set of coveralls, identical save for the silvery color of the oak leaf patches sewn onto the shoulders. "My God, I never had such a pinning ceremony in my life," he muttered.

"It'll be worth it when you see your paycheck," Morrill informed him heartily.

The officers weren't the only ones who seemed to be having a lot of fun. Muro's Skytrain got under way shortly after the ceremony and stopped for fuel at the tiny airstrip in Salina, Kansas. Aviation Storekeeper 2d Class Sarah Leslie climbed down a stairway below the plane's tail. An executive assistant with a consulting firm, Leslie was taking a vacation from her civilian job to fly with the Taskmasters. In the terminal's bright front room, the airport's genial owners offered her free popcorn and apples. Demurring, the flight attendant strolled back to the airplane. "We do it because we love it," said Leslie, a reservist with VR-52 for eleven years. "Even if it's just a different runway, you can say, 'I've been there.'"

Under the aircraft's wing, Aviation Survival Equipmentman 1st Class Michael Lee Foster plugged in a fuel hose and eyed a flow gauge. A semiretired businessman from New York, Foster believes he holds the record for most C-9 flight hours in a single year: 1,009 in 1997. "We're the best-kept secret in the navy," the crew chief said. "It's great because we have these great jobs to ourselves."

Their Skytrain stopped to top off its tanks at Travis Air Force Base in California, then leapt across two thousand miles of pearly pink clouds to Hawaii. Leslie, Foster, and the rest of the crew retired for the night in a Honolulu hotel. In the morning, they mustered at the airfield—and found that a leaky fuel bladder had brought their mission to a screaming halt.

Ducking under the plane's belly during the preflight, Foster twisted a test valve and recoiled in disbelief. Instead of a trickle of pink-tinted liquid, the crew chief drew a rush of fluid that quickly filled a quart jar. The gusher indicated a leak in one of the plane's five rubber fuel bladders.

"It's hard down," said Senior Chief Aviation Structural Mechanic (AW) Julio Franjul, the squadron maintenance chief. "We'll have to drain the whole aircraft."

Foster and Franjul talked it over with Muro, the officer in charge of the detachment. They made some phone calls. The nearest replacement bladder was in Texas.

"The only way we'll make this mission is to get Fifty-four to fly out here," Franjul said, referring to VR-52's other ready aircraft—which, of course, was back in Pennsylvania. But it would be faster to wait for the replacement plane to arrive from Willow Grove than to get the bladder from Texas and fix their own bird. Repairs would be left to the ferry crew, who would wait for the bladder and fly the ailing aircraft home.

The crew lost two days out of a two-week mission. The Seventh Fleet would have to do without a logistics bird for a few days. Worst of all, this was the second time in as many weeks that the plane had sprung a fuel leak. "This is a perfect example of why fleet air logistics needs the [Boeing] 737," said Foster, pulling his bags from the plane and walking away.

The Navy's Skytrains average twenty-five years old, and the eldest is thirty-one. Although they've always been meticulously maintained, more time and money is spent on Skytrain maintenance every year. In fiscal 1997, the Naval Air Reserve spent nearly one-third of its contract maintenance budget on overhauling and reworking its twenty-seven C-9s, say officials for the Naval Reserve Association, an advocate group for the reserves.

It's affecting both the reservists and their customers—the fleet. "The squadron's working harder than eight years ago because of maintenance," said Muro, VR-52's maintenance officer. "The active-duty squadrons are putting in lift requests and being denied or waiting longer."

The aging aircraft will soon be unable to meet the needs of modern aviation without major changes requiring a vast investment. The Skytrains don't have the quiet engines that are required to land at many urban airports. Although their cockpits have GPS autopilots, they don't have the extra gear necessary to fly some types of approaches prescribed by upcoming civil air regulations. Even the current missions tax the limits of the aircraft. It's not unusual for Hawaii-bound C-9s to turn back to the mainland after battling winter headwinds for an hour.

The bottom line in summer 1998: Everybody was waiting for a new cargo-and-passenger aircraft to replace the three-decade-old Skytrains. The Fleet Logistics Support Wing officials were waiting to see whether they would get the money to buy them. "The C-9 has done it admirably for the past thirty years," said wing commander Capt. Chip White. "It's just getting old."

The navy has already purchased three Boeing 737-700s, which were slated to arrive in December 2000. Still in production, the newer plane, unlike the DC-9, will be more easily serviced in far-flung airfields, and its parts easier to come by.

But three aircraft are just a fraction of the number it will take to replace the C-9 fleet. White was realistic about his prospects for a huge new group of planes. There is a pecking order to naval aviation: carrier planes first, land-based second. "You're not going to cancel an F-18 to buy a 737. It ain't going to happen," the wing commander said.

There is also the fear that reserve aviation might be given short shrift, and that would constitute a disservice to the entire fleet, said Morrill. "It's our active-duty brothers and sisters that don't always understand how much a part we are of what they do. They want gas for the Hornets, ice cream for the ships, it comes through us."

Morrill said wing leaders had been arguing their case throughout 1998 with presentations to the four-star regional commanders in chief. "We are very much in the process of selling ourselves to the c-in-cs. We need to be included in their budget," Morrill said. "We had a full-court press going on for six months."

The wing commander summed it up. "We're looking to buy the planes, but moreover, [the active-duty navy] should be looking to help us buy them," White said. "What do we do with them? Haul navy stuff."

It made sense to the crew of VR-52, even if they did manage to find a silver lining in the delay.

"If we were spending money on new planes instead of pouring it into old ones," Leslie began. A crewmate interrupted her, gestured at the green ridge of Oahu's tropical mountain ranges. "We wouldn't be staying here," said Aviation Electrician's Mate 2d Class Scott Silva.

---

Tacalhuano, Chile, September 1998

On a naval base's stone-paved pier, Storekeeper 1st Class Tim Abbuhl picked through a haystack of brown packages and orange sacks. The jumbled pile represented more than ten tons of supplies and mail flown in from Norfolk, Virginia, the previous night. Covered with fluorescent stickers, the parcels held parts and equipment for the flotilla of American ships making its slow way around the South American continent.

Abbuhl marshaled the items belonging to his ship, the frigate *Doyle,* and marveled at the cornucopia of express-delivered goods.

"This is my first Unitas cruise, and I've been amazed," said Abbuhl, a veteran of four previous deployments. "It really would be nice if you could get this kind of support in the Persian Gulf or the Med or on counterdrug ops in the Caribbean."

For rushing important repair parts to a flotilla of exercising warships, no one does the job better than the navy's VR squadrons. Commercial freight services such as Federal Express can get parcels quickly to the airports, but clearing customs can take three weeks. Military flights have no such problem. "The way Unitas has evolved over the years, we wouldn't be able to do this without them," said Cdr. Fritz Joh, the exercise's logistics coordinator.

But the supply effort is expensive, and that's one reason why the exercise was about to evolve again. When Unitas started, thirty-nine years ago, it consisted of blue-water antisubmarine exercises. But as the games grew more complex, so did the logistics. When littoral operations were added in the early 1990s, the SEAL teams, explosive ordnance disposal squads, and other new players sent supply requirements skyward.

In 1997, the navy airlifted 175 tons of cargo and 836 people to support Unitas, Joh said. Supply ships delivered 325 tons of cargo plus thirty thousand gallons of fuel for ships and helicopters. Much of it was dispatched months before the Unitas ships headed south across the Equator. Containers of lubricants and nonperishable food were shipped to wharves around South America to await the northerners' arrival.

Joh's team stepped into overdrive when the four ships left their home ports. The speedy movement of planners, mail, and emergency parts began to fill their days and nights—everything from thousands of care packages to a replacement periscope for the attack sub *Boston.*

Chief Storekeeper (SW) Kenneth Williams said that replacing broken parts takes just one satellite phone call or e-mail message, and new ones are often on their way before the official supply request goes out. "Anything we ask for, it's pretty much here," said *Doyle's* supply chief, a broad smile spreading across his face. "I'm overwhelmed by the support."

It's only what's necessary, said Joh, who called the lack of bases and supply depots on the South American continent "a logistics nightmare." "You don't do anything there without taking it there yourself," he said. Joh's system can get a part from Virginia to Chile in three days.

But supplying four ships for five months in an area nearly triple the size of the Mediterranean Sea costs more than the navy wants to spend. Supporting ten separate exercises costs about $500,000 for the VR logistics flights alone. And that's too much, said Rear Adm. David R. Ellison, the commander of the navy's southern Atlantic forces. Logistics costs were a big reason that Ellison was pushing to consolidate some of the events into a larger session off Puerto Rico. "We're trying to make it a more efficient exercise," the admiral said.

Even the VR Navy has its limitations.

# 11. THE MINESWEEPERS

---

Aboard the USS *Dextrous* in Manama, Bahrain, August 1998

When Adm. David Farragut cried, "Damn the torpedoes" at the Battle of Mobile Bay in 1864, he was actually talking about the underwater weapons known today as naval mines. Bellowing for full speed, Farragut rallied a flotilla that had just watched a single explosive sink the Union monitor *Tecumseh*. "Eighty of the crew of one hundred perished in a catastrophe that suggested for the first time the real vulnerability of ironclads to weapons lurking below the waterline," writes historian Kenneth J. Hagan in his 1991 book *This People's Navy*.

The mine retains the power to rattle even the stoutest nautical hearts. In the Great War, the spiky black globes hid below the surface, waiting for the brush of an unlucky hull. World War II introduced several variants: contact mines with thousand-yard tripwires, acoustic versions that listened for a ship's screws, magnetic mines that sensed the passing of steel hulls, the seismic kind that exploded at the feathery pressure of a bow wave. Modern technology has created mines that track their prey miles away and strike with torpedoes.

These underwater weapons provide a measure of sea control on the cheap. Dollar for dollar, nothing beats their power to cripple seagoing operations. Clearing underwater minefields is a hazardous, exhausting business, and the smart, stealthy new weapons make it tougher. They're bad news for today's navy, whose new coastal missions bring ships, subs, and sailors squarely into harm's way. By the late 1990s, defense analysts were sounding alarms, and bargain-minded militaries were taking note.

Yet for years, navy leaders have kicked minesweeping to the rear of the budget line. Witness the four-crew system of the mine counter-measures ship *Dextrous*. In a unique arrangement, the ship stays in the Persian Gulf while a new crew flies in from Texas every six months. It's the only way the mine warfare commanders could clear the dangerous waters on a penny-pinching budget.

The crew of a mine-hunting ship may spend hours circling a sus-pected mine, sniffing with sonar from one direction, then another. Divers or remote-controlled drones may be dispatched for a closer look, then recalled to let the ship's sensors have another shot. The ship inches across the ocean's surface, skirting an invisible "danger circle" around the contact below. Computers and inertial navigation systems help keep the vessel on target, but it takes sweat and practice.

All in all, it's a slow, deliberate process. "You have to understand what mine hunting is: the minute examination of the bottom of the ocean," said Capt. Gary Belcher, the navy's deputy commander of mine warfare.

But for the eighty-four members of Crew Golf, the first few days aboard *Dextrous* were nothing short of hectic. Within hours of touch-ing down at Manama International Airport on 1 July 1998, the crew scrambled to check out their new ship. At a glance, it resembled the ones they had trained on at mine warfare headquarters in Ingleside, Texas.

Launched in 1992, *Dextrous* is the penultimate of the fourteen *Avenger*-class mine countermeasures ships. The vessel was designed from the keel for the job. Its 224-foot hull is constructed of oaken beams lapped with Douglas fir planks and sheathed with fiberglass against the elements. The wooden construction eludes mines that hunt for iron. Four diesel engines power the ship—until it enters a mine zone. Then the crew starts the twin electric motors; less noise, less vibration, less danger.

The ship is stuffed to the rails with all manner of gear for finding and disabling its explosive quarry. In the parlance of the trade, "mine hunting" is the painstaking identification and disposal of suspected mines, one at a time. "Mine sweeping," on the other hand, is the attempt to clear vast swaths of ocean at a single pass. *Dextrous* carries equipment for both.

A giant winch rising on the forecastle—nearly obstructing the view from the bridge—controls a towed sonar array. Like underwater radar, sonar alerts the crew to suspicious contacts floating in the water or resting on the bottom.

Along one side, the ship carries a twelve-foot, torpedo-shaped drone called a mine neutralization vehicle. A pair of pilots in the ship's control center "fly" the craft underwater, guided by its sonar and television cameras. The orange beast clips the tethers of floating mines, bringing them to surface for easy disposal. Bottom-dwelling mines can be dispatched with small explosive charges.

*Dextrous* carries its minesweeping gear on the fantail. Giant speakers—essentially big bass drums—are designed to trip acoustic fuzes at a safe distance. The ship also carries two long cables and hundreds of pieces of associated equipment. When the crew goes sweeping, they pay out four thousand feet of steel wires in a giant submerged V. Along the way, they attach buoys, sinkers, steering vanes, and cable-cutters to help *Dextrous* troll the ocean for mines.

Crew Golf arrived aboard *Dextrous* on 1 July and, swiftly and methodically, the new crew turned the ship inside out. The engineers scrutinized the diesels. The navigators checked off computers and charts. The deck department cleared a space on the sun-scorched concrete pier and lifted the sweep gear over the side. Piece by piece, they checked it against an inventory list and restowed it aboard.

Crew Golf's haste wasn't entirely eagerness to start their six-month deployment. It was also a race to pick the brains of the outgoing crew, and, as if renting a car, to note any dings before taking the keys. Soon, there wouldn't be a single member of the old crew left on the ship. "There is a period of five days of turnover, the other crew leaves and—boom—you've got it," said Lt. Dan Colman, Golf's executive officer.

The mine-hunting force first dabbled with rotating crews around 1987, when it became painfully obvious that Persian Gulf operations required more support. That year, an Iranian contact mine damaged the oil tanker *Bridgeton*. The 400,000-ton ship contained the flooding to a few compartments and sailed on. But the American warships assigned to guard the tanker huddled in its wake, defanged and defenseless against the underwater threat. Less than a year later, another Iranian mine put an exclamation point on the lesson. A Soviet-made weapon built to a ninety-year-old design nearly sank the guided missile frigate *Samuel B. Roberts* as it sailed from Qatar to Kuwait. Detonating under the frigate's keel, the 250-pound charge set blazes throughout the ship and jolted both gas turbine engines from their mounts. The two-year-old frigate was later hauled back to the United States aboard a heavy-lift cargo ship. Repairs totaled $37 million. The value of the mine was reckoned at $1,500.

By rotating crews among a pair of ships, mine warfare officials hoped to increase the total amount of time their ships spent on station. The idea wasn't new; the navy's ballistic missile submarines have for decades rotated between Blue and Gold crews to keep them at sea. The way the mine czars saw it, rotation could eliminate the gaps that developed during the three-week transits between American home ports and the Persian Gulf.

In practice, the concept proved promising but difficult. Rotation could keep mine hunters on station year-round, but the scheme could not be sustained without substantial changes in the way the crews prepared back home. As the tanker escort missions ended, the mine hunters reverted to one-ship, one-crew operations.

But Operation Desert Storm renewed the demand for antimine forces, and the mine warfare command set up rotating crews for the duration of the Gulf War. Despite their efforts, Iraqi mines caused virtually all the combat damage sustained by American surface ships. In February 1991, a weapon fuzed to explode at low tide punched a twenty-foot hole in the hull of the helicopter landing ship *Tripoli*. The amphib, which was leading the American minesweeping effort, sat dead in the water for seven hours. The same day, the billion-dollar cruiser *Princeton* fell victim to a magnetic mine. The three-hundred-pound warhead took out half of the cruiser's engines. *Princeton* was towed to port and repaired at a cost of millions. The mine's purchase price was about $35,000.

In 1996, shrinking budgets prompted a third try at rotating crews. Drawing on past lessons, the mine warfare command invested heavily in training for the nondeployed crews. Four *Avenger*-class ships were permanently assigned as full-time training support in Ingleside, and a cyclical curriculum was drawn up for the eight crews who would operate *Dextrous* and its sister ship *Ardent* in the Persian Gulf.

For Crew Golf—named for the radio call sign, not the little white tees on their ball caps—the cruise that began on 1 July would wrap up on 16 December. After a harried turnover with the next crew, they would hop the next flight home from Manama airport.

Then, after a few weeks' postdeployment leave—a treasured tradition throughout the navy—the crew would start to prepare for their next deployment. Some would get basic "trailer training" in Ingleside's portable classrooms; others would scatter across the country for advanced schools in their specialties. In April 1999, the crew would embark aboard the Ingleside-based *Warrior* for a year of workups. And in April 2000, Crew Golf would once again board an airliner and fly halfway around the world to *Dextrous*.

"When you look at the complexity of the turnover process, I think it works pretty well," Belcher said. "What we send over there is a crew that is a ready round." They have to be. While the crew of the average navy ship spends its transit polishing their skills, the mine hunters have to be ready for their lethal job when they arrive at the pier.

The turnover schedule left Crew Golf with little time to recover from eight hours' jet lag, or to adjust to the breezeless, humid gulf weather. The sailors learned quickly to baby the diesel engines and to take it easy in the 115-degree heat. Meanwhile, they struggled to locate everything from training manuals to toolboxes. Most of it was aboard, but it wasn't where Crew Golf wanted it, not where they had learned to use it aboard *Warrior.* "The first couple of weeks are a disaster for us, getting it set up the way we want," said Operations Specialist 1st Class (SW) Steve Greenlaw.

Occasionally, a crew will arrive to discover that their duty ship's electronic equipment—sonar systems, training computers—is different from the stuff they trained on back at Ingleside. It's simply the law of operational primacy: when the mine command acquires new gear, the deployed ships get it first. Besides, it's generally easier to jump from older to newer systems. "We work hard at configuration control over six ships, but it's not a perfect world," Belcher said.

Above all, the new crew scopes out the warship to see what works and what doesn't. Full disclosure occasionally suffers when the outgoing crew's desire to go home overcomes the incoming crew's need to know. "It's human nature. If I know I've got a piece of gear that's down and I'm getting ready to leave, am I going to jump up and talk about it?" said Master Chief Gunner's Mate (SW) Robert Eisenberg, Mine Countermeasures Squadron Three's command master chief.

The community has "sort of overcome" the problem, Eisenberg said, through training and a rotation schedule in which each crew relieves the same predecessor. With four crews sharing a ship, the relationships are looser than the missile subs' Blue-and-Gold system. But minesweeper crewmen say their system works. "You can screw someone once, but not twice," said Eisenberg, adding, "You build up a level of trust."

Perhaps 95 percent of the turnovers run quite smoothly, thanks to the long memories of the chiefs and senior petty officers. "Your professional reputation follows you back to Texas. The mine warfare community isn't a big community," Belcher said.

But moving in requires more than storekeeping, more than technical evaluation. There is no checklist for building the intangible bond that connects sailor and ship. It's part pride and part morale, and its lack all but ensures a dreary deployment. "If I were a junior engineman, I would have spent a whole year loving one engine. It's just like a sports car," said Capt. Mike Simpson, the commanding officer of Mine Countermeasures Squadron Three. "Now I've got to fly to another ship. And, incidentally, develop that affection. And give up my ship to someone else."

Crew Golf's skipper tries to ease the transition by emphasizing a clean break between the training vessel and the deployed one. "After one year you have accomplished your mission," said Cdr. John Bowie. "You have trained up for the deployment." Better than switching ships, Belcher said, would be switching from the deployed ship to a simulator ashore, as ballistic missile sub crews do. "If you're going to be in the rotational crew business, you want shore-based trainers," he said. "If you look at the submarine method of doing rotational crews, they don't have the ownership problem." But ships need to be designed with trainers in mind. Belcher realizes, however, that building a useful simulator for the *Avenger* class is "not technically feasible."

The mine-hunting community may eventually discard their crew rotation system. Although it provides maximum coverage with U.S.-based vessels, it would be cheaper simply to base the ships in the gulf. "That's the way these ships were built to be manned," Belcher said. That would uproot crews and possibly their families, Belcher said, but it would likely also improve morale, the quality of life for the crew, and the sense of ownership. It might even save time; there's a certain amount of redundancy when a crew boards a new ship. "You go over the same ground less often" when crews don't rotate, Belcher said.

The idea, which is still under consideration by top navy brass, would mean giving up easy access to U.S.-based training schools. It would also incur the expense of building several new training and repair facilities. And Belcher cautioned that the hefty political considerations to homeporting U.S. ships in the gulf may keep the idea from becoming reality.

A former Fifth Fleet commander is more optimistic. "After the Persian Gulf War, we looked at Oman, the United Arab Emirates, and Kuwait, but nobody wanted to have a permanent U.S. presence on their soil," said retired Vice Adm. Doug Katz, who commanded the U.S. Central Command's naval forces after the war. "We're really pushing now, and I think that Bahrain will be the place."

Even if the mine warfare community abandons crew rotation for a third time, the lessons learned will likely influence the way the navy does business in the twenty-first century. With shipbuilding money growing scarcer, the navy is looking for ways to squeeze more forward presence from a smaller fleet. Officials have said that the DD-21 destroyer class, slated for launch in 2008, will be built for rotating crews.

But Katz, for one, doesn't see it as a cure-all. "Rotating crews make a lot of sense on small ships. It's awfully hard on larger ones," he said. But it could give new meaning to the mine warfare command's slogan: "Where the fleet goes, we've already gone."

Just how difficult is it to get rid of mines? The effort to clear the Persian Gulf's international waters began in 1990. It ended in May 1998. Even then, navy officials said there was still plenty of work to do.

Mine hunting—the art of finding objects obscured by the sea's watery veil—requires information, and the more the better. With their most urgent task complete, *Ardent, Dextrous,* and the rest of the navy's mine countermeasures forces turned to preparing for the next time mines threaten safe passage. To this end, they are meticulously building a database about the world's seas—seabed elevation, currents, geology, and more. Officials say the database will speed up the clearing of sea lanes closed by mines, and indicate whether ships, helicopters, or divers would be most effective in pursuing a suspected mine. "Each has its own strengths and weaknesses. The better you know your battle space, the better you're able to direct your efforts," Belcher said.

And even when they're not collecting information, the navy vessels send an important signal, officials say. "Two mine countermeasures ships make the U.S. point that we will not tolerate the Strait of Hormuz to be closed," Simpson said. "The U.S. Navy presence is our commitment to the world that we will keep oil flowing through the strait."

But critics of the navy's mine countermeasures policy—including Secretary of Defense William Cohen—say the navy is woefully unprepared for a growing threat. Mines are cheap to build, effective, and tremendously expensive to defend against. Like poison gas or airplane bombs or computer hackers, they are the weapons of a smaller country against a larger one. "A widespread or sophisticated mine threat can readily thwart, halt or forestall many naval operations," concluded a 1997 study by the National Academy of Sciences in Washington, D.C.

Furthermore, "Technology will continue to favor those who deploy mines over those who attempt to detect and destroy them."

Cohen has repeatedly pressed for more countermine capability. Navy officials have responded with plans to pack it into cruisers, destroyers, and other ships. There are plenty of gee-whiz systems in laboratories and on drawing boards. Soon, planners say, helicopter pilots will use blue-green lasers to find tethered mines, then dispatch them with twenty-millimeter exploding shells. Mine neutralization vehicles will get smarter and more capable, and they can deploy from subs and surface ships.

But if past is prologue, the navy could be in for trouble. In early 1998, the minesweeping force received unpleasant news. Facing a $10.5 million budget shortfall, the commander of Atlantic surface forces severely cut back repairs aboard a dozen of the navy's twenty-five countermine ships.

On 31 January, Vice Adm. Henry Giffin III prohibited the ships' commanders from fixing sonars, using satellite communications, authorizing travel for training, purchasing computers, and repairing some other shipboard items. Navy officials told a *Defense News* reporter that the surface warfare budget—which provided Giffin the only money he had to repair and operate the ships—contained only 57 percent of the amount required.

At the time, Crew Golf was preparing for six months of life-threatening work in the Persian Gulf's unearthly heat. For all of their nerveless skill, they were powerless against bombshells from Washington.

# 12. THE BASES

The end of the cold war drastically shrank the number of U.S. Navy bases overseas. The fabled naval facility at Subic Bay has been turned over to the Philippine government. Rodman Naval Station outside Panama City, a prime staging area for counterdrug operations, has preceded the canal into the hands of the Panamanians. The submarine maintainers at Holy Loch, Scotland, have been called home from their North Sea haven.

Nevertheless, the navy maintains foreign installations of all shapes and sizes, and sailors who stick around for a few enlistments will likely do a tour or two on foreign soil. The Japan-based Seventh Fleet alone is home to one in twenty U.S. Navy sailors. Most of its ships operate from the giant Fleet Activities Yokosuka naval base—home to thirteen thousand sailors, civilians, and dependents.

The majority of the navy's foreign posts are not so large. It would be hard to get much smaller than the desert outpost known as Fleet Logistic Site Hurghada, Egypt, where one officer and one sailor coordinate the supply of U.S. warships sailing through the Red Sea.

Each of these far-flung islands of naval presence brews its own mix of cultures and tradition. The ethoses that evolve are predominantly American, to be sure. Hamburger joints and brand-name fast-food restaurants far outnumber restaurants serving local fare on U.S. bases. And quite a few sailors and their families never venture outside the military ghetto. But the surrounding cultures inevitably work their way past the gates, insinuating themselves into the lives of those who dwell within. Sometimes they get no deeper than a toehold among the household furnishings—a Japanese print, perhaps, or a piece of Sicilian pottery. But sometimes the American sojourners learn new mores and behaviors—and must unlearn them on leaving.

Culture shock works both ways. Sailors who serve in Iceland or Japan learn to relax in these virtually crime-free societies, but on returning home they face the sad task of teaching their children to be more wary. Their own country is more dangerous than the foreign place they are leaving.

And sometimes the strange cultures leave deep marks on the souls of those exposed to them. Those who voyage to faraway lands often find love—a new spouse, an affinity for a foreign country, a renewed passion for their native land.

One thing doesn't change, though: the navy is the navy no matter where you put it. Or is it?

Naval Air Station Keflavik, June 1998

It's obvious, looking out the airplane window on the weekly rotator from Norfolk, that Iceland is no typical duty station. Maybe it's the twin steam plumes that rise like exclamation points from a peninsula of cooled lava. Maybe it's the lunar desolation of the treeless Keflavik peninsula. Or maybe it's the appearance of the base commander and a few dozen shipmates to welcome you early on a Saturday to the navy's northernmost air base. "It's the social event of the week," said Capt. Al Efraimson, the commander of Keflavik Naval Air Station.

The base is home to some 1,850 American servicemen and women —navy, marine, and air force—and their families. The homey, small-town greeting is part of the commanding officer's survival strategy for newcomers. It's designed to boost morale and motivation early on, and prepare them for the wintry days ahead. "We let 'em know they're in a tough place, a physically challenging place, get them feeling special about themselves," said the avuncular Efraimson, a P-3 pilot making his third Keflavik tour.

Winters in Iceland, which sits just below the Arctic Circle, are not so much oppressively cold and snowy as they are windy and dark. The average winter temperature is about thirty-two degrees, but the wind chill factor can make it feel like forty below. In midwinter, the feeble sun struggles into the late-morning sky, then drops like a stone by 4:00 P.M. Seventy-knot Arctic winds scream across the peninsula's lava fields, unimpeded by flora taller than moss. Off-duty marines from the base's security unit ride the school buses to make sure youngsters don't sail away between shelter and vehicle. "We have dumpsters around here that weigh a thousand pounds, full, and they blow around parking lots like empty sardine cans," said 1st Sgt. Keith English.

Then there are the earthquakes—more than two hundred a day— which spring from the same tectonic forces that power the island's volcanoes, geysers, and hot springs. Few of the quakes rattle hard enough to notice, but one June temblor registered 5.3 on the Richter scale.

That quake left the plaques hanging askew in Chief Warrant Officer-4 Thomas E. Jones's office. Jones runs the base's media center, which provides forty cable television channels and ten radio stations to the American community. The channels include CNN, the Cartoon Network, American movies subtitled in Norwegian, and plenty more. The base's journalists produce a daily half hour of news coverage.

Jones's staff has an appreciative audience. "Television here is a lot more important than it is in Bermuda," the warrant officer said. "The only complaint we get is that sporting events come on too late at night."

But Keflavik residents don't survive the Icelandic winter by hibernating in front of the TV. Keeping busy is the key to keeping happy on sunlight-deprived days. The bars and restaurants of Reykjavik, Iceland's capital, are less than an hour's drive away, although the high cost of island living makes eating out a rare treat. A Coke, burger, and fries at the downtown McDonald's costs about ten dollars. Two submarine sandwiches and a small soda cost twice that. "If we go out to eat dinner, it looks like a car payment," said Capt. Ray Olafson, the base hospital's executive officer, who lives in a base apartment with his wife and their three youngest daughters.

So most wintertime life takes place on the base. "NAS Kef" is a scattering of a hundred prefab buildings painted in flat shades: red, pink, yellow, green. A retired P-3 Orion looms near a major intersection; old Iceland hands say it used to be a handy source of spare parts. There are almost no plants except for the imported grass sod. As one local wag put it, "If you get lost in the forest, stand up." People take up new hobbies or get out to the gym, the navy-sponsored recreation halls, or just down to the barracks' rec rooms.

Although the dark winter has ruined its share of marriages, many families thrive on Keflavik's simple, small-town lifestyle. "Up here, you've got the time to do things with your family," said Marcia Olafson. And no worries about crime. Newly arrived Americans who venture into town are often shocked by grocery-shopping Icelanders, who leave their children unattended in strollers outside.

When the brilliant days of summertime arrive, people grab their camping gear and head for the hills, waterfalls, and wildflowers of Iceland's all-but-uninhabited interior. "If you're into photography, this is the place to come," said Aerographer's Mate 2d Class David Halpern, checking charts one June day at the airfield's weather shack.

Yet even the sun causes problems when it keeps shining at 2:00 A.M. Twenty-one hours of sunlight can lure the unwary to stay out far later than advisable on work nights. "We have to make sure people are getting enough sleep," said marine sergeant Bo Lancaster.

The jobs they do in this cold land have not fundamentally changed since World War II, when more than forty-five thousand Americans guarded, maintained, and flew the aircraft that protected Allied convoys from German U-boats. After the war, those forces learned to find and track Soviet submarines instead.

As the cold war withered, so did the American presence on Iceland. Today's American presence is a scant 4 percent of its World War II strength. The 1,850 people on the air station include half a squadron of P-3C patrol planes, a security force of about sixty marines, and several air force fighter jets, early warning aircraft, and airborne tankers.

Officials say the work remains vital. The base still touts itself as "the antisubmarine warfare capital of the world," and the air ops officer argued that point during a briefing in the base's windowless tactical support center. "It's one of the last bastions of what we do," said Cdr.

A. J. Johnson, the operations officer for Fleet Air Keflavik. Most of the world's new submarines are built by countries that operate in the North Atlantic: Holland, Sweden, Russia. "Subs we're going to see around the world, we're going to see here," Johnson said.

The marines, too, receive unique training in winter warfare skills that they take back to the fleet marine force. "We take kids who have never had skis on in their life and teach them to move with a pack," said marine captain Hank Brown, the commander of the base's marine contingent.

Asked to predict the base's future, Capt. Efraimson reckoned that the arrangement of forces on Iceland—small and integrated with the local community—might provide a road map for NATO garrisons in the twenty-first century. "I think we're here to stay," he said.

------

Singapore, July 1998

A month into their western Pacific cruise, the *Essex* Amphibious Ready Group pulled into Singapore. A game of musical piers broke out by the Sembawang cargo terminal's docks.

Stuffed to the lifelines with marines, the dock landing ship *Fort McHenry* raised its brow and headed for Malaysia. The frigate *Sides* moved into the nearby channel. This allowed *Anchorage* to tie up pierside, bow to bow with the cruiser *Mobile Bay*. *Duluth* anchored out in the strait that separates this island country from the Malaysian mainland. *Essex* itself was forced to tie up downtown, miles away from the navy's leased pier. Late in the day, the attack submarine *Jefferson City*, en route to the Persian Gulf, slipped into Sembawang's last vacancy.

When the navy's western Pacific logistics hub gets as crowded as it was on 25 July, the parking problems can make ship drivers long for the wide-open spaces of Subic Bay. Established in 1992 to replace the repatriated base in the Philippines, Commander, Logistics Group, Western Pacific, consists of sixty-five active-duty souls, a few warehouses, and a single pier that used to belong to the British Royal Navy.

The U.S. military doesn't own a scrap of land in this island country, an arrangement that keeps local feathers unruffled. Newcomers who refer to the navy housing as a "base" are quickly corrected. "We generally call it 'the place,'" said Lt. Cdr. Cate Mueller, the local public affairs officer.

Sembawang isn't Subic, and Singapore is no Olangapo, the legendary fleshpots that sprawled outside the Philippine base. As U.S. Navy warships approach Singapore, skippers pass the word: Don't mess around. The citizens of this thirty-by-eighteen-mile island country have handed their democratic government far-reaching power to keep things orderly and clean.

Drug dealers here are put to death—one strike and you're out. Pitching a candy wrapper among the ubiquitous fan palms or flowering hedges risks a thousand-Singapore-dollar fine. And leave that Wrigley's in your coffin locker. "The import, sale and possession of chewing gum is prohibited," reads the customs declaration. "The high costs and difficulty in removing discarded chewing gum were the reasons for the prohibition."

Even the cab drivers apparently need a little help staying inside the law. Taxi dashboards start beeping when their speedometers hit forty-eight miles per hour.

For all the restrictions—and the eight-dollar beers—Singapore remains a popular port of call for sailors passing through this part of the world. It's a happening place: bars, shopping, and nightlife in a squeaky-clean urban environment of high-rises and indoor shopping malls. The tourism industry is highly developed, if, like many things Singaporean, a bit off to the Western ear. A Chinese mythology theme park advertises: "We promise to make your vacation a living hell."

Yet, for all the modern buildings, Singapore's multiethnic population reflects a thousand years of coming and going. The street names are Chinese, Malay, and a dozen different dialects. The cuisine in the "hawker stalls"—not quite farmers' markets, not quite food courts—is even more varied. U.S. Navy personnel live in bungalows and duplexes built before the island gained its independence from the British Empire three decades ago. Many apartments still bear the royal initials of Queen Elizabeth II; others, even older, were occupied by the Japanese army during World War II. Just offshore, scores of ships jockey for position in the Strait of Malacca, the busiest waterway in the world.

Amid this historic jumble, the men and women of COMLOG WESTPAC coordinate the supply and repair of Seventh Fleet ships from the central Pacific Ocean to eastern Africa, from Siberia to the Antarctic.

They are also in charge of coordinating naval exercises with the countries of Southeast Asia: Brunei, Indonesia, Malaysia, Thailand, the Philippines, and Singapore itself. For many of these nations, the U.S.-led Cooperation Afloat Readiness and Training exercises are the largest events on their calendars. The annual event sends American ships on a three-month swing around Southeast Asia. "CARAT's a big deal out here," said Mueller. "It's pretty much the premier exercise these nations do with the U.S. Navy."

The traffic of 28 July was not terribly unusual for a summer day. *Essex, Duluth, Anchorage,* and *Jefferson City*—all based in San Diego—were taking a break from their month-long transit to the Persian Gulf. The rest of the ships—and more besides—were finishing up the Singaporean phase of CARAT 1998.

One of these, *Salvor,* hadn't been caught in the Sembawang traffic jam. The salvage-and-rescue ship was anchored in the Strait of Johor, the mile-wide passage between the island and the Malaysian shore. Nearby, a team of American divers and their Singaporean counterparts worked to hoist a five-thousand-pound concrete block half-buried in the strait's oily bottom.

Clad in dive shorts and sneakers, Engineman 3d Class (DV) Jay Ryan watched his foreign teammates dive and surface, dive and surface. "These guys are probably the best we've worked with," said Ryan, who was perched on a nearby dock. "They're really knowledgeable and really good." Ryan, who has been diving for three years, said he got into it for the cool uniforms. "We're in the navy and we hang out in tennis shoes and T-shirts," he said, grinning.

Working in pairs twenty-five feet below the surface, the divers used a stout, U-shaped shackle to attach a rubberized bag to the block. They resurfaced, and a compressor began to pump air into the yellow sack. "It's a soft, silty mud, so it either pops right out or you get a real nice suction," said Chief Hospitalman (SW/DV/IDC) Jon Sanders, who watched from a nearby dock.

This time, it was the latter. The sand held tight. Under constant inflation, the bag's buoyancy eventually exceeded the fabric's strength. A strap ripped. A Singaporean diver ran off to fetch another lifting sack.

Sanders shrugged. "In salvage, you learn as you go. What worked last time doesn't necessarily work this time," he said.

A gathering thunderstorm sent a far-off bolt into the Malaysian jungle, and Master Chief Machinist's Mate (SW/MDV) John Schnoerring called his team from the water. A good day's work, he reckoned. "This training's important, because if we ever have to work together, at least we'll have an idea of how we do it," Schnoerring said.

The next day, the Singaporean divers were working again—this time with divers from Explosive Ordnance Disposal Mobile Unit Five. While U.S. Navy divers are trained in either salvage or EOD, Singaporean navy divers do both. This time, the divers defused a practice bomb by clamping a pair of rockets on its fuze and firing them off. With a flash and a bang, the pyrotechnic device spun the arming mechanism clear of the "bomb."

The EOD drill took place on the top floor of Singapore's state-of-the-art damage control trainer. Thirty feet high, it looks like a tiny three-deck ship squared off at bow and stern and mounted in a giant cradle. The thing is a virtual house of horrors for naval firefighters. Some spaces catch on fire, others flood—and the entire assembly can rock back and forth fifteen degrees. After the "bomb" was safely dispatched, several groups of American sailors came by to practice patching pipes as the "ship" rocked and rolled.

More than one wished they had something similar on American soil. "The water drops away, and then comes back, and suddenly you're neck deep. We got a lot out of it," said *Fort McHenry* sailor Damage Controlman 1st Class (SW) James Bovender.

Life isn't all work on the tropical isle, which is located eighty miles north of the Equator. Later that day, as dusk crept across Rear Adm. Stephen R. Loeffler's yard, an informal gathering of officers assembled. The admiral had invited the wardrooms of the *Essex* ARG to his grand two-story house, and so they came, wearing military haircuts and casual shirts, for an hour of chit-chat and hors d'oeuvres.

The darkness concealed the monsoon drains surrounding the admiral's house. Like tiny moats, these foot-deep concrete troughs encircle most of the American houses and apartment buildings. The British architects who built these houses meant the drains to keep torrents of water from eating away the foundations during the rainy season. They work well, the admiral informed his guests, but they invite skulking by geckos, monitors, and other local fauna.

A few blocks away, past winding streets and verdant lawns, the ARG's sailors and marines were kicking their own party into gear at the all-hands club. Named the Terror Club, a reference to a long-departed British warship, it resembles a tropical resort. The long slopes hold a saloon; a swimming pool; courts for tennis, volleyball, and basketball; and fields for softball and soccer. The club also features cheap beer, not easy to find at Singapore's exchange rates.

*Essex*'s own four-man rock band, Namespace, blasted music from the club's stage. The band featured two petty officers, a corporal, and a sergeant. During deployments, they said, they practiced in the "tiniest, grungiest space on the ship." Sailors moshed next to the low stage as the band ground its way through alt-rock hits.

The crowd was overwhelmingly male, although that would change after the ships had been in port for a few days and the sailors had rounded up some dates. "The best gosh-darned club I've been to in my nineteen years in," said diver Jon Sanders, relaxing on one of the giant steps above the pool. "The best-kept secret in Westpac."

Naval Support Activity, Naples, Italy, June 1998

In Italy, where the Fiat dealerships have marble steps, it's no surprise to find a grand cobblestoned piazza enfolded by elegant tan buildings and accented with Mediterranean orange tile. It is, perhaps, surprising to find it on a navy installation, though—and especially in Naples, long derided in the fleet for its rundown facilities.

In the base's sparkling new gym, Michele Hartley power-walked on a deluxe treadmill. "It's almost as if we'd gone from the ridiculous to the sublime," said Hartley, the wife of a navy investigator.

Snuggled up against the Capodochino municipal airport in the shadow of Mount Vesuvius, the new regional administrative center is getting much of the half-billion dollars the navy is pouring into the metropolitan area. The service presence here is big—some twenty-eight tenant commands.

In summer 1998, navy families began to move into a brand-new American-style housing development some twenty minutes away from the Capo complex. The attractive three-story apartment buildings, built to replace the eight crumbling concrete towers that used to house sailors and dependents, will eventually be home to 850 families. Surrounded by acres of southern Italian farmland and a stout fence, the American compound will eventually include a hospital, navy exchange, schools, movie theater, gym, and more.

Naples's physical plant had been decaying for years, but it accelerated in the 1980s with the reawakening of a not-sufficiently-extinct volcano. The seismic activity weakened the structures at the navy's Agnano complex, long the center of navy activity in Naples. A navy progress report on the "Naples Improvement Initiative" says it best: "Although quality of life improvements are an important facet of NII, the initial rationale behind the move is life safety."

The Capodochino gym had already received the ultimate in military construction accolades from a visiting basketball team. "It's better than anything we have in the air force," said one airman.

---

Fleet Activities Yokosuka, Japan, July 1998

"Last dog!" cried a sailor in blue coveralls. He flipped the final lever on a waterproof hatch. It sprang open, releasing a wave of water from the flooded compartment.

A red-helmeted casualty inspector pushed forward into the flooded space. A dozen shipmates plowed in after him, yelling above the din of rushing water. On one side of the compartment, the damage control team hurried to brace a buckled hatch; on another, they struggled to patch holes in the bulkhead. Faces twisting with effort, they eventually lost the battle with the rising sea and duck-walked from the space, noses just above water level.

Moments later, Damage Control Chief (SW) David Russell gleefully relived the drill. "I had those mothers scrambling to keep those holes covered," the instructor said, flashing a toothy grin. Mocking his students' predicament, he cried, "I got three holes and two hands!"

It's all in a day's work at the concrete training building of Afloat Training Group Westpac Fire Fighting School, stuck way out next to Tokyo Bay on the far side of Fleet Activities Yokosuka, Japan. The damage control team had come ashore from the amphibious command ship *Blue Ridge,* the Seventh Fleet flagship that makes its home at a nearby pier. "This is the best training they can get, right here," Russell said.

If so, it puts the school on par with the rest of the base, which won an impressive number of navy awards in 1997 and 1998. The long list includes security department of the year; navy fire department of the year, its second consecutive prize; navy exchange of the year, for an unprecedented three straight years; "five-star" status for the bachelor quarters, a grade currently held by only three other navy bases; and an award for outstanding physical plant improvement by volunteers, for the second year running.

Yokosuka topped it off with the 1998 Commander-in-Chief Installation Excellence Award—essentially the Pentagon's prize for the best navy facility. Ask base spokesman Michael Chase, and he'll go even further. "This is the best naval base ever," he said.

It's not hard to elicit the same reaction from visiting sailors. When the attack sub *Batfish* pulled up to a pier in July, its crew members were flabbergasted. Instead of being forced to sleep on their sub during the port visit—the routine in most places—the crew was offered berthing in Yokosuka's guest quarters. "I think the facilities here are the best I've seen anywhere, in any fleet. The barracks are phenomenal and the rec center is unsurpassed," said Machinist's Mate 1st Class (SS/DV) Hoy Weissinger.

There's a reason for all the effort. Japan isn't exactly right around the corner from Main Street, USA. In fact, the country is ten time zones from Washington, D.C. The distance makes it hard to get sailors to sign up for an overseas tour. "This is one of the hardest places to get people to come. Consequently, the leadership has worked really hard to improve the quality of life," said Master Chief (SW) Tom Sheppard, the Seventh Fleet's command master chief.

Strange, then, that the forward-based fleet also has the best retention in the navy. "Once they're out here, they like it, and that's not just me talking, that's the numbers," said Vice Adm. Robert J. Natter, the fleet's commander between 1996 and 1998.

Indeed, many sailors will tell you the same, citing everything from the superb base facilities to the infinitesimal crime rate in the city outside the gates. There are plenty of stories like the one related by a base worker who forgot her purse on a city bus. "The police tracked me down and returned it two days later. They were apologizing that it took so long," she said.

Yokosuka is one of the few growing bases in the shrinking navy. Its population has grown 40 percent over the 1990s. Some thirteen thousand sailors serve on the base—which has a ship repair facility, fleet and industrial supply center, public works center, naval hospital, and the fleet staff—or aboard one of the eleven ships homeported here. "If you go to boot camp today and you serve twenty years, the chance that you'll come here is excellent," Chase said.

Life isn't perfect at Yokosuka. Base housing hasn't caught up with demand, which forces nearly half the population to live outside the installation. It was worse a few years ago—nearly three quarters of them lived off-base—before the navy began the gradual replacement of old houses with residential high-rises.

Those who live "on the economy"—outside the base's gates—find that Japanese buildings are, as a rule, drafty and scarcely insulated. Some have been discomfited by Yokosuka winters that froze their toothpaste. Others manage just fine with Japanese customs like placing heat lamps under blanket-draped tables and taking lots of hot baths. "It's different; that's why they call it 'Japan' and not 'California,'" growled Jon Nylander, a retired lieutenant commander who settled in Yokosuka and now works for the Seventh Fleet's staff.

Yokosuka can't match the elegance of Pearl Harbor, but the Japanese base is every bit the Hawaiian port's equal in historical ambiance. Located forty-three miles south of the Japanese capital at the mouth of Tokyo Bay, the naval base has six working dry docks, including three that date from the 1800s. During World War II, the Japanese riddled the base's hills with more than 260 caves and bunkers. The tunnel networks concealed a five-hundred-bed hospital, a power plant, and an underground submarine factory that launched midget subs through a secret underwater passage. Today, the commander of U.S. Naval Forces Japan makes his headquarters in the wood-paneled buildings that were built for the Japanese Imperial Navy. More recently, the base high school counted among its graduates Mark Hamill, better known as Luke Skywalker in the *Star Wars* series.

The Seventh Fleet itself is run from *Blue Ridge,* which is tied up nearby as a communications hub. The navy's largest forward-deployed force, the fleet included at midsummer of 1998 some 51 ships, 186 aircraft, 26,000 sailors, and 20,400 marines. The fleet's staff is responsible for deploying and supporting the personnel and machines over a vast operational area. On a map of the western Pacific, an outline of the continental United States looks lost amid the vast distances.

Once a frontier unit whose sentries kept watch over the Soviet Pacific Fleet, the fleet now deals with a maturing China, the Korean peninsula powder keg, and dozens of Pacific Rim countries whose dramatic growth has not inured them to instability. In the name of engagement—and honing the sword's edge—Seventh Fleet forces perform one hundred exercises a year.

It's a mission that requires ships to be ready to go at a moment's notice. Seventh Fleet ships are in and out of port constantly; no six-month deployments, and no extended stops for repair. The cruises are shorter and more numerous. One of the navy's most cherished regulations—the one stating that operating tempo will keep a ship from home no more than half the year—gets a workout from the fleet planners. "We bump right up against the ceiling of op tempo," Natter said.

The sailors of the Seventh Fleet visit some of the world's most beautiful and intriguing countries. But there is a flip side to the exotic liberty ports. "I think being forward-deployed, people are more stressed out, because it's a foreign country, and you've got to make a good impression," said Aviation Boatswain's Mate Airman (Fuels) Phillip Evans, a fuel line repairman on *Independence.*

Being a good ambassador is high on the list of Natter's priorities. He has tried to limit unpleasant experiences by ending non-home-port liberty at midnight for E-3s and below. "I tell them, that's my policy, it works, and if you're unhappy with it, make E-4," Natter said.

As forward-based units, the Seventh Fleet gets top priority for personnel and ports, which eases the impact of the navy's shortages. Still, Yokosuka doesn't escape them. In 1998, the fire-fighting school, for example, was down four instructors from its full complement of seventeen. The school was forced to close down for two weeks when the trainers traveled to the naval base at Sasebo.

But things are only looking up, said Boatswain's Mate 3d Class Chris Caldwell. Homeported here with the destroyer *Fife* in the early 1990s, Caldwell found Japan even better the second time around. "Since my first time here, everything has gotten better. Yokosuka has blossomed," he said.

---

### Naval Air Facility Atsugi, Japan, July 1998

If Japan's streets are squeaky clean of crime, the same is not always true of the air. Take Naval Air Facility Atsugi, the home airfield for the navy's Carrier Air Wing Five, located about an hour north of Yokosuka. When the wind is wrong—about six months out of the year—a toxic haze spills from a nearby private incinerator's low smokestacks and blankets the installation's runways and residential buildings.

Hunched in a river valley just beyond the airfield's chain-link perimeter, the Jinkanpo incinerator burns everything the municipal trash dump can't: plastic, chemicals, even chromium car bumpers. Built in 1985 by a Japanese businessman, the incinerator has become one of the biggest quality-of-life problems at the Atsugi base, which supports about eight thousand members of Carrier Air Wing Five, support personnel, and family members.

"It smells like tar burning, some days," said Journalist 3d Class Anna Melzer, who works in the base's headquarters. She and her husband live off base so their seven-month-old baby won't be exposed to the smoke.

A 1994 navy study found arsenic, mercury, chromium, and other heavy metals in the smoke, but more recent efforts to determine the gray clouds' content have been thwarted by maneuvers that could have come from *Mad* magazine's "Spy vs. Spy" cartoon. When the navy placed a spectrometer atop its nearby residential towers, the incinerator owner erected twenty-foot-tall barricades to block the reflections. When the navy attached a video camera to a base telephone pole, up went a blinding white spotlight, trained on the lens.

Tactics like these have kept navy officials from discerning the precise risk to base personnel. "It's difficult to say whether Johnny's rash is from Jinkanpo," said Capt. Frank Sweigart, the base commander. "The branch medical center is looking into it."

Nevertheless, the command in 1998 briefed every person and family living on base, telling them what was known about the dangers. "We are really trying to make people understand the health risk," said Cdr. Frederic Henney, a spokesman for Naval Forces Japan.

Meanwhile, navy officials are trying to persuade the owner—or Japanese government officials—to reduce the amount of smoke that blows onto the base. But it's slow going. The incinerator stacks have scrubbers, but the owner leaves them turned off much of the time to save money. The local mayors don't want to shut down the incinerator because it would mean paying to send their trash farther afield. Regional and federal bodies are hamstrung by the lack of strong environmental laws. "Over here, it's Japan, Inc.: industry first, everything else second," Henney said.

A good compromise, Henney said, would be construction of one-hundred-foot smokestacks, which would carry the fumes past the base before they settle to earth. Navy officials estimate the new stacks would cost the incinerator owner about $10 million. "We're doing everything we can possibly do to get this resolved," Henney said. "We are trying to make it a topic every time we have a U.S. official over here."

One minor success: The Japanese government denied the incinerator owner's request to increase the allowable amount of trash burned from thirty to ninety tons per day. But the victory may be more symbolic than real. "Our monitors have observed the burning of one hundred tons a day of trash," Henney said.

Still, the base commander doesn't expect to have to deal forever with the incinerator, whose name translates to "God protects the environment." "People say Japan is twenty-five years behind the U.S. in EPA matters, but they are moving quickly in the right direction," Sweigart said.

---

Naval Air Station Sigonella, Italy, June 1998

When the brush fires that plagued Sicily threatened to level the small city of Catania, the folks at Sigonella Naval Air Station did what came naturally: delivering heavy loads under perilous circumstances.

Aloft within ninety minutes of a local official's distress call, a giant MH-53E Sea Dragon helicopter roared toward the conflagration in the nearby city of 850,000. "It looked like a Hollywood disaster movie," pilot Cdr. Chris Real told the base newspaper. "I couldn't believe the size of the fires in the downtown area."

Dipping a giant bucket into the nearby Ionian Sea, the helicopter's crew hauled thirteen hundred gallons of water to the nearest fire and released a smothering shower of seawater. For four hours, the powerful helicopter ran its airborne bucket brigade, extinguishing five separate blazes and earning the gratitude of Catania's citizens.

The circumstances aren't usually so dramatic, but the men and women who work at Sigonella are forever rushing passengers, mail, parts, and other cargo to navy ships and bases. Located on Sicily's eastern coast in the shadow of Mount Etna, the airfield is perfectly placed to support Mediterranean operations. And with the closure of U.S. bases in the Philippines, Sigonella has become the busiest hub for people and cargo headed for southwest Asia and the Indian Ocean.

On a single June day, the flight line featured a smorgasbord of military aircraft in light gray paint. Most were just passing through: two long rows of air force attack jets, a passel of giant cargo planes and tankers, a pair of F-15 Eagles that touched down, taxied over for some gas, and screamed off.

Taxiing out for takeoff, a group of aviators marveled at the cargo jets spread across the tarmac. "That must be half the C-17s in the air force," one remarked.

Most of the navy aircraft at Sigonella carry cargo or passengers:

there are C-2 Greyhounds to fly onto the heaving decks of aircraft carriers, C-12F Hurons to ferry small groups around the theater, and C9-B Skytrains to handle much of the fleet's heavy lifting. Mail and parts headed for smaller ships often fly with the HC-4 Black Stallions and their MH-53Es, the world's largest helicopter. The navy's only heavy-lift combat support squadron, HC-4's squadron mates spend much of their deployment following carriers around the Med or even the Persian Gulf. "No one can lift what we do," said Lt. Bruce Nolan, citing the Sea Dragon's unique ability to loft a jet engine onto a carrier. "Ships are eternally grateful for us."

A recent transfer, Aviation Machinist's Mate 2d Class (AW) Angel Adorno, found life in a logistics squadron nearly as fast-paced as his old strike fighter unit. In August, Adorno and thirty other HC-4 squadron mates returned to Sig after a broiling six weeks in Bahrain. "Even if it's one bag of mail, these guys'll bust tail and work twenty hours to fly that," Adorno said.

There is always a brace of P-3C Orions deployed here to shoulder the multiplying missions heaped on the navy's patrol squadrons: tracking refugees near Kosovo, monitoring evacuation of Americans from Albania, and hunting suspected smugglers in the western Med. "The intel community lights up, and they say, 'Go find them,'" said Lt. Tony Parton, whose VP-26 Tridents recently completed their Sigonella deployment.

Sigonella Naval Air Station is actually two chunks of land separated by eight miles of sun-baked olive groves, fruit orchards, and pastures roamed by herds of interbred goats and sheep, dubbed "geep." Travel between the base's two parts is accomplished via shuttle bus or hitchhiking: hold up one finger to beg a ride to NAS I , the personnel support area; two fingers for NAS II and the flight line. Three fingers gets you to Motta St. Anastasia, the nearby town that's home to many navy people who live on the local economy.

More than $140 million in new construction is going up on the base, including a set of new barracks. The recent arrival of a Subway sandwich shop drew cheers, and many view the imminent replacement of the base Wendy's with a Burger King as another big step up.

"Little things like this get us pretty excited," said Journalist's Mate 1st Class (SW) Anthony Falcone.

Falcone works tirelessly to get his shipmates out into the history-drenched countryside. But as everywhere, local laws and customs often present unusual challenges. Take the local drinking age. There isn't one, which Utilityman 2d Class Dave Pedreira said makes it too easy for American youths to imbibe. Pedreira, who has a sixteen-year-old cousin as a dependent, began in June to mount an informal campaign to persuade bars and stores not to sell alcohol to minors.

"We're going to gently back them into a wall," he said, by writing letters informing them that if they don't start carding, their names will be distributed in a message encouraging other Americans to take their business elsewhere. Several months later, a base spokesman said Pedreira's unofficial efforts had met with some success. And some of the bars have changed their newspaper ads to say, "No alcoholic beverages will be served to anyone under 18."

Pedreira said it's just his way of serving the community, carrying the water for his shipmates. "They say the ultimate responsibility lies with the parents, but how do you expect your parents to do their jobs and still chase their kids all over creation?" he said. "I'm no square, and I'm no angel, but now that I'm responsible for a sixteen-year-old girl and my career's on the line for every move she makes, it's gotten me thinking about the situation in a whole new way."

---

### Fleet Logistics Site Hurghada, Egypt, August 1998

*Desolate* is a good word for the navy's logistics outpost at Hurghada, Egypt. Caught between a knifelike mountain ridge and the Windex blue Red Sea, the flatness of the land is broken only by the ersatz dirt mesas of bunkers around the airstrip. Sunset turns the desert mountains a dozen dusty shades of orange and tan, throwing shadows across a battered collection of white shacks.

A sign supported by sandbags proclaims "Welcome To Fleet Logistic Site Hurghada, Egypt, Headquarters For North Red Sea Readiness," but this is hardly a welcoming locale.

Yet people are climbing all over each other to get here. "Every time I go to Bahrain, people are asking me whether I need a replacement for my assistant," said Lt. James Farrens.

The officer in charge of one of the navy's smallest outposts, Farrens and his lone subordinate help support carrier battle groups and amphibious ready groups as they transit the Red Sea. Cargo arrives in C-9s or C-130s, then leaves for the ships aboard C-2s and helicopters. "When there's a carrier in the Red Sea, we're the hardest-working guys in the navy," said Storekeeper 2d Class Daniel Mincica.

That goes for the supply corps officer as well, who earned his fork-lift license after arriving last October. But when nobody is cruising through, their schedule is enviably empty—and the scuba diving nearby is great. Farrens gestured to a whiteboard calendar that was much more free space than filled.

"I'm doing admin work for the sake of work," Farrens said. "I've totally automated the billing system. I've done next year's bills already. The next guy who comes along just has to print them out. They've already got his name on them."

Originally detailed to Bahrain, Mincica was so overjoyed with his temporary duty that he extended his twelve-month tour another year. "Everyone talks about the best-kept secret in the navy, and they're completely wrong, because they've never been stationed here," he said. "Once I saw my paycheck, my request was in to extend."

The extra payments that bulk up his bank account include imminent danger pay, cost of living allowance, foreign duty pay, overseas housing allowance, basic assistance for quarters, commuted rations, and a per diem. Plus overseas income tax exemptions. Plus a civilian clothing allowance because Farrens and Mincica are required to wear clothes that don't stick out when they go into nearby towns on business. To top it off, they live in and work out of a seaside hotel a few miles from the terminal. Food, lodging, and laundry are all paid for. "I'm the luckiest guy in the navy," Mincica exulted.

## 13. THE SAILORS

Another brutal day of flight operations ended aboard the carrier *Abraham Lincoln.* Temperatures still topped 110 degrees. The flight deck crew was wrapping up, descending into the air-conditioned hull, and peeling off sweat-soaked layers of safety equipment. In eight hours of sweltering work, Catapult Crew Three had reprised the deadly dance of launch and recover more than one hundred times.

Many of them would spend much of the night taking care of their equipment, then rise, bleary-eyed, to risk their lives once again on too little sleep. It wasn't the ideal situation, but ABE Todd Gray and his teammates had little choice. Like almost every division aboard, Cat Three was short-handed. On the previous deployment *Lincoln* had embarked forty-four greenshirts to operate the catapult. In summer 1998, Gray's team numbered twenty-five.

It takes a minimum of thirteen sailors to launch an aircraft, not counting the ones standing watches, keeping logs, and turning wrenches below. Over the long summer, Gray's teammates were on deck for almost every flight. "We're stretched to the limit right now," he said.

Cat Three was hardly unique. The mighty *Abe* was missing a sailor for one out of every seven jobs.

"We left port with four hundred fewer than we did in 1995," acknowledged Master Chief Electrician's Mate (AW/SW/SS) Gary Weir, the ship's top enlisted sailor. Indeed, *Lincoln* had lifted sailors from other ships in order to make the cruise.

*Abe* was not alone. As *George Washington* and *Nimitz* prepared for war with Iraq in January, neither was close to the navy's recommended manning levels. *GW* was supposed to have a crew of 5,680; there were actually 1,000 fewer aboard. A month later, *Independence* dashed into the area with a crew of 4,200, having snatched seventy-five specialists from other ships in order to meet combat readiness standards.

The 1998 shortages were hardly limited to the navy's marquee warships. By year's end, the fleet was missing a sailor for roughly one of every fifteen jobs. The navy had roughly 328,000 billets for enlisted sailors but was short about twenty-two thousand people to fill them. More than three quarters of the jobs were shipboard positions, which meant that most of the fleet was putting to sea with less-than-ideal personnel levels.

What was going on?

Simple. Too few sailors coming in and too many getting out.

The fleet's personnel specialists had hoped for fifty-five thousand new sailors in 1998, but navy recruiters missed their quotas by nearly eight thousand. There were several reasons, they believed. More high school graduates were heading straight to college. Young people didn't see the military as a good way to start their careers. There were fewer veterans around to talk up the service, and several traditional reasons to join had gone by the wayside.

"Years ago, it used to be the patriotic thing to join the navy. Next, it was unemployment that was so bad," said Bernard Heffernan, *Eisenhower*'s command master chief. "Most sailors that I've interviewed said they joined for the education money. I have yet to meet anyone who said, 'It was my duty to God and country.'"

One effect of the shortfall: If you were a mid-grade petty officer coming off sea duty in 1998, you were quite likely heading to a recruiting station. The navy recruiting command added hundreds of sailors in the hope that more recruiters would mean more recruits. Some relished the opportunity to sell the navy; many dreaded it.

Another effect: the fleet was short about eight thousand general detail sailors, the technically unskilled seamen who chip paint and keep its vessels shipshape. This led to a trickle-up of labor, and petty officers who imagined that they had advanced beyond such menial tasks found themselves down on the deck with a chipping hammer. This was not a morale booster.

There weren't enough people coming in, but there weren't enough staying, either. Part of this was the result of the red-hot economy. Many of the navy's highly trained technicians discovered that they could triple their government paychecks overnight by walking out the door. "Too much money to be made out there," one *Wasp* fire control-man said.

The navy and the other service branches tried to address this issue by pushing for large pay raises in the fiscal 1999 and 2000 budgets. Reenlistment and retention bonuses soared for many officers and enlisted specialties. But most officials realized that money wasn't the whole reason people were leaving the service. Usually, it wasn't even the main reason. The main reason was frustration: too few parts, too few ships, too few people. "It's not money. It helps. But it won't substitute for job satisfaction," said Mike Zieser, skipper of the submarine *Houston*. The civilian economy might be pulling them, but the navy was also driving people away.

Everywhere, there were too few sailors doing too many jobs. As *Wasp* cruised off the Albanian coast during the 1998 Kosovo tensions, there were only thirty-five mess specialists to prepare meals—twenty fewer than the last time the ship deployed. The gator's fire control division—the sailors who operate the guns and missiles—numbered about twenty-five. "We should have thirty or thirty-five," said fire control officer Lt. Homer Denius. "But everybody sucks it up for each other. They really come together well."

The shortages hit certain ratings harder than others. Fleetwide, one of every three slots went unfilled for junior ship's serviceman—the rating that gives haircuts, does laundry, runs the ship's store, and more. Many ship's barbers hung "Barbers Wanted" signs outside their shops, begging shipmates to come in and learn to cut hair.

Yet because of the peculiarities of the drawdown that had lasted nearly a decade, it was hard for junior sailors in some ratings to move up. There were few shortages among the more senior levels of enlisted jobs, and hence little chance to advance. Taking the advancement exam had become a dreary biannual ritual for many sailors. "You keep finding ways to recognize them and keep picking them up and dusting them off and helping them to move on after the disappointment of not advancing," said *Shiloh*'s Chief John Norrell.

Other issues led to frustration as well. Seemingly endless inspections meant more time away from home, even in home port. Yet it wasn't the long hours that had Isidoro Madrigal, *Duluth*'s "best boilerman," half convinced to leave the navy after his contract expired. It was the shriveled retirement benefits that offered him so much less than the sailors who had served before him in the three-decades-old steam plant. "If I stay in twenty years, I only get 35 percent, versus the 50 percent of veterans," he said.

The frequent confrontations with Iraq engendered another complaint: really lousy liberty stops. "What they want is port visits. What the troops want is to be sailors," said *Princeton* skipper James Moseman. "You give a sailor Cartajena, Colombia, and that goes a long way. Every sailor hopes for Australia. In the Persian Gulf, it's rough, because there's only sand."

Difficulties in getting repair parts heaped insult on injury. "Not only is there not any time for family, not only are they not able to get advanced, on top of that, you're not letting them do the job they're trained to do. They're going to vote with their feet," said Mark Butler, *Halyburton*'s command master chief. And that's too bad, said Butler, because it's quite clear why young people stay in or get out. "The thing about the navy is reaching your potential. Those who can't reach their potential are dissatisfied. Those that can are tremendously satisfied."

But if 1998 had the worst personnel situation in many years, there were also signs that the top brass was starting to understand—and solve—some of the problems. In September, the chief of naval operations began hacking away at obsolete or simply needless inspections, training requirements, and regulations. Adm. Jay Johnson limited the number of days a ship could spend out of home port during a training cycle. In one fell swoop, he whacked the number of shipboard inspections in half. In early 1999, he eliminated the Propulsion Evaluation

Board—one of the most feared of all inspections, an exam that could make or break careers. It had been established two decades ago, when engineering standards had become so lax that sailors were getting killed by steam-related accidents in their engine rooms. But as standards rose in the 1980s and generally safer gas turbine engines replaced steam in the navy's ships, the board became obsolete. It is a revealing commentary on naval bureaucracy that it took a crisis to eliminate its needless burden.

Urged on by new navy secretary Richard Danzig, navy engineers began looking for ways to reduce the sailors' burdens: new low-maintenance watertight doors, new power tools to speed paint stripping. By early 1999 there was even a plan to bring civilian painters aboard navy vessels in port to relieve highly trained sailors—and even the not-so-highly trained ones—of the menial, if time-honored, labor of painting the ships' hulls. "We acted for so long as if labor were a free good," Danzig said. The navy began coating its amphib well decks with a new kind of paint that lasts not one year but ten, saving millions of dollars and hundreds of man-hours. Why hadn't this happened earlier? Didn't have to. "In the early nineties we were fat, dumb, and happy," said an official with the navy's engineering branch.

As personnel shortages and money problems got worse in the late 1990s, the military's top officers still reported each year to Congress that, however shaky rear-echelon readiness might be, the frontline troops were ready to go. The strike team aboard the guided-missile destroyer *Stout* seemed to prove it during the winter strikes on Iraq dubbed Operation Desert Fox.

At 11:18 P.M. on 16 December, a cruise missile bearing a thousand-pound warhead rose from a burst of flame on *Stout*'s forecastle and headed off toward its target. Through the night and into the muggy Persian Gulf dawn, Tomahawk after Tomahawk streaked from the destroyer's vertical tubes, wreathing the bridge in smoke with each launch. When the firing ceased nine hours after it began, *Stout* and seven other ships had laid down the biggest cruise missile strike in history.

Remarkably, *Stout*'s sailors had never launched a real Tomahawk before they received the order to fire.

"Before the strikes, there was a little apprehension among my Tom-ahawk strike team," said Cdr. Dave Jackson, *Stout*'s skipper. "But the butterflies went away after the first missile left the rail." Intense train-ing during workups enabled the crew members, about half of whom were making their first deployment, to perform flawlessly in combat, Jackson said.

Capt. Ray Pilcher, who heads up the navy's land attack planning and development office, lauded the sailors and their flawless exe-cution of their duties. Despite all the navy's problems, its sailors per-formed when it counted. "I mean, how much more ready do you want them to be?" he said.

It may seem a small thing to landlubbers, but to many sailors, 1998 was the year of e-mail. In dozens of ways, the ability to send free mes-sages that arrived in hours and not weeks helped close the gap between sailors and their loved ones. Most of the fleet's aircraft car-riers were equipped with the capacity for instantaneous e-mail in 1998. Sailors on smaller ships, which were less well endowed with communications links, nevertheless usually managed to send and receive every few hours. Captains and crews alike touted e-mail as the biggest single quality-of-life improvement they'd seen in years.

Aviation Electronics Technician 3d Class Michael Eccles would agree. In July, he burst into the carrier *Eisenhower*'s television studio waving a pair of floppy disks. "My wife had our baby, and I got her pic-ture on e-mail," the dungareed sailor exclaimed, hopping with excite-ment.

As with the rest of the fleet's carriers, *Ike* was wired with an onboard computer network and e-mail capability just before its last deploy-ment. Unfortunately, Eccles's own workstation wasn't set up to handle pictures, so the technician came running into the studio after he got off work around 3:00 A.M.

Eccles waited anxiously as Journalist 3d Class Stacy Clark shoved the disk into his computer and pulled the image up on the screen. There she was, eight pounds and twenty inches of chubby, pink, naked Morgan Brook Eccles, born to Jessica Eccles on 28 June in Houston, Texas. It's no fun being six thousand miles away on a ship in the Adriatic Sea when your first child is born, but the digital picture eased the new father's pain.

"Wow," Eccles said, nearly speechless with joy and wonder and pride.

Yet even in the age of technology, nothing matters more than good leadership. The skipper, or commander, or officer in charge affects the entire unit more than anything else within or without it. As the ever-more-technical navy moves into the twenty-first century, John Paul Jones's example is not obsolete. It's more important than ever.

"Sailors aren't worried about how many days off they get if you show them you care for them," said *Houston* skipper Zieser.

Moseman echoed the thought. "The most powerful thing a commander can do to boost retention is one simple thing: you have to ask the sailor what he wants to do. Then say, 'I'll show you your future, and it looks pretty good.'"

An aviation machinist's mate second class from the *Eisenhower* summed it up. "Morale goes up because someone gives a damn," he said.

The navy demands much of its sailors. Toil. Sweat. Nights. Weekends. Repetition. Responsibility. Commitment. Isolation. "You go three weeks without mail, you feel forgotten. You don't feel part of the universe anymore," said Photographer's Mate 3d Class Tim Altevogt, who served his deployments aboard *Abraham Lincoln.*

Holidays missed. Children's first words, first steps. Six-month holes carved from family life. Long watches when nothing happens. Long watches when everything happens. Long watches followed by three hours of fire drills followed by ten-hour workdays followed by . . . when did I last sleep?

Courage in battle. Sometimes, life itself.

Yet there are rewards. Some are mundane. A paycheck. Health benefits for the family. College tuition. A pension for twenty years' service.

Some are exciting. Travel. Adventure. Crewing and commanding powerful warships and warplanes.

Some are sublime. The chance to do what few do. The camaraderie of an elite. The not-so-old-fashioned notion of service to one's country.

When everything goes right, a sailor's sacrifice becomes an investment returned many times. Ask Anthony Batz.

At age twenty-five, Batz was flying high, figuratively and literally. The aviation warfare systems operator, third class, was several thousand feet above the Black Sea in one of VP-26's P-3 Orions. He was sensor two, the junior operator of the patrol plane's sonar equipment.

For a week, his twelve-person crew had operated from a Romanian airfield, flying exercises with forces from many countries. On this particular mission Batz hadn't even bothered to power up the monochrome screens of his sonar equipment. The pilots were teaching various Eastern European ships about the Orion's surveillance capabilities, lessons that didn't require the particular skills of the sensor operator.

Batz sat on the cabin deck in his flight gear, wedged against a metal bulkhead. He cracked a training manual to bone up for his aviation warfare qualifying exams, but his mind kept wandering back to the bus trip to Transylvania a few days before.

"I saw Dracula's castle," the young petty officer said, recalling the ride through the Romanian hills. "It blew my mind. I can't believe this used to be a communist country. I wish we could stay some more."

Two years ago, the Lebanon, Pennsylvania, native was working fifty hours a week in a convenience store. The pay was lousy. His life was lousier. "I was living at home at age twenty-three. I needed a new direction," he said. A recruiter's pitch, dimly remembered from high school days, steered him toward the navy. At boot camp, the instructors handed Batz his first taste of responsibility: simple things, positions of authority in his company of recruits. Batz was startled, and then pleasantly surprised, to find himself bearing up well under its weight. "Someone saw something inside of me that I didn't," he said, wonderingly.

In fact, the navy saw the potential for a highly skilled air warfare specialist. After boot camp turned Batz into a sailor, the service invested thousands more dollars training him to hunt subs. It was a perfect match. As Batz learned to recognize the sonic patterns that would enable him to find a quiet boat in noisy seas, something clicked. In a yearlong stab at college, Batz had studied criminal justice. His favorite part was fingerprinting.

"No submarine looks the same as any other, even in the same class-es," he explained as the P-3's engines droned outside. "They have sim-ilarities, but each one's different, like a fingerprint."

When he arrived at VP-26, fresh from school, he found that prying submarines from their watery hiding places was even more fun that he'd expected. "It really gets my heart pumping," he said.

The surveillance flights over Bosnia, keeping a protective eye on things for the ground troops below, were even better. "That job brought it home to me. This is the real world. I'm helping people. I'm doing the right thing," he said. "It was the warm fuzzy that everyone needs."

Batz's first deployment was coming to an end. In a month, the squadron would head home to Maine. He would not return quite the same person who left. "I'm learning to rely on myself far more than I ever thought I could," he said. "Younger guys are leaning on me for support."

And he has goals now. He's going after his air warfare pin. Then he'll look to move up in his rating. Above all, he's determined to finish his college education. "I promised myself I wouldn't get out of the navy without a bachelor's degree. Whether that takes five years or twenty."

The navy's no free ride. But for Batz, the trip is well worth the fare.

"You work hard, you get recognized, and you get what you want," he said. "Right now, I'm loving it. I couldn't have asked for better."

---

Naval Air Station Brunswick, Maine, 6 August 1998

A chartered airliner touched down on a quiet tarmac at 3:50 P.M. The three hundred white-garbed sailors in the cabin erupted in cheers and whistles. Outside, children and wives and husbands, friends and lovers and squadron mates impatiently toed a line on the tarmac.

After six months on deployment, VP-26 had come home.

Eleven hours before, skipper Andy Johnson had bid good-bye to his departing flock, shaking hands in the air terminal at Sigonella Naval Air Station in Sicily. For six months, his crews had flown and maintained their P-3s all over Europe.

"These guys have done such a good job," he said, pride welling in his voice. He almost looked sad to see it end. Almost.

Aboard the plane, outward bound after a refueling stop in Ireland, Aviation Machinist's Mate Airman Terrence Pinnock fingered his car keys.

"First thing I do, I'm going to bring up my car," he said. Well, maybe right after he met his girlfriend, he amended. And maybe even after he traveled to New York City to see his family on Monday. But one thing was certain. There was no end to the reasons he was glad to be home.

"I miss English," the Jamaican-born sailor said. "I miss going out in town and hearing English."

As the plane taxied across the Maine airfield, a flight attendant came on the intercom. "Thanks for flying with us and we hope we can fly you to some better vacation destinations soon," she said.

The passengers exchanged a few incredulous looks. What, exactly, did she think this mass of sailors was doing? Where did she think they'd been?

"We spent six months busting our ass," Pinnock said without rancor. "She ought to be informed about what's going on."

But soon the sailors had more pressing things to think about. At the bottom of the boarding ladder they fumbled proffered roses and miniature American flags. Then they looked up to the roiling Technicolor mass that broke from the painted line with peals of laughter and squeals of joy.

One of the squadron hangar's painted banners spelled it out in navy blue and gold: "It's finally over."